THE
BEST
OF
SAIL

THE
BEST
OF
SAIL

Paintings by J. SPURLING

Text by BASIL LUBBOCK

Edited by F.A. HOOK, F.R.G.S.

With an Introduction by ALAN VILLIERS

GROSSET & DUNLAP

Publishers New York

1977 Printing

ISBN: 0-448-11840-8
Library of Congress Catalog Card Number: 74–7554

Text reprinted with the permission of the Estate of the
late Basil Lubbock.

Printed in the United States of America.

INTRODUCTION

The reissue of the three-volume edition of Jack Spurling and Basil Lubbock's classic *Sail: The Romance of the Clipper Ships* was such an instant and complete success that thought had to be given to providing a shorter volume containing a careful selection of some of those fascinating Spurling paintings, accompanied by the interesting Lubbock stories of the ships portrayed. The result is this volume—no easy task, for the problem was what to leave out when all the candidates were uniquely beautiful and interesting both in painting and in story. What I have tried to do is to make a representative selection of the periods, the trades, the lines, the rigs—the old regular passenger carriers; the Australian gold rush racers; the famous tea clippers in their brief reign of glory (among these the famous *Cutty Sark*—still with us—and her great rival, the fleet *Thermopylae*); the wool clippers (including that old flyer *The Tweed,* which began life as an auxiliary frigate for the Honourable East India Company and went like a scalded cat from the day her unnecessary engines were removed); the Devitt & Moore sailing liners; then the "medium" clippers which had to be sailed with an eye on costs and were the harder on their tough, tireless masters for that sad fact; and then at last the splendid big carriers which really were no "clippers" at all but larger square-riggers with greater sail areas and smaller crews, ships which had to be driven *all* the time, by a breed of hardy, able men now utterly gone.

Among all these were many splendid ships, though their studding-sails area had been incorporated in longer yards with deeper hoist to spread more and more canvas, without those old-fashioned, awkward kites. The cut-down crews worked harder than ever, the old masters drove ships harder, and planned their passages better as knowledge grew of the behavior patterns of the ocean winds—the more or less steady trades, the seasonal monsoons, the doldrums belts of catspaws and the calms of the horse latitudes at the trade winds' edge. Many of these new-style square-riggers, being often larger and stronger than their clipper predecessors, could be driven even harder than the smaller tea-racers ever were, for they were the swift "dollies" of the azure winds, the pampered queens of tropic sailing, the Good Hope users—the "flying-fish" sailers as the tough Cape Horn lads used to know them.

By comparison, the big iron and later steel 1,500–1,900-ton full-rigged ships and 2,500–3,000-ton four-masted barques were powerful, massive ships with all-steel masts and yards and standing rigging of iron wire, which could and did stand the determined driving essential to force those great hulls full of heavy cargo to windward past the Horn, down toward the ice-line towards 60° South latitude. On their way they fought gale after gale with a gutful of heavy coal and a handful of the toughest merchant seamen the world has known, and the bravest, most skilful, most fully extended masters the sea world has bred.

All these had their glory, too, and their triumphs—though the loss-rate also grew, both of the brave ships and the brave men. As the years passed, they were forced into these dreadful runs which had to include the savage war with the winter's Horn: for steadily the steamship first cut in, then spread and soon monopolised the other, more reliable, simpler trades, since they could pass through Suez—a thing the ocean square-rigged ship never did because for her it made no sense. Not only was it costly but it was no kind of ocean sailing route at all, with all the Red Sea and the Mediterranean to take on every voyage. Calms and doldrums airs were always a greater curse to the square-rigged ship than any storm. She could fight the gale up to full-storm strength, but she could only roll, sweat and wallow in the useless calm. And auxiliary power was ruin, not answer.

So at the end came those last "clippers"—the great Horn fighters, the powerful wind'ard sloggers, British and German, French and American. Writer Lubbock and artist Spurling, probably wisely, did not concern themselves much with these, though they covered some splendid metal ships which took on any charter that offered—strong powerful beauties like the *Mermerus,* the newer *Lochs* like Conrad's *Loch Etive* (he was third mate, a "pier-head jump" in that good Glasgow ship back in the 1880s) and the strong, splendid *Tamar* of over 2,000 tons, which was perhaps just a little on the over-large size for a three-mast full-rigger. She would have been easier to work as a four-masted barque, but many owners had learned (or chose) to be conservative.

Considering the inevitability of a more or less complete turnover to large powered ships in at least the important trades (hastened also by the equal inevitability of a successful Panama Canal to give swift access for the steamers to the west coast of all the Americas), it was obvious that, even in the dawn of the twentieth century, the great and beautiful square-rigged ship was doomed, though some—very few, like the *Preussen* and the *France,* both huge five-masters—were products of the twentieth century. But these few remained unique. It is only now, in the mid-1970s, that the idea of using oceangoing square-riggers, engineless and splendidly efficient, is finding perhaps some favour again. In the meantime the real skills have largely been thrown away, along with the ships, and the know-how has departed too—and this could be fatal.

It is a pity, for those ships were beautiful and quietly effective. And, after all, the wind-blown ship did *all* the world's seafaring work—the longer haul freighting and the passenger carrying, and the fighting too—for at least 2,000 years.

We must be grateful to the far-sighted team of three plain men who, feeling these things, put their talents together to produce the uniquely attractive volumes of *Sail* for, among much else, these offer a striking record of at least the culmination of the era, more particularly from the British point of view. There were others, especially the French, and Germans, the Americans of later days, the Semitic seamen of the Arab peninsula and Near East, the Chinese and Indians over thousands of years, and Polynesians, Mexicans and Peruvians too—so far back into antiquity that records are scant and the works of any possible Lubbock-Spurling team have unfortunately been lost, save for a very little in stone.

Those three competent and able men were the talented marine artist John Robert (Jack) Spurling and the chronicler Basil Lubbock, old Etonian who had seen some active deepwater seafaring in a ship or two and from that foundation maintained a lifelong interest; and, third, F. A. Hook, the editor of the monthly sea-and-ships magazine known at the time as *Blue Peter*. It was his idea to get the Spurling-Lubbock team together and to commission them to produce one painting and its accompanying story for each monthly edition of the magazine. So the wonderful series began, and *Blue Peter* became the most attractively presented specialised magazine, at any rate in the English-speaking world. For all three men knew ships: the Spurling and Lubbock contributions were thorough, accurate and complementary, and for years a succession of gloriously attractive great ships brought a breath of stimulating sea air to at least the news-stands of most of the great rail termini in the world, brightened a thousand stately homes, and the libraries, masters' quarters and lounges of a thousand ships. In those days the ship-masters in great lines had *all* begun in deepwater sail, for no all-steam training was acceptable to their selection boards. Every wandering lime-juice tramp (or liner) "windjammer" had her half-deck of four, six or eight strong and able boys, indentured apprentices learning their tough profession in that rigorous but highly effective school, and some great lines ran their own square-rigged cargo school-ships as well, White Star and Devitt & Moore among them.

So there was a great, firmly entrenched and widespread tradition of more than just the beauty of Square Sail, so deeply rooted that it seemed impossible that it could ever die. (Nor has it yet by any means, for in the mid-1970s a fleet of at least forty sailing-ships still provides the *ab initio* professional sea training of the embryo officers of over a score of great seafaring nations, among them Soviet Russia, Spain, Portugal, Italy, Germany, Japan, France, Norway, Sweden, Poland, Denmark, Chile and Argentina.) As well as the appeal of beauty there was the lasting value of coping with the fundamental challenge of the sea, and it is ever thus. So the square-rigged ship survives, evolved from the swift clippers and the great Horn-fighters of earlier eras: and the interest of red-blooded men in them not only continues but is increasing. It is no mere nostalgia that stops grown men in their stride to admire some painting of a great square-rigged ship blending so perfectly in her natural environment: in any good sailing conditions the ship herself is an eye-stopper too, even such widely differing square-riggers as Italy's *Amerigo Vespucci,* Denmark's *Danmark* and the Argentine's *Libertad.*

The young John Robert Spurling was born with a considerable artistic talent which, perhaps oddly, found its first outlet in a stage career, after a nasty fall from aloft in a former big Canadian wooden barque named the *Astoria*—an old drogher with a considerable thirst for the sea, and little sign about her of clipper (or much other) grace. It could have been a family hope that she would sicken him of the sea: she did indeed, in her own way, by trying her best to kill him as a sixteen-year-old apprentice on his first voyage. Few survived any fall from aloft; but young Spurling had the luck to land on a flaked-out long brace made up on deck—not much of a shock absorber but it saved his life. He was five months recovering slowly in a hospital at Singapore, and that was the end of his active seafaring. He had already been a precocious art student in his early youth and had shown considerable talent. He drew well and had a fine sense of color.

"I can teach him no more," his old art teacher said before he went to sea—a profession in which he was particularly interested as his father was a jute merchant, using chartered big square-riggers (like old "Brace-winch" Jarvis's four-masted barque *Lawhill*) to bring Indian jute to his mills at Dundee. Young Spurling knew ships (as far as a landsman may) before he went to sea, and he learned fast when at last he got afloat. He was also something of a musician, with an excellent singing voice which he could turn to earning a living on the London stage: so he did that, too, and was a considerable success. All this took years, of course: success in such fields never comes quickly. He was no dilettante flitting between attractive professions. Indeed, when he recovered from that fall in the wooden *Astoria,* he insisted on going back to sea in other large square-rigged ships and finished his "time" in the fine Devitt & Moore ships *Sobraon* and *Hesperus,* splendid big full-riggers, as gracefully distinguished and perfect in their seaworthy qualities as the elderly *Astoria* may have been the other way. The Devitt & Moore ships were in the classic square-rigger trade, the Australian run—out round Good Hope, home round the Horn, a great wind-driven circumnavigation every voyage. This was magnificent experience, stirring and splendid. An aspiring artist could not have chosen better, for these were ships of grace and beauty, and superb sailing qualities. Wherever his eye glanced aloft, or aft, or for'ard along the length of such ships, it filled with the wonder of that perfect composition which the graceful ships embodied in their being, or they could not be true wind-ships at all.

Such impressions were for life. Yet it was the stage that first claimed young Spurling when at last he was home from sea. He was also painting, but there were other marine artists so much more experienced and better known: England had been served well by naval painters, both Dutch like the Van der Veldes and English like Turner. So Spurling sang on the West End stage, and crowds of enthralled admirers had not the slightest idea that their songful, stage-lit spellbinder was a Cape Horn seaman and a considerable artist, too.

But that fall in the *Astoria* had been a body-twister, and the stage life was arduous and quite a strain. Spurling began full-time painting—always of ships, square-rigged ships, those classic, strong, unique beauties: and he caught them in deep-sea stance perfectly, technically correct as ships and at the same time artistically appealing. For years the bright cover of the seafaring monthly first known as *Blue Peter* (later *Trident*) shone the brighter for the wonderful Spurling representations of glorious great ships, even while the ships themselves were sold foreign, reduced in rig, forced to carry what they might find at the most barren and unlovely ends of the earth, staggering about still bravely and with grace untarnished, but threadbare in the rising winds, not of the sea but of economic storm. Great ships! And beautiful—and the better remembered because a brave lad named Spurling once sailed in them, and survived being flung from the rigging.

He died in 1933, aged sixty-three, in the Seamen's Hospital at Greenwich beside the Thames, where James Cook was a Governor briefly between his epochal voyages, and where the green English turf is shroud for hundreds of Nelson's Trafalgar veterans. His stirring, glorious paintings remain his lasting memorial.

Basil Lubbock, sailing-ship chronicler, methodical, thorough and industrious, was different in most ways, though a kindred spirit both in his admiration for the beautiful square-rigged ships and his determination to get on record whatever he might still be able to discover about them, for he came near the end of the British Cape Horning era. He was a member of a well-known, distinguished English family whose sons were educated at Eton and usually went on to Cambridge to distinguish themselves later in many fields, from the Services to Law and the Universities. Young Lubbock chose adventure rather than any great university, however distinguished, and the goldfields of the Yukon attracted him in the late 1890s rather than the sounder merits of King's College, Cambridge. Finding (like most) little if any gold, he picked up a berth in the apprentices' half-deck of the four-masted barque *Ross-shire,* as a privileged passage-worker from the West Coast of the United States back to Britain in 1899. Privilege may have helped get him the berth, but stout young men willing to work a passage were very welcome aboard lime-juice square-riggers in West Coast U.S. ports in those bad days, when those cowardly criminals called crimps controlled manning of outward-bounders for their own illicit but considerable profit. The more old Etonians or new Board-School boys who turned up healthy, sober and willing to work passages homewards in any lime-juice or other Cape Horn ship then the better, though official influence with consuls was a help in preventing the crimps from making trouble.

Lubbock was 123 days homewards from San Francisco round the Horn, which was excellent experience. This, and his close association with the splendid young Scots in her 'prentices' half-deck, formed a good foundation for his lifetime interest in and study of deepwater sailing-ships from that time onwards. He was not the first but he was perhaps the most thorough chronicler of that stirring age, and his *Round the Horn before the Mast* set something of a pattern for such books. This was good for maritime history, for he could gain ready access to records: for him, all doors might open. Soon he was working with Mr. Hook and artist Spurling for the outstanding

Blue Peter sailing-ship painting-and-story series—outstanding because both artist and chronicler worked at first hand from primary sources and their own indelible experience.

Hence, among other achievements—a long line of them—came the *Blue Peter* paintings and chronicles, then the Spurling and Lubbock *Sail,* in several editions, the latest in 1972, and now—in response to great demand—this shorter edition, to fill what has already become an otherwise unclosed and considerable gap. These ships were a great achievement on the part of Man, both as inspired shipbuilder and indefatigably competent seaman, of infinite courage, skill and endurance. Only from his mind, with pencil and skill and scales and rules, did he produce these glorious, lovely and efficient ships: only with his tremendous courage and vast endurance, his infinite store of inspired know-how and the good qualities of brave crews under his leadership, could they make great voyages, or indeed hope to survive at sea at all.

This they did, and gloriously. This book is both tribute and memorial to the Men and the Ships.

OXFORD
January 4, 1975

Alan Villiers

CONTENTS.

THE "JAMES BAINES."

OUR grandfathers have always been severely criticized for their conception of artistic beauty. The mid-Victorian even went to the length of perpetuating his drooping whiskers, his peg-top trousers and his chimney-pot hat, in all their ugliness, on the bows of his ships; and all through the great clipper-ship days of sail allegorical and classical figure-heads found themselves the neighbours of grim gentlemen in severe broad-cloth and silk top-hats. One of the first of the Victorian shipping magnates to put his effigy on the bows of a ship was James Baines.

It must have come as a great shock to the graceful lady who pointed her golden thunderbolt from the bows of the *Lightning*, when she recognized the features of her little red-haired owner at the bows of her new rival. She had been cheek by jowl with that proud grandee, *Marco Polo*, with that famous Indian chief, *Red Jacket*, and even with the curly-haired sailor-boy who called himself *Champion of the Seas*, but to hobnob with her owner in the same way must have been somewhat disconcerting, even to a woman of her impetuosity. But the example of Mr. James Baines was soon followed, and carved portraits of distinguished men soon became very popular as figure-heads. Two very famous ships, the *Thomas Stephens* and the *Samuel Plimsoll*, had to put up with these unsightly headpieces.

I fear these top-hatted effigies were entirely British. Donald McKay, the builder of the *James Baines*, was no party to anything so inartistic, and when Mr. James Baines announced that he was going to call the fourth of these mighty Boston-built Black-Ballers after her designer, it is noticeable that a magnificent Highlander in the McKay tartan became her figure-head, and not a black-coated, top-hatted Donald McKay.

* * *

The *James Baines* was in many ways the finest of all Donald McKay's creations. Though not so sharp, or as hollow-lined, as the *Lightning*, she was not so full as either the *Champion of the Seas* or the *Donald Mackay*. Whether she was really faster than the *Lightning* it is extremely hard to decide. From the evidence of their performances, I should say that the *James Baines* was a trifle more powerful in heavy weather, and a trifle slower in light breezes. Amongst old seamen favouritism discounts most opinions, but I believe the critical shipping fraternity of Liverpool considered the *James Baines* to be the greater masterpiece. Donald McKay was an artist, who always improved on his latest creation; and there were many small faults in the design of the *Lightning* which were eradicated in that of the *James Baines*. We cannot compare the latter with either the *Champion of the Seas* or the *Donald Mackay*, for these two ships were not intended to be record-breakers like the *Lightning* and *James Baines*, and thus had decidedly fuller lines.

Perhaps it would be of interest to put down the chief measurements of the *James Baines* against those of the *Lightning* :

Chief Measurements.	*James Baines*.	*Lightning*.
Registered tonnage .. (American)	2,525⁶⁵⁄₉₅	2,096
Registered tonnage .. (British)	2,275 (old)	1,468 (new)
Length overall ..	266 feet	244 feet
Beam	44¾ feet	44 feet
Depth of hold.. ..	29 feet	23 feet
Height of 'tween-decks	8 feet	8 feet
Dead rise at half floor	18 inches	20 inches
Sail area	13,000 yards 18 inches wide	13,000 yards 18 inches wide
Mainyard	100 feet	95 feet

The *James Baines* had Donald McKay's usual sheer, bold and buoyant, with lavishly carved trail-boards.

The experts considered her stern to be perfect, and " surpassing in neatness that of any vessel her talented builder has yet produced." It was rounded, and ornamented with a carved representation of the globe set between the arms of Great Britain and the United States. She had a full poop and a topgallant-fo'c'sle, which extended to the foremast. Abaft the foremast was a house, which contained the galleys, store-rooms, ice-rooms, and a companion-way. Forward of the poop another large house held the first-saloon dining-room.

The interior fittings of the McKay Black-Ballers were completed in Liverpool. Those of the *James Baines* were supplied by James H. Beal and Brother, and are described as being of " lavish splendour, with innumerable pilasters and mirrors."

Donald McKay gave both the *Lightning* and *James Baines* three skysails, but the two ships proved themselves so powerful that the main-skysail masts of both ships were lengthened and moonsail-yards crossed. The sails were all strengthened to stand driving by every possible means, even to diagonal roping across the cloths from earing to clew.

The Australian Black-Ballers were all painted black outside and white inside, with blue waterways. Mastheads and yards were black, lower masts white, and all stunsail-booms bright, with black ends.

Though each ship built by Donald McKay produced a chorus of praise, the *James Baines* was pronounced to be the most perfect sailing ship that had ever entered the Mersey. And when Queen Victoria inspected her at Portsmouth in 1857 she declared that she did not know her Mercantile Marine possessed such a fine ship.

Her first passage, from Boston to Liverpool, was claimed as a record, and the abstract log is therefore worth recording :

1854.
Sept. 12.—At noon parted with steamboat and pilot. Wind, S.W., light.
  ,, 13.—Lat. 42° 10′ N., long. 66° 33′ W. Distance 225 miles. Light airs and calms, increasing in the evening to brisk winds and clear weather.
  ,, 14.—Lat. 40° 18′ N., long. 62° 45′ W. Distance 238 miles. Light breezes and clear.
  ,, 15.—Lat. 42° 26′ N., long. 59° 53′ W. Distance 218 miles. Strong breezes, S.S.W.
  ,, 16.—Lat. 43° 15′ N., long. 53° 9′ W. Distance 305 miles. Strong gales from S.S.W. to N.W.
  ,, 17.—Lat. 44° 54′ N., long. 48° 48′ W. Distance 280 miles. Strong breezes from N.W. 4 a.m., passed several vessels fishing.
  ,, 18.—Lat. 45° 42′ N., long. 44° 16′ W. Distance 198 miles. Light breezes and hazy weather. 10 a.m., brisk breezes and cloudy. Wind West.

"James Baines"
Built 1854 American built Clipper Ship.

Sept. 19.—Lat. 47° 22′ N., long. 36° 42′ W.   Distance 342 miles.   Strong breezes and
     squally.
  „   20.—Lat. 48° 39′ N., long. 33° 12′ W.   Distance 200 miles.   Light breezes and
     hazy.   Variable.
  „   21.—Lat. 49° 34′ N., long. 28° 38′ W.   Distance 230 miles.   Light breezes and
     clear.   Wind S.W.
  „   22.—Lat. 50° 12′ N., long. 21° 00′ W.   Distance 291 miles.   Brisk S.S.W. winds
     and cloudy weather.   Passed several sail standing eastward.
  „   23.—Lat. 50° 37′ N., long. 13° 39′ W.   Distance 337 miles.   Strong breezes and
     cloudy weather.   Wind S.W.
  „   24.—Strong breezes and gloomy weather.   At 6 a.m. made the land, and at 8 a.m.
     passed Cork.   Distance 296 miles.   Passed Tuskar at 3 p.m., and Holyhead
     at 9 p.m.

Time, 12 days 6 hours from Boston Light to Rock Light.   As the ship raced along the Irish coast, with the wind strong, and very squally, she was timed as making 20 knots between points on several occasions.

Captain Charles McDonald, who had given up the command of the *Marco Polo* in order to take over the *James Baines*, was very much impressed by her power in hard breezes, and declared that if she had only had a fair share of wind she would have made the passage in 8 days.

On December 9th, 1854, the *James Baines* sailed from Liverpool with 700 passengers, 1,400 tons of cargo, and 350 sacks of mails for Melbourne.   Owing to the usual mail steamer being taken up by the Government for trooping to the Crimea, the mail contract to Australia was given the great Black Ball and White Star sailing ships, which agreed to accept a forfeit of so much a day for every day which they took over 65 on the passage.

The great McKay clipper actually fulfilled this severe contract on her first passage, with a day or two to spare.   The start was far from being propitious.   Light head winds so held her up that the *James Baines* was only off St. Ives Head on the seventh day out.   Then the wind came strong and fair.   Off Cape St. Vincent she again had to tack, on the tenth day out, and the N.E. trades did not favour her, for in 19° N. the wind came out of the S.S.E., set her to leeward of Cape San Roque, and she was 18 hours beating round that dreaded point. In spite of these delays she was spoken in 3° N. 28′ W., only 19 days out.   On the whole it was a light weather passage, as Captain McDonald declared that the main-skysail was only taken in three times between Liverpool and Melbourne.   Nevertheless, she made some big 24-hour runs in the " roaring forties," the best being :

1855.
Jan. 26.—Lat. 48° 02′ S., long.   50° 46′ E.   Distance 391 miles.
  „   27.—Lat. 48° 56′ S., long.   60° 46′ E.   Distance 407 miles.
Feb. 6.—Lat. 50° 09′ S., long. 123° 40′ E.   Distance 423 miles.

This magnificent run was made under main-skysail and stunsails.   Her position on the previous day, February 5th, was lat. 50° 19′ S., long. 113° E., which shows 10° 40′ difference of longitude.

Captain McDonald, in a letter to his owners, declared that he was off the Otway on the 54th day from Liverpool.   If this was the case, the ship was very unlucky to be held up for over a week within a day's sail of her port, for she did not anchor in Port Phillip till February 12th, when she was 63 days 18 hours and 15 minutes out from the Rock Light.

This record passage made a great stir in Melbourne, and many were unwilling to believe the times of the *James Baines*.   The *Argo*, which had steamed the whole way, had taken 62 days, and another steamer, the *Pacific*, which had left Plymouth 15 days before the departure of the *James Baines*, had not yet arrived, whilst the crack clipper, *Indian Queen*, which had arrived 12 days before, had been 79 days on the passage.   The *James Baines* had sailed 14,034 miles in 63½ days, averaged 221 miles a day and 9·2 miles an hour.

On March 12th, 1855, she left Melbourne for Liverpool, and made the run home in 69½ days—a truly wonderful voyage of 5 months 10 days, 27 of which were spent in port. She brought home 360 passengers and 40,000 ounces of gold.   Many of her passengers spun lurid yarns of young McDonald's sail-carrying.   They declared that when beating to windward off the Irish coast, under a heavy press of sail, McDonald tacked so close to the rocks, on three occasions, that a stone could be thrown ashore.   This daring navigation on a lee shore evidently produced something like a panic, for every passenger recognized that if the ship missed stays she was lost.   Many remonstrated angrily with the captain, but he replied calmly : " We have to make a good passage."

After such a maiden voyage, both owner and captain confidently expected further records on the part of the great clipper, but they were sadly disappointed, for she never made another passage which was in any way out of the common.   This is shown by the following abstract of her remaining voyages :

2nd Voyage, 1855–6	Left Liverpool August 5, arrived Melbourne October 23—79 days.
	Left Melbourne November 25, arrived Liverpool March 4—99 days.
3rd Voyage, 1856.	Left Liverpool April 6, arrived Melbourne June 24—79 days.
	Left Melbourne August 8, arrived Liverpool November 21—105 days.
4th Voyage, 1857.	Left Liverpool January 5, arrived Melbourne March 23—77 days.
	Left Melbourne April 26, arrived Liverpool July 12—77 days.
5th Voyage, 1857–8.	Left Portsmouth August 8, arrived Calcutta November 19—103 days.
	Left Calcutta January 1, arrived Liverpool April 12—101 days.

These records show a steady average, which was being equalled and even surpassed by many of her rivals.   It is, therefore, evident that she was either very unlucky with her winds, or else she lacked speed in light weather, as, in the " roaring forties " not even the *Lightning* could surpass her ; witness the following abstracts from her third outward passage :

May 25.—Lat. 37° 40′ S., long. 3° 28′ E. Distance 328 miles. Winds S.E. 8, S.S.E. 10, S. 11, S.S.W. 10. Begins with heavy gale and heavy squalls. At 4 p.m. double-reefed mainsail and crossjack. Midnight, similar wind and weather, heavy sea, ship labouring very heavy and shipping great quantities of water. Noon, very heavy sea, sun obscured. (Wind true and in Beaufort scale.)

May 26.—Lat. 38° 38′ S., long. 10° 0′ E. Distance 320 miles. Winds S.W. 9, 8, W.S.W. 7, 6. Begins with strong gale and heavy sea, squalls, and showers of rain, dark gloomy weather ; midnight, gale decreasing, reef out of courses and set staysails ; 4 a.m., still moderating, out all reefs, set royals and skysail ; 8 a.m., set all starboard studding sails ; noon, gentle breeze, fine clear weather. Wind westering all the time and sea going down.

May 27.—Lat. 40° 2′ S., long. 17° 41′ E. Distance 384 miles. Winds W.S.W. 6, 7, S.W. 10. Fine gentle breeze and fine clear weather, all sail set ; midnight, same wind and weather ; a.m., breeze freshening and heavy black clouds driving up from S.W. ; noon, same wind and weather.

May 28.—Lat. 42° 44′ S., long. 25° 48′ E. Distance 404 miles. Winds W.S.W. 10, 9, West 7. Begins with brisk gale and occasional heavy squalls, accompanied with heavy rain ; 4 p.m., handed small sails and double-reefed fore and mizen courses ; midnight, still increasing ; noon, as previously.

May 29.—Lat. 44° 15′ S., long. 30° S. 51′ E. Distance 240 miles. Winds West 7, 5, 3, 2. First part strong gales and fine clear weather, heavy sea, ship rolling ; midnight, less wind, sea going down, set all small sails ; 4 a.m., set all starboard studding sails ; noon, light breeze, dark gloomy weather.

May 30.—Lat. 46° 16′ S., long. 36° 56′ E. Distance 300 miles. Winds W.N.W. 3, 4, W.S.W. 5, S.S.W. 8. First part light breezes and dark gloomy weather; 8 p.m., sky clearing and wind increasing, barometer falling; midnight, fresh gales, took in royal and skysail studding sails; 8 a.m., heavy snow squall, took in topgallant studding sails; noon, fresh gales and clear weather with snow showers and squalls.

May 31.—Lat. 46° 52′ S., long. 43° 54′ E. Distance 300 miles. Winds W.N.W. 5, 6, W.S.W. 3, S.S.W. 6. First part fresh breeze and squalls; 10 p.m., ran through between Petit and Grande, Prince Edward's Islands; midnight, dark with snow squalls; noon, as midnight.

This week's work amounts to the splendid total of 2,276 miles.

In the same abstract we have the famous statement, " Ship going 21 knots, with main-skysail set." On June 17th the *James Baines* was in lat. 43° 31′ S., long. 106° 15′ E., running before a freshening S.W. gale, with squalls of sleet and snow and high sea. The entry for June 18th reads :

June 18.—Lat. 42° 47′ S., long. 115° 54′ E. Distance 420 miles. Winds W. to S.W. Breeze freshening; 8.30 p.m., in all starboard studding sails; *ship going 21 knots, with main-skysail set ;* midnight, fresh gale and fine clear night ; noon, less wind, attended with snow squalls.

Four days later, in 41° 40′ S., 134° 58′ E., the *James Baines* had a very nasty experience. Again I will quote Captain McDonald :

At 5 p.m. ship was struck with a most terrific squall, which lasted in full strength only about three minutes. The ship broached to, blew away all head sails, fore topsail, fore topgallant sail, main topmast and middle staysails, main sail, main topgallant sail, mizen lower and topmast staysails ; and carried away main topgallant mast and main yard. I never before experienced such a terrific gust of wind. The barometer gave no indication whatever of the approach of the squall.

The long homeward passage in the autumn of 1856 caused great anxiety in Liverpool. When the *James Baines* was 99 days out she was reinsured at £8 per cent., and the day before she arrived another £15 per cent. was paid. She had 174,000 ounces of gold on board, and the usual terms for specie at that time were 35s. to 40s. per cent. Light and baffling winds accounted for this long passage. In spite of two runs of 356 and 340 miles, the *James Baines* was 36 days to the Horn, and she was actually 65 days to the Equator.

On October 30th, in lat. 29° 03′ N., long. 33° 14′ W., when beating against a head wind, she was overhauled by the *Lightning*, which had left Melbourne three weeks after her, and for the next six days the two great rivals were together, striving against very light head winds. In the end the *Lightning* had the best of it, and arrived in the Mersey 24 hours before the overdue *James Baines*.

In 1857 the *James Baines*, together with the *Lightning, Champion of the Seas*, and many another famous clipper, was taken up by the Government to load troops for India, owing to the outbreak of the Mutiny.

The *James Baines* took the 97th Regiment on board at Portsmouth, and before sailing was visited by Queen Victoria and Prince Albert. As showing the terrible anxiety which weighed upon the Queen, the following anecdote is worth recording. Before leaving the ship she took Captain McDonald on one side, and privately offered him £100 a day for every day that he saved on his contract time. The *Champion of the Seas* sailed a day or two before the *James Baines*. On August 17th both ships were spoken by the homeward-bound *Oneida*, surging along under a cloud of canvas—the *James Baines*, with 34 sails set, including three skysails, sky-stunsails, and moonsail, and her rail red with the jackets of the cheering troops.

The two ships arrived off the pilot brig together, but neither was built for such light weather passages, and their times were therefore disappointing.

The *James Baines* loaded a cargo in Calcutta, consisting of 2,200 bales of jute, 6,213 bales of linseed, 6,682 bags of rice, and 40 bales of cowhides. She docked in Liverpool on a Sunday, and discharging began on the next day. But when the stevedores removed the lower hatches on Thursday, April 22nd, volumes of smoke poured from the afterpart of the main hold. Though eight fire-engines were soon playing upon the burning ship, they made no headway, and, as a last resort, the *James Baines* was scuttled. At first this had a delaying effect on the fire, for there was plenty of water in the Huskisson Dock, but as the tide ebbed the ship grounded, and the fire gained so rapidly that the vessel was soon alight from end to end. About 11 a.m. the main and mizen masts fell, crushing the roofs of the dock sheds ; they were followed at 3.15 p.m. by the foremast, and by 6 p.m. the ship was burnt to the water's edge.

This sudden end of the mighty *James Baines* not only stunned Liverpool, but was spoken of as a national disaster. The hull was auctioned, and sold to a Mr. Pace for £1,080, the value of the ship and her cargo being estimated at £170,000 on her arrival from Calcutta. A use was found for the hull, and thousands of people have boarded the *James Baines* without knowing it, for the old Liverpool landing-stage rested upon the remains of the great Black-Baller.

Captain McDonald did not long survive his ship. He retired broken-hearted to the cottage of his widowed mother at Glengarriff. Then, when suffering from a bad cold, he went out in a bitter N.E. gale to help in the salvage of a brig which had gone ashore ; came home, after a long day, worn out and wet through, contracted pneumonia, and died a few days later. The mother survived her son for many years, her two most valued possessions being a saucy Australian magpie, which had been brought home by the captain, and a huge painting of the *James Baines*, which had been presented to her son by the Black Ball Line.

THE "LIGHTNING."

THE clipper ship *Lightning* was undoubtedly one of the most remarkable wooden vessels ever built. Her designer and builder, Donald McKay, of East Boston, is now recognized as the greatest shipbuilder that the United States ever had; indeed, many Americans claim that he was a genius, who stood head and shoulders above every other naval architect of his day. Certainly he never made a failure, unless that untried leviathan, the *Great Republic*, can be counted as a failure. Every one of his ships had her own peculiar characteristics, but they resembled each other in one great quality, which was tremendous speed in hard winds. And if her performances may speak for her, the *Lightning* possessed this quality to a greater degree than any other ship, either before or since. Twice she made 24-hour runs at an average of 18 knots, the day's work being on these occasions 436 and 430 miles.

And here are a few extracts from the log of her second outward passage to show her speed through the water when she had sufficient wind :

February 9th, 1855.—" Going 14 knots upon a bowline with the yards braced sharp up."

February 20th, 1855.—" Going 15 knots with royals set, yards slightly checked."

February 21st, 1855.—" Going 15 and occasionally 16 knots with main skysail and fore-topmast stunsail set, the yards slightly checked."

February 27th, 1855.—" Fresh gale with heavy squalls and occasional showers of hail and snow, the sea running high. During six hours in the morning the ship logged 18 knots with royals, main skysail and topgallant studding sails set."

March 11th, 1855.—" Fresh gale. Ship going 17 knots with single-reefed topsails, foresail, trysail and fore-topmast staysail, wind abeam."

When making this speed we must remember to note that the *Lightning* was carrying emigrants and not a heavy dead-weight cargo; thus she could not have been in better trim for making big runs. The *Lightning* was the first of four very famous emigrant ships, designed and built by Donald McKay to the order of that remarkable shipping personality James Baines, the founder of the Liverpool Black Ball Line of Australian packets.

It is a curious fact that there were two well-known lines of passenger ships flying the red flag with the black ball in the centre—both of which sailed out of Liverpool. The senior line was the New York packet-ship line, belonging to Marshall & Co., which was founded as far back as 1816. This line was entirely American, and was at the very height of its prosperity when that energetic son of an old wife, who kept a cake and sweet shop in Upper Duke Street, Liverpool, started the equally famous Australian Black Ball Line.

How James Baines came to appropriate the name and house flag of the American packet-ship line I have never been able to find out. There is generally an interesting story attaching to the choice of a house flag and this case of the two black balls holds a mystery which may possibly be known to some old retired skipper or shipping clerk in Liverpool ; but the story, so far as I know, has never found its way into print.

To return to the *Lightning*, she was built at Donald McKay's yard in East Boston during the winter of 1853–4, and cost £30,000, without her internal decoration, which was carried out in Liverpool at a further cost of £2,000.

Her most important measurements were as follows : Tonnage—builder's, 2,096 tons, registered, 1,468 tons ; length 244 feet, beam 44 feet, depth 23 feet ; her poop was 92 feet long and her main saloon 86 feet long, the height between decks under the beams being 8 feet, a very liberal allowance for those days.

As regards her spars, when she came from the builder's hands, her masts from deck to truck measured as follows : Main 164 feet, fore 151 feet, mizen 115 feet. Her mainyard was 95 feet long, and her lower stunsail-booms 65 feet. Her sail plan was considerably increased after her first voyage. Donald McKay gave her 13,000 yards of canvas, without flying kites. To this James Baines added a moonsail over the skysail at the main, besides a host of ringtails and watersails. Altogether, when under all plain sail, without her stunsails, she set 30 sails, a veritable cloud of canvas.

The most remarkable point about her design was her concave bow lines ; she was, in fact, almost as sharp forward as a modern destroyer, and from her stem to her fore-rigging along her water-line she had a concavity of 16 feet. She was probably the most extreme example of what were called " hollow lines." This innovation in design was not the invention of Donald McKay, but of a man named John W. Griffiths, a draughtsman in the drawing-office of the New York shipbuilders, Smith & Dimon.

This man designed the *Rainbow*, the first true American clipper ship, in 1844, and in spite of the most pessimistic prophecies from his fellow-craftsmen, gave the *Rainbow* a hollow bow. The *Rainbow* at once proved a success, and hollow lines became the rage, though her success was really due to other improvements in shipbuilding, invented by Griffiths, rather than to the hollow lines, which for a sailing ship are undoubtedly all wrong. Yet Donald McKay was very angry when in 1855 Captain Anthony Enright persuaded James Baines to have the *Lightning's* hollow bow filled in. He wrote sarcastically about the " wood butchers of Liverpool," and when on her third voyage to Australia the ship washed away her false bow in the " roaring forties," he could hardly withhold his glee.

James Baines sent his senior captain, the notorious Bully Forbes, across the Atlantic to take command of the new clipper. Forbes, with the aid and advice of Captain Lauchlan McKay, the brother of the designer, raced the *Lightning* across to Liverpool in 13 days 19½ hours.

The most remarkable part of this passage was the record run made on March 1st. Forbes's log records it as follows :

" Wind south. Strong gales, bore away for the North Channel ; carried away the fore-topsail and lost jib ; hove the log several times and found the ship going through the water at the rate of 18 to 18½ knots ; lee rail under water and rigging slack. Distance 436 miles."

At noon on February 28th the *Lightning* was in lat. 52° 30′ N., long. 13° 50′ W., but owing to the fact that she had made her landfall, no position is given for noon on March 1st, thus some modern critics have doubted this run, though no single voice was raised against it at the time.

With Bully Forbes in command, and the almost equally famous Bully Bragg as first officer, the *Lightning* left Liverpool on May 14th for Melbourne. But with a light weather

"*Lightning*"

Built 1854. American built Clipper Ship.

passage, during which her topgallant yards were never lowered, the new clipper had no chance to break records, her best run being 348 miles and her time 77 days.

At 4 p.m. on August 20th, 1854, she dropped her tug off the Heads, homeward bound, and raced for the Horn with Forbes carrying on in the most desperate manner. During the night of August 28th the fore-topmast went over the side in a violent squall, when the ship was under all plain sail to a fore-topmast stunsail. The log records that the stunsail blew away, breaking the boom, whilst the fore-royal, topgallant sail and topsail were all blown out of the bolt ropes. For the next four days Forbes had to restrain his impatience and keep his ship under small canvas until a new fore-topmast could be sent up. Yet in spite of this delay the *Lightning* was only 19 days 1 hour from the Heads to the Horn, a record for that traverse which still stands.

The run to the Line was not favoured by the wind, nor were things much better in the North Atlantic; nevertheless, the *Lightning* was off the Old Head of Kinsale at 4 p.m. on October 22nd, and anchored in the Mersey at 9.30 a.m. on October 23rd, her actual time being 64 days 3 hours 10 minutes. As this is another sailing record which has never yet been broken, I will give the times between points:

Port Phillip Heads to Cape Horn, August 20th to September 8th	..	19 days.
Cape Horn to Equator, September 8th to September 30th ..	..	22 ,,
Equator to Azores, September 30th to October 12th	..	12 ,,
Azores to Liverpool, October 12th to October 23rd	..	11 ,,

On his arrival in Liverpool Bully Forbes found that James Baines had a new ship for him, and the command of the *Lightning* was handed over to Anthony Enright, who had just made a reputation for sail-carrying and quick passages in the Liverpool tea clipper *Chrysolite*. Enright, as a matter of fact, had the choice of either the *Lightning* or her great White Star rival, the *Red Jacket*, and he chose the *Lightning*, though he insisted on the almost unheard-of salary for a Liverpool shipmaster of £1,000 a year.

Under Enright the *Lightning* became a very favourite ship with passengers. Forbes, indeed, scared his passengers to death with his desperate carrying of sail, and he was also a skipper who did not worry much about their comfort. Enright, on the other hand, though he also carried sail hard, had some caution in his disposition, and was really the better seaman of the two; added to this he was extraordinarily tactful and clever with his passengers, and went to endless trouble in order to keep them amused, so that the usual testimonials were showered upon him.

He had the famous clipper for four voyages, from January, 1855, to August, 1857, her passages being:

Liverpool to Melbourne	..	73, 81, 68 and 69 days.
Melbourne to Liverpool	..	79, 86, 84 and 82 ,,

During this time the *Lightning's* best week's run was as follows:

1856.	Lat.	Long.	Distance.
June 28th.	44.25 S.	42.58 E.	232 miles.
,, 29th.	43.36	50.07	312 ,,
,, 30th.	44.02	56.35	281 ,,
July 1st.	44.39	63.27	298 ,,
,, 2nd.	45.07	70.55	319 ,,
,, 3rd.	45.07	79.55	382 ,,
,, 4th.	45.07	88.30	364 ,,
		Total	2,188 miles.

This, to the best of my belief, is the biggest 7-day run in her whole career.

Her best 48-hour run was made in March, 1857, and it called forth the following letter from Captain Enright to his passengers :

" 21st March, 1857.

" Ladies and Gentlemen,—I cannot help informing you of the extraordinary run we have made during the last 48 hours—or rather, allowing for change of time, 46 hours 48 minutes.   During this time we have run, by thoroughly good and trustworthy observation, no less than 790 knots, or 920 statute miles, being an average of nearly 17 knots, or more than 19½ statute miles per hour.   Yesterday our noble ship made no less than 430 knots, amounting to an average during the 24 (23½) hours of more than 18 knots.   Our change of longitude has amounted to 18 degrees, each degree being equal to 44 miles.

" I firmly believe this to be the greatest performance a sailing ship has ever accomplished.   I hope this information will in some degree compensate you for the inconvenience which the heavy weather has occasioned you."

These wonderful speeds were, of course, made in hard, favourable winds.   If the *Lightning* had only been as fast as the *Thermopylæ* or *Cutty Sark* in light and moderate winds, all her passages would have been a week to 10 days better than they were ; but, like all vessels with hollow lines, she had no speed until it was blowing fresh, nor was she as weatherly as the little tea clippers.

On account of the illness of his wife, Captain Enright was obliged to give up his command in August, 1857.   He was succeeded by Captain Byrne.   Owing to the Indian Mutiny, the *Lightning*, together with the *James Baines* and the *Champion of the Seas*, was taken up as a trooper by the Government.   On August 24th, the day before she sailed from the Thames, a dinner was given on board to her old commander, at which Benjamin Disraeli paid his tribute to Anthony Enright, as one of the most respected master mariners under the Red Ensign.

Captain Byrne took the *Lightning* out to the Sandheads in 87 days ; though he beat the times of the *James Baines* and the *Champion of the Seas* by nearly a fortnight, this light weather sailing was not that for which the *Lightning* was designed, and Byrne must have been glad to get her back to the Melbourne run.

For the next 12 years the old ship ran steadily between Liverpool and the Colonies. But we do not hear of any very wonderful performances ; no doubt she was getting strained and water-soaked.   During most of this time she was commanded by Captain Tom Robertson, the marine painter.

On October 31st, 1869, Captain Henry Jones being in command, she had just finished loading wool at Geelong, and was preparing to haul off from the wharf, when smoke and flames suddenly burst forth from the forehold.   Though every effort was made to put out the fire, in which the crews of the *Argo*, *Aboukir* and *Lanarkshire*, the town fire-engines and the ship's force-pump all played their part, the famous old ship was soon in flames.

The *Lightning* was then towed away from the wharf, and anchored two cable-lengths away, and, whilst a party of carpenters were trying to scuttle her, stevedores were breaking out the wool in the 'tween-decks and the crew were saving what they could of furniture, stores, sails, boats and gear.   These men were presently driven over the side by the fall of the foremast and the main topmast.

An attempt was next made to sink her by firing two small cannon from the wharf. This was in vain.   Finally, Captain Jones and a number of ship's carpenters succeeded in scuttling her, and she sank at her anchors in 24 feet of water.   Thus ended the *Lightning*, one of the most wonderful ships in the whole history of sail.

THE "FLYING CLOUD."

OF all the famous American clipper ships which were launched from New York, Boston and other Down East yards between 1850 and 1860, the *Flying Cloud* had by far the best record. In strong whole sail winds she could not be beaten, though like all McKay's designs she was not a fast ship in light airs. Unfortunately, like all soft wood clippers, she soon became strained and water-soaked, and she was only at her best for about five years, after which her passages lengthened and she dropped out of the first flight.

The *Flying Cloud* was designed and built by Donald McKay of Boston to the order of Enoch Train, the owner of the White Diamond packets; but, to his lasting regret, Train sold her whilst on the stocks to Grinnell, Minturn & Co., of the Swallow Tail Line, for their New York–San Francisco service.

Flying Cloud registered 1,783 tons, and her chief measurements were as follows :— Length on keel, 208 feet; length on deck, 225 feet; length overall, 235 feet; extreme beam, 40 feet 8 inches; depth of hold, 21 feet 6 inches; height between decks, 7 feet 8 inches; dead rise at half floor, 20 inches; rounding of sides, 6 inches; sheer, about 3 feet. With regard to her deck plan, she had a full poop, on the level of the main rail, 5 feet above the main-deck. This poop was 68 feet long; beneath it there was ample cabin accommodation, which, in the language of that day, was described as " most elegant and tastefully wainscoted with satinwood, mahogany and rosewood, set off by gilded pilasters, etc."

Besides a topgallant fo'c'sle, 30 feet long, the *Flying Cloud* had the usual midship-house, which was 41 feet long and 18 feet wide. Her figure-head was a finely carved angel blowing a trumpet—Donald McKay was as celebrated for his artistic figure-heads as for his superb models, and *Flying Cloud's* was always greatly admired.

The famous clipper had the well-known McKay bow and stern with small overhangs, the curve of the cutwater being very slight, whilst the stern was elliptical in shape and the taffrail was only just behind the rudder post.

The sail plan of the *Flying Cloud* had height rather than breadth, which in those days was usually gained by long stunsail-booms. The following measurements give one an idea of her sail spread :

Mainmast, step to truck, 200 feet; main lower mast, 88 feet; rake of masts, $1\frac{1}{4}$ inches to the foot; bowsprit and jib-boom outboard, 58 feet; mainyard, 82 feet. She crossed three skysail yards with every imaginable flying kite, from watersails under her swinging booms to royal stunsails. Her single topsails had four bands of reef points and her topgallant sails were also fitted with a reef-band.

The command of the new flyer was given to Captain Joe Cressy of Marblehead, who had made his reputation with the *Oneida* in the East India trade.

On June 3rd, 1851, the *Flying Cloud* sailed from New York for San Francisco on her record-breaking maiden passage. From the first it was a case of " what she can't carry, she must drag," and the following extracts from Cressy's log speak plainly of his desperate sail-carrying :

June   6.—Lost main-topsail yard, and main and mizen topgallant masts.
  „   7.—Sent up topgallant masts and yards.
  „   8.—Sent up main-topsail yard, and set all possible sail.
  „   14.—Discovered mainmast badly sprung about a foot from the hounds and fished it.
  „   15–18—Doldrum weather.
  „   24.—Crossed the Equator, 21 days out.
July   11.—Very severe thunder and lightning. Double-reefed topsails. Latter part, blowing a hard
             gale, close-reefed topsails, split fore and main-topmast staysails.
             At 1 p.m. discovered mainmast had sprung. Sent down royal and topgallant yards and
             studding sail booms off lower and topsail yards to relieve the mast.
             Heavy sea running and shipping large quantities of water over lee rail.
  „   12.—Heavy South-West gales and sea. Distance 40 miles.
  „   13.—Let men out of irons in consequence of wanting their services, with the understanding that
             they would be taken care of on arriving at San Francisco.

        (These men had been put in irons soon after crossing the Line. The usual belaying
pin and knuckle-duster warfare had been going on between officers and men.)

             At 6 p.m. carried away main-topsail tye and truss band round mainmast. Single-reefed
             topsails.
July   19.—Crossed latitude 50° South.
  „   20.—At 4 a.m. close-reefed topsails and furled courses. Hard gale with thick weather and snow.
  „   23.—Passed through the Straits of Le Maire. At 8 a.m. Cape Horn North 5 miles distant, the
             whole coast covered with snow
  „   26.—Crossed latitude 50° South in the Pacific, 7 days from same latitude in Atlantic. (This was
             a record passage of the Horn.)
  „   31.—Fresh breezes and fine weather. All sail set. At 2 p.m. wind South-East. At 6 p.m.
             squally ; in lower and topgallant studding sails ; 7 p.m. in royals, 2 a.m. in fore topmast
             studding sail. Latter part, strong gales and high sea running, ship very wet fore and
             aft. Distance run this day by observation 374 miles. During the squalls 18 knots of
             line were not sufficient to measure the rate of speed. Topgallant sails set.
Aug.   1.—Strong gales and squally. At 6 p.m. in topgallant sails, double-reefed fore and mizen
             topsails. Heavy sea running. At 4 a.m. made sail again. Distance 334 miles.
  „   3.—Suspended first officer from duty, in consequence of his arrogating to himself the privilege
             of cutting up rigging contrary to my orders, and long-continued neglect of duty.
  „   25.—Spoke barque *Amelia Pacquet*, 180 days out from London, bound to San Francisco.
  „   29.—Lost fore-topgallant mast.
  „   30.—Sent up fore-topgallant mast. Night strong and squally. 6 a.m. made South Farallones
             bearing North-East half East. 7 a.m. took a pilot. Anchored in San Francisco Harbour
             at 11.30 a.m. after a passage of 89 days 21 hours.

             Sandy Hook to Equator   ..   ..   21 days.
             Equator to 50° South   ..   ..   25 „
             50° S. Atlantic to 50° S. Pacific   ..   7 „
             50° S. Pacific to Equator ..   ..   17 „
             Equator to San Francisco   ..   ..   19 „
             Distance Run   ..   ..   ..   17,597 statute miles.
             Daily Average..   ..   ..   ..   222 statute miles.

        The arrival of the *Flying Cloud* aroused a stir of enthusiasm in San Francisco. Crowds of people came off to see the new wonder. Old seamen pointed significantly to the state of her rigging with its extra seizings, rackings and stopper knots, to the fishings on her spars, and to the crushed and broken topmast fids and chain frappings round the mast doublings. All these scars of victory bore testimony to desperate sail-carrying. Captain Cressy was fêted right and left, but he found time to discharge his unsatisfactory mate, who immediately got in touch with a " shyster " lawyer with a view to making trouble, but dropped his proceedings on hearing a false report of the captain's death.

        The *Flying Cloud*, like most of the Californian clippers in those early days of San Francisco, had to cross the Pacific to China in order to get a cargo home. On her first day

"Flying Cloud"
Built 1851 American built Clipper Ship

out on this passage she proved that her record run was no fluke, for she covered 374 miles in the 24 hours under skysails and stunsails. And she was only 12 days from the Pacific Coast to Honolulu.

Tea was loaded at Macao, from which place sail was made on January 6th, 1852. Although she had a favourable monsoon and made a very quick run down the China sea, the *Flying Cloud* was not well suited by the light winds of the East, and the beautiful *N. B. Palmer*, sailing 3 days after her, beat her home by 10 days, the *Flying Cloud's* time being 96 days.

On her second voyage round the Horn, the Swallow Tail clipper had a chance to wipe out her defeat by the *N. B. Palmer*.

Leaving New York in May, *Flying Cloud* had very light winds down the Atlantic, and took 30 days to the Line. The *N. B. Palmer*, sailing 8 days behind the *Flying Cloud*, came along with strong winds. When off the coast of Brazil, in a very light wind, the *Flying Cloud* gradually overhauled a vessel which was lying becalmed ahead. To his amazement Cressy recognized the *N. B. Palmer*. The *Flying Cloud* crept up until the two ships were within hail of each other, then she too lost the wind, and from noon until 4 p.m. the two clippers lay side by side without steerage way. At last a ripple on the water ahead warned them to prepare for a southerly breeze. In came all stunsails as quick as the men could work— Cressy had a splendid crew, but Low was having trouble with his ; however, both ships stood away, close-hauled on the starboard tack, and with the wind steady and freshening, it was a fine test.

Slowly but surely, the *Flying Cloud* fore-reached and weathered on the *N. B. Palmer* amidst intense excitement, and by the following morning the light weather flyer was hull down to leeward. Both ships experienced a rough time off the Horn, and the *Flying Cloud* was 113 days out when she reached San Francisco. The *N. B. Palmer* did not arrive until three weeks later. Captain Low had to put into Valparaiso on account of his refractory crew. Here he was delayed nearly a week by the difficulty of replacing those who were landed in irons and others who deserted. This voyage the *Flying Cloud* again loaded Canton tea and, sailing for home on December 1st, made the same time of 96 days from China to New York.

On her third outward passage the *Flying Cloud* made San Francisco in 106 days, after an exciting race with the 1,400-ton clipper *Hornet*, built by Jacob Westervelt in 1851. The two ships left New York on the same day and both arrived in San Francisco Bay on August 12th.

Both clippers made good runs to the Line, which was crossed by the *Flying Cloud* on the 17th day out and by the *Hornet* on her 18th day out. In the S.E. trades the *Hornet* had the best of it, crossing 50° S. in the Atlantic 3 days ahead of *Flying Cloud*, but in the winter gales off the Horn, Cressy, with the more powerful ship, got round the corner in 9 days against the *Hornet's* 14, and crossed 50° S. in the Pacific two days ahead of his rival. However, the smaller ship made up the two days in the run up the Pacific, and so honours were even. The skipper of the *Hornet* was justly proud of himself, but Joe Cressy complained of want of wind.

On his next Cape Horn passage, in 1854, Cressy got the wind he wanted, with the result that the *Flying Cloud* came within two hours of her record maiden passage. She sailed from New York 8 days behind the new clipper ship *Archer*, 1,098 tons, which was on her maiden voyage.

Both skippers followed the tracks laid down in Maury's Wind and Current Charts, and *Flying Cloud* came up with the *Archer* off the Horn.

As the Cape Horn weather happened to be taking a breather, Cressy, after giving Thomas of the *Archer* the latest New York news, invited him to come aboard and dine ; but it is not wise to go ship-visiting in the neighbourhood of Cape Stiff, and Thomas reported that he was reluctantly compelled to decline.

The following table shows the way in which the *Flying Cloud* overhauled and out-distanced the *Archer* :

	Archer.			*Flying Cloud*.		
	Date. 1854.			Date. 1854.		
Left New York	Jan. 13			Jan. 21		
Crossed Equator ..	Feb. 2	20 days out		Feb. 7	17 days out	
Passed Cape San Roque	Feb. 5	23	,,	Feb. 10	20	,,
Passed 50° S. (Atlantic)	Mar. 4	50	,,	Mar. 4	42	,,
Passed 50° S. (Pacific) ..	Mar. 18	64	,,	Mar. 16	54	,,
Crossed Equator.. ..	Apr. 7	84	,,	Apr. 5	74	,,
Arrived San Francisco ..	Apr. 29	106	,,	Apr. 20	89	,,

Once more the passage of the *Flying Cloud* filled the San Francisco papers with enthusiasm, and Captain Cressy was again lavishly entertained.

On her homeward passage from China this voyage, the famous ship was very nearly lost. On August 7th, in foggy weather, the *Flying Cloud* ran with such force upon a coral reef that her bow was lifted 3 or 4 feet.   Cressy managed to back his ship off into deep water, but she was leaking badly, and it was found afterwards that the sharp coral had stripped off the shoe and cut right through her keel.   Nevertheless the indomitable Cressy, refusing to put into the expensive Eastern ports for repairs, managed to bring her home to New York, thus saving the underwriters some 30,000 dollars.   For this service he was banqueted at the Astor House and presented by the Board of Underwriters with some valuable plate.

On her fifth voyage the *Flying Cloud* reached San Francisco on June 6th, 1855, 108 days out from New York.   For five passages between New York and San Francisco *Flying Cloud*'s average was 101 days 7 hours, a record which has never been broken.

On the passage home this year, whilst the *Flying Cloud* was running 12 knots off the coast of Madagascar, a man fell overboard.   The captain's wife was the only person to see the accident ; as the man was swept astern she saw him through her cabin window.   Rushing on deck, she threw over a life-buoy and gave the alarm.   The ship was hove to and a boat lowered.   After a long row it returned without finding the man.   Whereupon Cressy, with characteristic determination, sent out two boats with orders to keep searching until dark. About four hours later the man was picked up some two miles from the ship, when at his last gasp.   Mrs. Cressy had him taken down to her cabin and nursed him back to health.

Her sixth was *Flying Cloud*'s last passage to San Francisco.   Captain Cressy, who was badly in need of a rest, handed over the command to Captain Reynard.

New York was left on March 13th, 1856, the Line was crossed on the 19th day out, and the ship was off Rio on the 31st day.   There is no doubt that Captain Reynard meant to uphold the ship's reputation, for she was credited with a 24-hour run of 402 miles, but by the time that she reached 40° S. the famous clipper had sprung her bowsprit, and was in such a shaky condition alow and aloft, that Captain Reynard reluctantly put back to Rio, where he arrived on May 10th.   It took six weeks to repair the *Flying Cloud*, and she did not reach San Francisco until September 14th, being then 82 days from Rio.   The year 1856 was one of great trade depression in the United States, and the *Flying Cloud* was laid up until January, 1857.   Then Captain Cressy once more took over the command, and made the run home to New York in 91 days.

The depression, however, still continued, and after the famous ship had been laid up for two and a half years at New York, Messrs. Grinnell, Minturn & Co. sold her.

Her new owners sent her across to London under Captain Winsor, who made the passage from Sandy Hook to Deal in 17 days. This was in December, 1859. The *Flying Cloud's* next voyage was from London to China and back.

On the outward passage, she arrived at Hong Kong on May 21st, 1860, 97 days from the Downs. Tea was loaded at Foochow, and the run home to the Thames, leaving the Min River on August 6th, was made in 123 days. On February 28th, 1861, *Flying Cloud* left again, for Melbourne this time, where she arrived on the 85th day out.

From Melbourne she crossed to Hong Kong in the average time of 67 days. Here the great American clipper was offered for sale, but she was finally chartered to bring troops home. Leaving Hong Kong on December 29th, 1861, she made a quick run to Anjer before the N.E. monsoon, being only 9 days down the China Sea. After making over a week's stay at St. Helena, *Flying Cloud* arrived in the Thames on April 20th, 1862, 112 days out.

She was now again in the sale list, but this time she was bought by James Baines, of Liverpool, who put her into the Queensland emigrant trade, along with such ships as *Young Australia*, *Royal Dane*, and *Sunda*.

In 1870, under Captain Owen, the *Flying Cloud* went from Liverpool to Hervey's Bay with 385 emigrants in 87 days, a fine performance for a strained and water-soaked soft wood clipper. On another occasion, in a four days' run round the Australian coast to Moreton Bay, she averaged just under 16 knots, though she was beaten by the *Sunda* by 18 miles.

In the early 'seventies the old ship was sold by the Black Ball Line, and her new owner put her into the North Atlantic timber trade, where most wooden ships ended their lives.

In 1874 the *Flying Cloud* got ashore on the New Brunswick coast. After bumping there for some time she was at length refloated and taken to St. John to be repaired. Whilst she was on the slip for this purpose a fire broke out aboard, and though it was got under, she was so damaged that it was decided to break her up for the sake of her metal.

Her old captain lived in retirement at his home in Salem until 1861, when he received a commission in the United States Navy on the outbreak of the North and South war. He first commanded the clipper ship *Ino*, with a crew of 80 men. On his second cruise in this ship, he sailed her across from New York to Cadiz in 12 days. This was in 1862. He left the *Ino* to take over his old adversary, the *Archer*, in which he made two China voyages. The famous shipmaster was only 57 when he died at Salem in 1871. Though in their latter years the record-breaking *Flying Cloud* and her captain were forgotten by their contemporaries, they have since been given their proper place in the history of the world's Mercantile Marine.

THE " SOVEREIGN OF THE SEAS."

PROGRESS in naval architecture has always proceeded in waves, each one of which has flung itself a little further up the steep shore of knowledge. These waves can always be traced, each in its turn, to the master-mind of some bold pioneer who was not afraid to brave the inborn conservatism of this short-sighted world with something new in the way of ship form. Within the last hundred years a number of these master-minds stand out a head and shoulders above their fellows; the first was Captain Sir William Symonds, R.N., who produced his *Symondites* between the years 1830 and 1850; then came Hall of the Aberdeen clipper, and Robert Steele of the Clyde tea clipper.

On the other side of the Atlantic one name stands pre-eminent amongst the many designers and builders of the famous American clipper, the name of Donald McKay. The boom in American clippers only lasted for a very short time—a bare ten years, from about 1848 to 1858. The first of these clippers, such as the *Rainbow* and *Sea Witch*, were small vessels of well under 1,000 tons. It was McKay who first began building bigger ships, and he launched the *Sovereign of the Seas* in June, 1852, in the face of the opinion of all the experts, who declared that she was much too big to fill her hold without so considerable a delay that all profits would be swallowed up by the lost time. But Donald McKay was a firm believer in big ships, and he actually built the *Sovereign of the Seas* " on spec." The choice of name shows what he thought of his new clipper; for he not only intended her to be the largest merchant ship in the world, but also the fastest.

No trouble was spared, to the smallest detail. Donald McKay, with his hawk-like eye, was continually hovering round his carpenters and shipwrights whilst the vessel was on the stocks; and directly she left the ways his younger brother, Captain Lauchlan McKay, took charge, and overlooked the riggers and sailmakers.

Her spar plan went a size larger than that of any previous American clipper. Her working suit of sails, without stunsails or flying kites, totalled 12,000 running yards of canvas. Her lower masts, from deck to cap, were :—foremast, 89 feet; mainmast, 93 feet; mizen-mast, 82 feet. These are tremendous sticks, and her yards were also very square for that date, her main-yard measuring 90 feet, her foreyard 80 feet, her cross-jack yard 70 feet; main topsail yard 70 feet, fore topsail yard 63 feet, and mizen topsail yard 56 feet. Her burthen, by American register, was 2,421 tons; length of keel, 245 feet; length between perpendiculars, 258 feet; length overall, 265 feet; breadth, 44 feet; depth of hold, 23 feet.

She was so sharp in her ends that she could not load 3,000 tons of cargo. She loaded in New York for San Francisco, and received 84,000 dollars in freight, sailing on August 4th, 1852, under the flag of Grinnell & Minturn's Swallow Tail Line. Captain Lauchlan McKay signed on a crew of 105 men and boys, consisting of 4 mates, 2 bos'ns, 2 carpenters, 2 sailmakers, 3 stewards, 2 cooks, 80 A.Bs., and 10 boys.

It was a bad time of year for the run down the Atlantic, but the new clipper did remarkably well, crossing the Equator in 25 days, and 50° South Latitude on the 48th day. Her time of 9 days between 50° S. and 50° S. was also very good for that difficult passage round the Horn from the eastward.

No doubt the *Sovereign of the Seas* was severely tested, for, shortly after a northerly course had been set, her fore and main topmasts went by the board and her foreyard was badly sprung. Such a dismasting would have induced the majority of skippers to put into a Chilean port, but Captain McKay at once started to refit his ship at sea. This operation took 14 days, during which time the vessel's large crew were tested to the utmost of their endurance, whilst it is related that the hard-driving captain never left the deck, taking what little sleep he allowed himself in a deck-chair. It must have been a magnificent piece of old-time seamanship, and when the *Sovereign of the Seas* sailed in through the Golden Gate, on the 103rd day out, Captain McKay was congratulated on what was considered to be a record passage for that season of the year.

In 1852 there was very little outward cargo to be obtained at San Francisco, and most of the clippers went across the Pacific in ballast, in order to load Canton tea home. The *Sovereign of the Seas* was, however, much too big for the tea trade, and Captain Lauchlan McKay had to look elsewhere for his homeward freight.

It so happened that just about this date the American South Sea whalers had begun the custom of landing their oil at Honolulu, so as to provide room in their holds for a cruise to the new Japan grounds, or a further try in the warm waters of the Line Islands. Fast ships were thus wanted to convey these landed barrels of sperm oil to the markets of Boston and New York, and this demand just suited the *Sovereign of the Seas*, which rushed across to Honolulu in ballast, and soon was homeward bound with a cargo which, being liquid, favoured a quick passage.

McKay's models were at their best in strong, quartering winds, and the *Sovereign of the Seas* astonished her crew by logging 19 knots whilst running for the Horn in the South Pacific. In 10 days she covered 3,144 miles; some of her 24-hour runs being :— March 11th, 332 miles; March 12th, 312 miles; March 16th, 396 miles; March 17th, 311 miles; March 18th, 411 miles; March 19th, 360 miles.

After rounding the Horn she had average weather in the Atlantic, and, in spite of being handicapped somewhat by a weak crew (most of her men had run in San Francisco), and by doubtful spars (her fore-topmast was badly sprung), she arrived at New York on May 6th, 1853, having made a record passage from Honolulu of 82 days.

The *Sovereign of the Seas* arrived to find Liverpool calling across the Atlantic to the American and Canadian builders for every big ship they could produce, this tonnage being required for the booming Australian emigrant trade. For such a trade the *Sovereign of the Seas* was just suited, and she crossed the Atlantic with her designer on board. The Liverpool shipowners, such as James Beazley, James Baines, Wilson, and others, wanted big ships and cheap ships, but also strongly built and fast-sailing clippers, and all these qualities Donald McKay had no doubt about being able to supply. Whilst crossing the Atlantic on the *Sovereign of the Seas* he spent most of his time on deck watching the behaviour of the vessel, and his vigil, without a doubt, gave him the ideas which he afterwards reproduced in such masterpieces of wooden shipbuilding as the *Lightning*, *James Baines*, and *Donald Mackay*.

The passage of the *Sovereign of the Seas* began very unfavourably. She passed Sandy Hook at 6.30 p.m. on June 18th, sighted Cape Race at 6 a.m. on June 24th, and two days later, when 8 days out, lay becalmed on the Banks. The wind at last came away strong

"Sovereign of the Seas"
Built 1852 American built Clipper Ship.

on the 27th, and by noon on the 28th the *Sovereign of the Seas*, close-hauled under single-reefed topsails, had run 344 miles. On the 30th the big clipper made a run of 340 miles under all sail to skysails and royal stunsails. That morning at 6 a.m. she was off Cape Clear, and two days later, at 10.30 p.m., she anchored in the Mersey.

The passage from New York to Liverpool, from dock to anchorage, was reckoned at 13 days 22 hours 50 minutes, but where she broke the record was from the Banks of Newfoundland, for she was only 5 days 17 hours from the time that she got the wind on the Banks to the Mersey. This was looked upon as the finest performance ever accomplished by a sailing ship in crossing the Atlantic, and the *Sovereign of the Seas* was immediately chartered by the Black Ball Line.

Captain Lauchlan McKay returned to Boston with his brother, and his place was taken by Captain Warner, who had been in the *Sovereign of the Seas* since her launch.

The new Black Ball Liner loaded a cargo valued at £200,000, and with 25 first cabin and 40 second cabin passengers sailed from Liverpool for Melbourne on September 7th, 1853. The run out to Melbourne was made in 77 days, which Captain Warner considered very disappointing. In his report he complained bitterly of light and contrary winds, declaring that he carried his skysails for 65 days out of the 77. The ship was certainly badly served, for she took 31 days to the Equator, and found no strength in the " roaring forties."

Captain Warner went to 53° 30' South, and wrote :—" I think if I had gone to 58° S. I would have had wind enough, but the crew were insufficiently clothed and about one-half disabled, together with the 1st mate."

Unfortunately there was nothing worthy of sailing against the *Sovereign of the Seas* amongst the August and September ships. She beat the little iron clipper *Gauntlet*, of 693 tons, by 10 days, and packets, such as the *Mobile* and *Chimera*, by 12 days.

For the passage home the *Sovereign of the Seas* took the mails, as well as a very large consignment of gold-dust. Captain Warner had the usual difficulty in shipping a crew ; and some of his new hands turned out to be old lags, who tried to seize the ship for the sake of the gold. However, Warner was too much for them, and they spent the rest of the passage in irons. This was by no means an unusual incident during the height of the Australian gold boom, when every ship leaving the Colony had her strong-room packed with gold-dust ; and there was always the suspicion of mutiny and murder on the high seas when one of these treasure ships failed to arrive.

Although her passage home was a splendid one, being only 68 days between Melbourne and Liverpool, we hear no more of the *Sovereign of the Seas* either on the Australian run or the Horn route to California.

She was sold at Liverpool to the Hamburg firm of J. C. Godeffroy & Son, and it seems pretty evident from her subsequent history, that the Germans expected too much of the ship.

Captain Müller claimed to have driven her at the rate of 22 knots an hour and made a 24-hour run of 410 miles on his way out to Sydney, but his passage time was no better than 84 days, owing to the loss of topmasts in a squall.

Her first voyage under the German flag was certainly very unfortunate. From Sydney she crossed to Shanghai with the usual cargo, but stuck on the bar of junks and had to be lightened—an expensive operation. Then on her passage home, cholera, brought aboard, as usual, after liberty day, accounted for nearly half her crew.

The end of this beautiful ship came in 1859; on her passage out to China from Hamburg, she ran on the Pyramid Shoal, a small patch of hard sand at the south-east end of the South Sands, Malacca Strait, where she became a total loss, though much of her cargo and gear was salved by an American ship.

Donald McKay built a second *Sovereign of the Seas* when the first changed her name and flag, but the new clipper only measured 1,226 tons, and was by no means the equal of the first *Sovereign of the Seas*. This second *Sovereign of the Seas*, whilst discharging at Campbell's Wharf, Sydney, in 1861, was " wilfully, maliciously, and feloniously set on fire on September 10th " by one of her foremast hands; she was scuttled, and finally abandoned. I mention this incident, as the vessel which was burnt in 1861 has been mistaken more than once for the first clipper of that name.

THE "DREADNOUGHT."

THE *Dreadnought* was one of those specially famous ships which were honoured in song :

> There's a saucy wild packet, a packet of fame,
> She belongs to New York, and the *Dreadnought's* her name,
> She is bound to the Westward, where the strong winds do blow,
> Bound away in the *Dreadnought* to the Westward we'll go.

So runs the first verse. The song was sung to the tune of " The Pique Frigate," which begins :

> O ! 'tis a fine frigate, the *Pique* was her name,
> All in the West Indies she bore a great fame,
> For cruel hard usage of every degree,
> Like slaves in the galley we ploughed the salt sea.

Both songs run to an interminable number of verses, but whilst the *Pique* is abused for her taut discipline and " spit and polish " routine, which are described in detail, the *Dreadnought* is worked across the Atlantic through storm and calm with a cheery goodwill, most of the verses ending with the stirring line :

> She's the Liverpool packet—O, Lord, let her go !

The *Dreadnought* was just ten years in the Atlantic packet service, but in that time she made such a name for herself that she is still remembered, whilst the other ships of her type are forgotten. Owing to the way in which she was driven by her remarkable Commander, Captain Samuel Samuels, she was nicknamed " The Wild Boat of the Atlantic."

Again and again ships which were lying hove to in a howling westerly gale reported sighting this New York packet plunging by under topgallant sails, her decks hidden in spray, and her keel showing to half its length, as she leaped from sea to sea. It was this sail-carrying, combined with a number of splendid passages, which spread her reputation far and wide, and made the name of her captain known not only amongst the shipping fraternity, but throughout America and the United Kingdom.

Samuels himself declared that he made his passages at night, by keeping sail on her throughout dark and windy nights, when other ships were snugged down. With regard to his daring navigation in crowded waters I find an interesting reference in the *Lightning Gazette*, the ship's newspaper, printed aboard the famous Australian Black-Baller *Lightning*.

In those days there were no strict rules about sidelights, and only the most careful shipmasters bothered to show a light, which was usually a two-colour lantern at the end of the jib-boom. This lack of sidelights made cross-tacking on a pitch-dark night in the Irish Sea or English Channel, when numbers of ships were about, a matter of great anxiety. On this occasion the daring Samuels forced a passage, although on the port tack. The entry in the *Lightning Gazette* runs as follows :

" January 7th, 1855. During the night we were nearly run into by a large American clipper, the *Dreadnought* of New York, which sailed from Liverpool a few hours before us (from Liverpool on January 6th). She being on the port tack, it was her duty to give way, but true to her name and with the independence of her nation, she held on her course, disdaining to turn aside. Our captain, with praiseworthy prudence, put his ship about and thus avoided a collision, which might have been serious to both vessels."

Curiously enough, on the very next night the *Lightning* was run into by a vessel on the port tack, but luckily the wind was light, the sea smooth, and the Australian liner received no damage, though the stranger lost her jib-boom.

To show the resolution of Captain Samuels, one might mention the shelf on which he was accustomed to lie down during the night. This was fixed in the after companion-way, and was purposely made too short, so that he could not stretch out upon it with any comfort ; by this means he was certain of keeping awake, and became aware of the least change in the weather.

★   ★   ★

The *Dreadnought* was designed and built by Currier & Townsend at Newburyport, Massachusetts. She was specially ordered by her owners, E. D. Morgan, Francis B. Cutting, David Ogden, and others of New York, for Captain Samuels, who had already made a great reputation on the Atlantic.

Samuels superintended her building, and it is probable that he had more than a little say not only in her rigging and sail plan, but in the design of her hull and internal arrangements. " The Wild Boat of the Atlantic " was not an out-and-out clipper such as her contemporaries, the *Flying Cloud, Sovereign of the Seas*, etc., but she was built to bear driving to the limit in the hard weather of the North Atlantic, and this quality she certainly possessed, for she would stand up to her canvas until the breaking strain of rope, spar, and sail was reached. In light winds she was nothing wonderful, and a tea clipper of the 'sixties could have sailed round her in anything under Beaufort Scale No. 5.

The " Flying Dutchman," as she was sometimes called, was originally intended to run under the flag of the Racehorse Line to California, but the loss of six of their ships and the good rates ruling between New York and Liverpool—it was a time when the emigrant trade to the States was booming—decided her owners to make a packet ship of her, and with a red cross in her fore-topsail she sailed for the next ten years as the only representative of the St. George's Cross Line, for all the other ships of the line came to grief shortly after the *Dreadnought* went afloat.

With a tonnage of 1,400 tons, the new packet ship measured 200 feet in length, 39 feet beam, and 26 feet in depth. She was launched before a large and enthusiastic crowd on October 6th, 1853. On November 3rd she left New York for Liverpool with a cargo consisting of 3,827 barrels of flour, 24,150 bushels of wheat, 12,750 bushels of corn, 304 bales of cotton, 198 barrels of potash, 150 boxes of bacon, and 5,600 staves ; this, together with a stiffening of 60 tons of pig iron, made up a total dead weight of 1,559·65 tons. The round trip was made in 58 days, 24 of which were taken on the maiden passage, and 19 days only for the much more difficult western run. The profits for the voyage came to 40,000 dollars, and the reputation of the vessel was made.

In those days there were only two regular steamship lines on the Atlantic, the Cunard and the Collins—the former British, and the latter American.

On her first passage to the westward, the *Dreadnought* left Liverpool the day after the Cunarder *Canada*, a flush-decked, paddle-wheel steamer of some 400 horse-power, which had been built in 1848. On the day that the *Canada* reached Boston the *Dreadnought* was

"Dreadnought"

Built 1853. American built Clipper Ship.

reported off the Highlands of New Jersey. This fine performance gave Samuels such confidence in his ship that he guaranteed to make deliveries in future within a specified time or forfeit freight charges, which bold undertaking induced shippers to offer the *Dreadnought* freight rates halfway between those of the other packets and the steamers. Another distinction was earned by the *Dreadnought* on her maiden voyage. She was the first full-rigged ship to pass through Hell Gate at night.

Her second and third voyages were nothing remarkable—18 and 30 days eastward, and 26 and 29 days westward, but the summer months were not those in which the *Dreadnought* made her best runs. Her fourth passage to Liverpool, however, was worthy of the ship. She passed Sandy Hook at 6.30 p.m. on November 20th, 1854, and her runs from day to day were as follows :—Nov. 21st, 120 miles ; Nov. 22nd, 57 miles ; Nov. 23rd, 225 miles ; Nov. 24th, 300 miles ; Nov. 25th, 175 miles ; Nov. 26th, 125 miles ; Nov. 27th, 250 miles ; Nov. 28th, 263 miles ; Nov. 29th, 240 miles ; Nov. 30th, 270 miles ; Dec. 1st, 242 miles ; Dec. 2nd, 222 miles ; Dec. 3rd, 212 miles ; Dec. 4th, 320 miles.

She was off Cape Clear on December 2nd, and took her pilot off Point Lynas at noon on the 4th ; then, after waiting eight hours for water to cross the bar, she anchored in the Mersey at 10 p.m., her actual time being 14 days 4 hours for a mileage of 3,071 miles.

The next eastward run of the Red Cross packet was almost as good ; she arrived at Liverpool on May 20th, 15 days 12 hours out.

In 1856 the *Dreadnought* made two very fine east-bound passages. On the first she averaged 222 miles a day, and, reaching Liverpool on February 9th, was 14 days 8 hours coming across. On the second she took 16 days in May. In February, 1857, *Dreadnought* only took 15 days from land to land in the terrible west-bound mid-winter passage, and she docked in New York 21 days out.

According to her skipper, her best passage was made in the early months of 1859. The details of this passage are as follows :

> Feb.   27.—At 3 p.m. discharged New York pilot.
> „   28.—Winds South to W.N.W., brisk breezes. Distance 200 miles.
> March 1.—Winds W.N.W., fresh breeze. Distance 293 miles.
> „   2.—Brisk gales and snow squalls from N.W. to N.N.W.   Distance 262 miles.
> „   3.—Heavy gales and snow squalls, N.N.W. to North. Distance 208 miles.
> „   4.—Heavy gales and snow squalls, N.N.E. to North. Distance 178 miles.
> „   5.—Heavy gales and snow squalls, North to N.N.E. Distance 218 miles.
> „   6.—Winds N.E. to South, light. Distance 133 miles.
> „   7.—Winds S.S.E., brisk breeze and clear. Distance 282 miles.
> „   8.—S.S.W. to South, fresh breeze and clear. Distance 313 miles.
> „   9.—Brisk gales, South to S.E. Distance 268 miles.
> „   10.—Wind S.E. to S.W., brisk breeze and squally. Distance 205 miles.
> „   11.—Wind South to S.W., strong breeze and squally. Distance 308 miles.
> „   12.—Wind S.W., thick weather. Distance 150 miles.

Abreast of the North-West Lightship, 3,018 miles from New York, in 13 days 8 hours, and anchored in the Mersey an hour later, at noon.

Referring to this passage, Captain Samuels, in his old age, declared that he made the run from Sandy Hook to Queenstown in 9 days 17 hours, and that the rest of the passage was held up by light and variable airs. This statement has caused a great deal of discussion and dispute. Unfortunately, the *Dreadnought*'s log-books have long since disappeared, and Captain Samuels lost his own records when his cabin was gutted by a sea in 1862. But it seems most likely that the old man mixed up two of his passages, and that the 9-day 17-hour record was made in June of the same year, when the *Dreadnought* anchored in the Mersey on July 2nd, 16 days out from New York.

On his return passage in July, Captain Samuels had his celebrated encounter with the Bloody Forty—a notorious gang of Liverpool " packet rats," who shipped aboard the *Dreadnought* on purpose to make trouble.   Captain Samuels, with the aid of his Newfoundland dog, " Wallace," and his plucky 2nd mate, managed to get the better of these desperadoes after an affray which terrified his passengers out of their wits.

In the year 1862, on her western passage, the *Dreadnought* was pooped by a sea which nearly killed her commander, stunning him and breaking his leg.   The helmsmen, in their fright, deserted the wheel, then the rudder was carried away, and the tiller broke off short, leaving the ship helpless.   After making a rough set of Samuels' broken leg, his officers, under the superintendence of their dauntless captain, managed to construct a jury-rudder ; but, in lowering it overboard, the tackle gave way, and their work went to the bottom.

By this time it was calm weather with a light westerly breeze.   The ship's head lay to the northward ;   Samuels wanted to steer for the nearest land, which was Fayal, bearing south by east.   By means of drags they tried for 10 hours to get the ship's head round in the right direction, but the *Dreadnought* was sulky without her rudder, and would not bear up.

At last her skipper, who all this time had been lying on the poop in a fever of impatience and pain, decided to sail the ship backwards.   The head-sails and all sails on the foremast were taken in, then with the main and mizen yards braced until every sail was flat aback, the *Dreadnought* gradually gathered stern way, and was actually sailed stern first for 280 miles in the direction of Fayal.   By this time a second jury-rudder had been made ; this was shipped successfully, and 14 days after the accident the *Dreadnought* came to anchor in Fayal Harbour.

For the next 52 days Samuels, with his leg so indifferently set in splints that the broken bones were not together, had to endure agonies of pain, whilst his ship was being repaired. In the end the *Dreadnought* reached New York, but she had to sail on her next passage without her famous skipper, Samuels having to keep his bed for 11 months.

However, the ship was saved, and that was all the old man cared about.

Captain Lytle now took command of the " Wild Boat of the Atlantic," but on his return trip in December, 1863, he, too, was knocked down by a heavy sea, and so badly injured that he died.

Once more the *Dreadnought* was headed for Fayal, and after repairs, was taken on to New York by her mate, Mr. Rockwell, arriving there on February 26th, 1864.   It was her last western ocean passage.   The day of the packet ships was almost over, and her owners decided to put her into the Cape Horn trade.

Captain Cushing was now given the command, and he took her out to San Francisco in 134 days.   From San Francisco the *Dreadnought* was sent across to Honolulu to load whale oil.

The *Dreadnought* brought her cargo of whale oil round the Horn to New Bedford in the splendid time of 84 days, though it is noted that her best 24-hour run was only 272 miles.

On her second Cape Horn voyage she took 127 days, arriving at San Francisco in January, 1866.   This time she went down to Callao and loaded guano home.

In 1868 Captain Cushing was replaced by Captain Callaghan, who made the run from New York to San Francisco in 149 days.   The *Dreadnought* left San Francisco on October 11th, 1868, with a grain cargo for Liverpool, which was reached in 125 days.

In 1869 the old ship left New York under Captain Mayhew, bound once more to San Francisco.   But she never arrived.   Whilst making for the Straits of Le Maire, Captain Mayhew got close in under the rock-bound coast of Tierra del Fuego.   A heavy swell was running, and the ship was just forging ahead under all sail to her main skysail when it fell calm.

Though the *Dreadnought* rolled until the sails threatened to flog themselves to tatters there was nothing to be done. Then it was noticed that a current was carrying the ship towards the land. One can imagine how her crew would employ every device for bringing up a wind that was known to seamen. The mainmast must have been stuck full of sheath-knives. But it was all in vain. Not a breath stirred aloft. At last, in desperation the boats were lowered, and they tried to tow the ship clear. To tow a fully-loaded 1,400-ton ship in a Cape Horn swell was, of course, an impossibility. As the *Dreadnought* was caught by the breakers, she was hove inshore with irresistible force ; then came the crash and all was over—the famous packet soon lay a battered wreck, which the angry surf slowly tore in pieces. Her crew were picked up by a passing ship, after three weeks of suffering, during which they ever had to be on their guard against the hostile Tierra del Fuegians.

Captain Samuels survived his famous ship by many years ; though he never went to sea again except on a yacht. In his later years he became President of the *New York Marine Journal*, in which capacity he was able to keep in close touch with sailors and the sea. It may be interesting to record that his broken leg made a wonderful mend, though the old captain always had a slight limp.

Captain Samuels died on May 18th, 1908, in his 85th year ; when he gained his first command, at the age of 21, the sea was covered with wooden sailing ships, few of which exceeded 1,000 tons, whilst the steamers were mostly small paddle-wheelers. When he died the sailing ship was so rare a sight that she was considered a curiosity, and great liners of 20,000 tons were doing the work of the *Dreadnought* and her sisters.

> Then a health to the *Dreadnought* and to her brave crew,
> To bold Captain Samuels and his officers too ;
> Talk about your flash packets, *Swallow Tail* and *Black-Ball*,
> The *Dreadnought's* the flier that can lick them all.

THE "CUTTY SARK."

I F any sailor of the present day wishes to see what real ship beauty is like, he should take train or boat to Falmouth, where he will find the famous *Cutty Sark* lying at her moorings as spick and span as in the days of her glory.

The *Cutty Sark* was launched as far back as 1869, right in the middle of the Victorian era, when man's taste in art was considered to be at its lowest ebb. Yet the ships of that date were a sheer delight to the eye, whilst those of the present day, with some notable exceptions, are so sacrificed to the exigencies of this material age that hardly a line runs true, hardly a curve shows sweet and wholesome, so that ships have mostly become monstrosities—mere floating workhouses, square-ended, wall-sided, and bristling with erections in the shape of derricks and ventilators, which often bear a close resemblance to the gallows.

The *Cutty Sark* was a composite tea clipper, built at Dumbarton to the order of Captain John Willis, the London shipowner, who with her hoped to lower the colours of that remarkable Aberdeen flyer, the *Thermopylæ*. Her registered measurements were as follows :—gross tons 963, net tons 921, length 212 feet 5 inches, breadth 36 feet, depth 21 feet, moulded depth 22 feet 5 inches. As regards the length of her spars, the extreme length of bowsprit and jib-booms was 60 feet; length of mainmast from deck to truck 145 feet 9 inches; mainyard 78 feet, and spanker-boom 52 feet. The distance from the end of the flying jib-boom to the end of the spanker-boom was 280 feet.

The *Cutty Sark* was by no means overhatted, the biggest sail plan in the tea fleet being that of *Spindrift*, whose mainyard was 84 feet long. Many of the China clippers had two suits of stunsails, large and small; but, though the *Cutty Sark* only had one set, these were big enough, and pretty nearly doubled the width of her spread on fore and main.

Hercules Linton, who had been apprenticed to Hall of Aberdeen, though a young and rising designer, had never given his contemporaries cause to expect that he would produce such a masterpiece as the *Cutty Sark*. I have received some interesting reminiscences from an ex-apprentice who was in the drawing office of Scott & Linton from the very start of the young firm. This man had the honour of journeying to Glasgow with the last of the three models, which were submitted to Captain Willis for his approval. He also remembers Hercules Linton and John Rennie arguing over tracings of suggested sail plans, when the former lengthened or shortened the yards on the plans with a soft blacklead pencil, to the dismay of the young apprentice, whose one thought at the time was that such pencil-marks were almost impossible to rub out and thus spoilt the beauty of the drawings. Before his death a few years ago, Mr. Rennie always proudly declared that he had designed the *Cutty Sark's* spar and sail plan, but the episode of the blacklead pencil certainly seems to prove that Linton corrected Rennie's work before giving it his full approval.

The *Cutty Sark* was by far the most powerful of the tea clippers; indeed, she seemed able to bear driving to an unlimited extent, which is more than can be said for any of the

Steele cracks, and even *Thermopylæ* had her limits. It is very difficult to decide on a vessel's capabilities from her records, for in sailing so much depends upon the skipper, and a certain amount upon the caprices of fortune. It has been argued that the *Cutty Sark* was slow in light winds. It is true that Captain Woodget, who had her for ten years after she had had her spars reduced, considered her a very ordinary ship in light weather ; yet, on the other hand, her masters in her China days, declared that she never lost way, because the mere flap of her sails kept her moving through the water. From the records, it would seem that she was not quite as fast as *Thermopylæ* or the Steele clippers in the light airs of the China Seas.

Captain Moodie, who was in command her first three voyages, though a superb seaman, was certainly not the man to take risks in navigation through waters which were not only studded with coral reefs, but had only been most indifferently surveyed. It would not be fair to call Moodie a timid navigator, yet he preferred to go round rather than to dash through a dangerous Channel such as Stolze's in Gaspar Straits : and he made no attempt to work the eddies in shore or the land and sea breezes on the Cochin China and Borneo coasts.

Captain F. W. Moore, who had Willis's crack on her fourth voyage, was up in years and far more concerned with a smart appearance in port than in making a record passage. Captain Tiptaft, who succeeded Moore, never had any reputation for carrying sail ; and the tragic Captain Wallace never had a chance to show what he could do with her on a tea passage.

Thus the *Cutty Sark*'s tea passages, which I give below, were nothing very remarkable :

										Days.
1870	Maiden Voyage		left Shanghai	June	25	Arrived	Beachy Head	Oct.	12	109
1871	Second	,,	,, ,,	Sept.	4	,,	N. Foreland	Dec.	20	107
1872	Third	,,	,, ,,	June	18	,,	Portland	Oct.	16	120
1873	Fourth	,,	,, ,,	July	9	,,	Deal	Nov.	2	116
1874	Fifth	,,	,, Woosung (loaded Hankow)	June	24	,,	,,	Oct.	20	118
1875	Sixth	,,	left Woosung (loaded Hankow)	June	21	,,	Deal	Oct.	21	122
1876	Seventh	,,	left Woosung (loaded Hankow)	June	9	,,	Start	Sept.	25	108
1877	Eighth	,,	left Woosung (loaded Hankow)	June	6	,,	Scilly	Oct.	6	122

Except in 1872, the *Cutty Sark* was never in company with another racing tea ship. But in that year she and her great rival, *Thermopylæ*, loaded together at Shanghai, and sailed within a few hours of each other. The two ships were constantly in company down the China sea, and owing to *Cutty Sark* having her way blocked by several waterspouts, she was led by *Thermopylæ* through Anjer Straits, the latter being 1½ miles ahead off Anjer, and when last seen outside Java Head was 3 miles W. by S. of Willis's clipper. However, Captain Moodie sent the *Cutty Sark* flying across the S.E. trades with three consecutive runs of 340, 327 and 320 miles, and he always contended that he was over 400 miles ahead of *Thermopylæ* when the *Cutty Sark* lost her rudder off the Cape coast.

Captain Kemball, of *Thermopylæ*, was one of those secretive navigators who would never allow anyone aboard to know the ship's position, and as he refused to compare his log-book with that of the *Cutty Sark*, after the two ships had arrived in London, one cannot say for certain which was leading when the *Cutty Sark* lost her rudder, though the generally credited belief in London at the time was that *Thermopylæ* was 600 miles astern.

The *Cutty Sark* never succeeded in loading China tea after 1877 ; and after a protracted voyage she loaded jute in 1879 at Manila for New York. Captain Tiptaft had died on the China coast, and his chief officer, Wallace, was appointed to the command.

"Cutty Sark"
Built 1869 Tea Clipper.

He was a hard sail-carrier, but though he got some fine bursts of speed out of the *Cutty Sark*, his passage of 111 days from Manila to New York was not quite worthy of the ship.

In March, 1880, the *Cutty Sark's* big sail plan was considerably reduced, as her owners considered that henceforward she would have to go a-seeking all over the world : and they were quite glad of a charter to load Welsh coal for the American fleet in Japan waters.

We now come to the most adventurous voyage in the whole of the *Cutty Sark's* career, in which she fell out of one disaster into another, and from one tragedy to another. The story of the voyage cannot be told in detail : the bare facts are as follows :—The mate, who was a typical bucko, killed a negro seaman with a handspike in the Indian ocean, and with the help of the captain managed to escape aboard an American ship, whilst the *Cutty Sark* lay at Anjer. This, and the resulting trouble with his crew, so worried Captain Wallace that he stepped over the stern one calm morning in the Java sea and was taken by sharks.

The *Cutty Sark*, under her 2nd mate, put back and eventually found her way to Singapore, where the coal was discharged and a new captain was appointed. For this purpose a man named Bruce, the mate of the *Hallowe'en*, was sent down by mail steamer from Shanghai. Bruce was the very opposite of Wallace, and only seems to have had one good point—he was a splendid navigator, notwithstanding which he suffered badly from land fever, and always started to shorten sail long before any land was in sight.

Under Bruce the *Cutty Sark* wandered up to Calcutta, and from thence to Australia ; loaded to Shanghai from Sydney, and finally took jute to New York from Cebu, Philippines. Bruce divided his time between drinking bouts and prayer meetings. A passenger, who paid £25 for a berth from Sydney to Shanghai, tells me that Bruce was convinced that the ship was haunted, and that this was the chief reason for his prayers. The tragedies of the voyage continued in spite of the captain's prayers. A foremast hand missed the she-oak net at Melbourne and was drowned the ship's first night alongside the wharf. Asiatic cholera attacked the ship's company at Shanghai, two of the men dying and one apprentice having to be invalided home. And on the passage home a seaman was lost overboard.

At New York Bruce was given the sack, along with his chief officer, after an official enquiry, and Captain E. Moore was shifted over from the *Blackadder*. Moore was a fine type of shipmaster and after a dull sugar voyage to Bengal, he made two fine Australian voyages, astonishing the wool fleet by his passages from Newcastle, N.S.W.

In 1885 Moore was promoted to *The Tweed*, which was always considered Willis's flagship. He was succeeded by Captain Woodget, one of the finest sailing-ship seamen of his age, and under Woodget the *Cutty Sark* not only broke all records, but was a supremely happy ship.

The following is a complete list of the *Cutty Sark's* wool passages :

Date.	Captain.	Wool Bales.	Left.				Arrived			Days.
1883/4	E. Moore	4,289	Newcastle, N.S.W.,	Dec.	28	Deal	Mar.	20	82
1884/5	,,	4,300	,,	Dec.	9	Dock	Feb.	27	80
1885	R. Woodget	4,465	Sydney, N.S.W.,	Oct.	16	Ushant	Dec.	22	67
						Downs	Dec.	28	73
1887	,,	4,296	,,	Mar.	26	Lizard	June	4	70
1887/8	,,	4,515	Newcastle, N.S.W.,	Dec.	28	,,	Mar.	7	69
1888/9	,,	4,496	Sydney	Oct.	26	London	Jan.	20	86
1889/90	,,	4,577	,,	Nov.	3	,,	Jan.	17	75
1890/1	,,	4,617	,,	Dec.	14	,,	Mar.	17	93
1891/2	,,	4,636	,,	Nov.	5	Lizard	Jan.	27	83
1893	,,	4,723	,,	Jan.	7	Bishops	April	7	90
						Antwerp	April	15	98
1893/4	,,	5,010	,,	Dec.	24	Scillies	Mar.	21	87
						Hull	Mar.	27	93
1894/5	,,	5,304	Brisbane	Dec.	29	London	Mar.	26	84

It will be noticed that the amount of bales screwed into the ship gradually increased. This was entirely owing to Captain Woodget, his sharp eye and his note-book of previous cargoes. It was on Woodget's first wool passage that the *Cutty Sark* beat the *Thermopylæ* by a week, and so delighted her owner that he presented her with the golden cutty sark which ever afterwards was seen at her main truck.

Whilst waiting at Sydney to load wool, Captain Woodget was ever ready for a bit of fun, and the *Cutty Sark* picnics were joyfully patronised by all the prettiest girls in Sydney. As a return for his hospitality, the captain's friends used to hire the Redfern Skating Rink for the evening in order to entertain the jovial skipper, his officers and apprentices.

One of Woodget's many Australian friends possessed a high bicycle with a big wheel. On one occasion this was embarked in the *Cutty Sark's* boat and taken aboard, and, one after the other, the apprentices rode the bicycle round the decks—no doubt to the secret anxiety of Selby, Woodget's smart chief officer, but to the great amusement of all hands, for heavy falls were frequent, and the bicycle was soon in need of repair. The next voyage the *Cutty's* carpenter managed to make a bicycle which was half hobby-horse. This, also, was ridden round the decks by everyone from the captain downwards. The *Cutty Sark* was always up-to-date, and this product of her carpenter's shop was probably one of the first safety bicycles.

One could ramble on with reminiscences, but space is lacking. Here is one, however, which was sent to me by a foremast hand :

" I can picture myself now, standing at her wheel one first watch from 8 to 12 p.m. Running our easting down somewhere about 55° South, wind well on port quarter, all sail on her except royals, the night as black as pitch, the only thing I could see was the binnacle light and the compass in front of me. The ship was tearing along about 15 knots an hour and griping, so that I could hardly hold her, one spoke of the wheel bearing down on my knee and making it bruised and sore. Although it was cold weather, I myself was wet with perspiration, owing to the strain she was putting me to. The wind was whistling up aloft, there was blackness everywhere, and I expected to see something go every time she gave a gripe to windward of her course.

" The captain himself was standing on the after end of the monkey poop—I could just see his dark form against the rail. He had his arms linked round the top rail and was quietly *whistling a jig*. Here was I expecting to see the sticks or something else go overboard and working myself into a perspiration to hold her on her course, and he calm and enjoying himself with a jig. I thought him mad. At last I yelled out to him :— ' Captain ! I want some help here. I can't hold her ! '

" His answer was :—' Stick her, lad ! You're doing all right, stick her.' And I stuck it until I was relieved." And the writer adds :—" Captain Woodget was the strongest and steadiest-nerved man ever I met—in fact, he did not know what nerves meant. Men with any nerves at all were no use in the *Cutty Sark*."

The passage home from Brisbane in 1895 was *Cutty Sark's* last under the Red Ensign. From August, 1895, until June, 1922, she sailed under the Portuguese flag and the name of *Ferreira*. During these years she had many strange adventures, though her usual round was from Lisbon to Rio and New Orleans, comfortable summer voyaging. Once, however, she got caught in a West Indian hurricane, dragged ashore, lost her rudder and had to be fitted with a new one at Key West.

Then, in the middle of the Great War, in May, 1916, she was towed into Table Bay dismasted, when bound with 1,142 tons of coal from Delagoa Bay to Mossamedes. Unable to get spars, her captain was compelled to refit her as a three-masted schooner, and under this rig she continued to sail the seas until bought by Captain Dowman in 1922.

The famous tea clipper is now used as a stationary training ship, and she has only once been under way since Captain Dowman reconditioned and re-rigged her. This was in August, 1924, when she was towed round to Fowey to act as flagship at the Royal Fowey Regatta. On this occasion she had three distinguished passengers : the sea poetess, Miss Fox Smith, Captain Vivian Millett of the Port of London Authority, who had served in her as an apprentice, and, lastly, her famous skipper, Captain Woodget.

Nothing has astonished me more than the world-wide interest which has been taken in this remarkable ship of a dead and gone era. Men and women, from all parts of the world, continue to write to me, asking interminable questions about the *Cutty Sark*. And I have had photographs of models of the ship sent me not only from many people in the British Isles, but from America and Canada, from Australia and New Zealand, and South Africa.

Only a couple of months ago an Italian sent me photographs of a model he had just made, and asked for criticism, and his letter was followed a week later by one from a Spaniard, also with photographs of his model, and soon afterwards came snapshots of a German model.

More people than one has any idea of, have an inherited love of ships, just as they have " desired the sea—the sight of salt water unbounded."

"THE TWEED."

IN the days of sail it was usual to find certain names cropping up wherever old seamen gathered together. These were either the names of men of outstanding character in their profession, such as Bully Forbes, or the names of ships, whose qualities or idiosyncrasies had brought them a wide notoriety.

Of these much-talked-of ships and captains, none were better known than *The Tweed*, and her famous Master, Captain W. Stuart. If the ship gave her captain his opportunity, it may equally be said that Captain Stuart did not allow *The Tweed* to suffer for want of an able hand at the helm. But the old ship's history stretches back before the days of Stuart, and her first years of service in the Indian Marine, under the name of *Punjaub*, were quite as remarkable as her later ones under Willis's house flag. Yet the exciting times of her paddle-wheel days have long been forgotten, though her fame as a sailing ship is still green in a thousand fo'c'sles.

In 1852 Cursetjee Rustomjee, master-builder, of the famous Parsee family of Wadia, laid down two paddle-wheel frigates for the Indian Marine in Bombay Dockyard. The first of these was the *Assaye*, and the second the *Punjaub*, afterwards Willis's flagship *The Tweed*. The *Punjaub* was designed by Oliver Lang, and the story goes that the wreck or hulk of an old French frigate aroused such enthusiasm in the famous naval architect that he reproduced her lines in the new ship. It has been said that the *Punjaub* was one of the most expensive wooden ships ever built, specially selected Malabar teak being the only material used in her construction.

The *Punjaub's* tonnage and dimensions were as follows : Tons net, 1,745 ; length overall, 285 feet ; length registered, 250 feet ; beam, 39 feet 6 inches ; depth, 25 feet. Her two cumbersome paddle-wheels were driven by engines of 700 horse-power, which were sent out from England, and her armament consisted of 10 8-inch 68-pounders. Years later, in her sailing-ship days, her apprentices, when cleaning the hold, found these same cannons down in her run, acting as ballast.

When the *Punjaub* was launched on April 21st, 1854, she was pronounced to be both the largest and finest frigate ever built in India. In those days nothing was ever hurried, and it was not until January 2nd, 1855, that the new ship was commissioned and Commander John W. Young appointed to the command. It happened, however, that there was now great cause for hurry, as reinforcements for the Crimea were being called for from India, and the *Punjaub* was actually fitted out as a transport in six days, and sailed on January 9th for Suez, with the Colonel and two squadrons of the 10th Hussars on board. In a fleet of a dozen transports, she at once proved herself so much faster than her consorts that she ran them hull down with her fires out and topsails on the cap.

We next hear of her in the Persian War of 1855, when she formed one of the ships of the Expeditionary Force, which left Bombay in November for the Persian Gulf. Commander Young had been transferred to the smaller *Semiramis*, and Acting-Commander A. Foulerton was now in charge of the *Punjaub*. After the fall of Bushire, he was ordered to convey the captured Governor and his staff back to Bombay, in company with the *Assaye*, which was acting as flagship of Rear-Admiral Sir Henry J. Leeke.

When the two ships were off the Island of Kishni they noticed that the British post there was being threatened by a Persian army. With the aid of their 68-pounders the two frigates forced the Persians to retire; but, not liking to leave the depot in such danger, the Admiral transferred his prisoners to the *Assaye*, and left the *Punjaub* on guard off the coast—thus she did not get back to Bombay until May 22nd, 1857.

When the *Punjaub* reached Bombay the mutiny had broken out, and every ship was engaged in rushing British reinforcements round the coast. In the wake of the *Assaye* and other ships, the *Punjaub* was raced to Calcutta. The transports arrived in the Hooghly on June 4th, and when their thunderous Viceroy's salute of 21 guns broke out, there were no complaints of broken windows, as was usually the case, for their arrival was just in time to stop the growing panic.

The *Assaye* and most of the transports turned short round and went back for more troops, but the *Punjaub* was detained with the *Semiramis*, and Commander Foulerton found himself the senior naval officer in port. He found the city in a veritable state of terror. Rumours of risings and massacres were flying through the bazaars. And every fresh rumour set a chattering, hysterical mob of Eurasians and Portuguese stampeding for safety to the ships in the river. Matters came to a head on June 14th, and Commander Foulerton was hastily summoned to the Viceroy's Council Chamber. The breezy sailor found the Council in a state of suppressed fright; with pale lips they told him that the Sepoys at Barrackpore had risen in the night and were marching to join the King of Oude's forces at Garden Reach, with the evident object of looting the city. The Council had decided to act with vigour; with the 53rd Regiment, the Viceroy's bodyguard, and seamen from the ships, they proposed to surprise the King of Oude and his rabble of 1,500 undisciplined men before the arrival of the Barrackpore mutineers. Foulerton was asked to drop down and anchor off the King of Oude's palace. He replied that he could not get steam up on the *Punjaub*, as her floats were off, but that he would take the *Semiramis*, with a landing force from the *Punjaub*, towing astern in her boats. This plan was agreed upon, and worked without a hitch, though it is said that Foulerton had to use rough measures with the pilot of the *Semiramis*, who wanted a formal order from the Council.

The rest is soon told. At daybreak the next morning the palace was completely taken by surprise. The King himself, surrounded by a mob of howling wives and officials, was found in a state of collapse in his bed by Mr. Edmonstone, the foreign secretary, Colonel Powell, commanding the 53rd Regiment, and the Captain of the *Punjaub*. The foreign secretary wished to remove the King and clear the palace, but the latter refused to budge. Foulerton suggested hoisting the wretched monarch aboard the *Semiramis* by means of a whip from the main yard-arm. This horrified Edmonstone, who was used to treating Indian potentates with ceremony, and in spite of the danger of delay, he insisted on sending back to Government House for a state carriage.

This capture of the King of Oude's palace was the first active service of the *Punjaub's* crew in the Indian Mutiny—but it was by no means the last. By the end of June detachments from the ships had been landed and sent out into the country in every direction. The *Punjaub's* detachment, under 1st Lieutenant T. E. Lewis, Acting-Master Connor, Midshipmen Arthur Mayo and W. Cuthell, and Mr. Brown, the bos'n, specially distinguished itself. Mayo gained a V.C. at the capture of Dacca. Lewis, though he never received any honour or reward, must have earned the V.C. over and over again. Both he and Mayo wore

"The Tweed"
Built 1854 Blackwall Passenger Ship.

themselves out in the hard service, and at the end had to be invalided home, their constitutions wrecked by wounds and fever.

Whilst the pick of her officers and men were fighting ashore, the *Punjaub* raced backwards and forwards round the coast. Her last service in the old Indian Navy was on the Muscat-Zanzibar Commission in June, 1860.

Early in 1862 the *Punjaub* and her sister ship, the *Assaye*, sailed for home in order to have their paddle-wheels removed and screws substituted. But by the time they arrived in the Thames, the Indian Marine had been merged into the Royal Navy and thus ceased to exist. The two warriors of the Persian War and Indian Mutiny were thereupon ordered to be sold.

John Willis, who had the keenest eye for a ship in the Port of London, bought both ships and converted them to sail. The *Assaye* he sold again for a large profit, but the *Punjaub*, which he rechristened *The Tweed*, was ever afterwards his pet ship, and the flagship of his fleet. He even gave her a new figure-head, representing Tam o' Shanter. It is needless to say that Willis hailed from the Tweed, and that Burns was his favourite poet. Captain W. Stuart, of Peterhead, Willis's most trusted captain, was given the command; and Moodie, afterwards the first skipper of the *Cutty Sark*, was put into the mate's berth.

The Tweed's first duty under Willis's house flag was a very arduous one; for, together with the *Assaye* and the *Cospatrick*, she took out and laid the Persian Gulf cable, under contract with the Government. This was in 1863, the passage out to Bombay being made in 77 days. After laying the cable up the gulf, Captain Stuart returned to Bombay, where the ship was refitted for carrying passengers and troops; she then took on board the Seaforth Highlanders at Vingorla and brought them home round the Cape in 78 days. After two such passages Willis at once realized that he had got a very exceptional ship.

The late Joseph Conrad in his " Mirror of the Sea " suggests that *The Tweed* did not look the clipper. He writes of her as " heavy to look at, with great sheer, high bows, and a clumsy stern." But he evidently confused her appearance with that of some other ship, for *The Tweed* had very little sheer, a by no means clumsy stern, and was a most majestic and handsome vessel, with her lofty masts and three skysail yards. Conrad goes on to remark : " There was something peculiarly lucky, perhaps, in the placing of her masts—who knows ? Officers of men-of-war used to come on board to take the exact dimensions of her sail plan. Perhaps there had been a touch of genius or the finger of good fortune in the fashioning of her lines at bow and stern. It is impossible to say."

Certainly *The Tweed* was very finely masted and sparred; she was very lofty without being over-sparred, and carried her canvas well. She was one of those vessels which were exceptionally fast under any condition of weather; bore hard driving and made big runs in the " roaring forties," but was also a flyer in light winds. Under Captain Stuart she made hardly a poor passage, whether in the Indian or Australian trade.

One has no space to give details, but the following were some of her best : 1873, Lizard to Melbourne 72 days; 1874, St. Catherine's Point to Otago 78 days; 1875, Sydney to Dungeness 69 days. On one occasion she beat the mail steamer between Hong Kong and Singapore. During the Indian famine, whilst carrying rice between Rangoon and Madras, she put up a most extraordinary record. And her Indian voyages were much on a par with her first.

In 1877 Captain Stuart handed his old ship over to Captain Byce, but Byce, who had been mate in her, failed to equal Stuart's passages, though it is but fair to say that the famous vessel was beginning to leak a bit and get water-soaked. Byce was followed by Gentleman White. Stuart had never carried away a spar, but under White *The Tweed* was caught aback running her easting down in 1882, and lost her jib-boom, fore topmast, with the foreyard, main topgallant mast and main topsail yards.   Yet the very next day, whilst her crew were busy jury-rigging her, she ran 240 miles under her mainsail and mizen canvas alone ; whilst under her jury-rig she covered 2,000 miles in a week, and reached Sydney only 93 days out.

On her passage home from Calcutta this voyage, she was nearly dismasted again whilst off the Western Isles.   She was running before a westerly blow, logging 16 knots under a goose-winged main topsail, when a sea was shipped over the quarter which gutted all the cabins on the port side of the poop.   This scared White into heaving her to.   He brought his ship to the wind successfully, but it was then found that the rigging was so badly stretched that the masts threatened to go over the side.   There was no chance of taking up the slack of the lanyards until the weather moderated, so the backstays were hastily frapped together.

The last Commander of *The Tweed* was Moore, who was promoted from the *Cutty Sark*. He had her from 1885 to the end, which came in July, 1888.   When bound from China to New York the old ship was dismasted off Algoa Bay.   The s.s. *Venice* got a rope aboard her and towed her into Port Elizabeth.   Here she was not considered worth repairing and so was broken up, her teak frames and timbers being taken for roofing a church in Port Elizabeth, where they may still be seen.   It may thus be said that the famous old teak-built frigate is still doing good and faithful work.

THE "MACQUARIE."

MANY good old-fashioned terms are gradually being lost to the Anglo-Saxon tongue owing to the extinction of sailing ships. Two of these, which express the way in which a ship is run by her captain and officers, are "Bristol fashion" and "Blackwall fashion." The same method of carrying on the work of a ship would undoubtedly be denoted in these days by the hard-used term "first class." Fifty or sixty years ago, anyone wishing to travel to the East under the very best conditions that money could buy always chose a ship which was run "Blackwall fashion." This meant engaging a cabin in one of Green's, Smith's, or Wigram's frigate-built Indiamen, known in the London river and the East as the Blackwall frigates. These frigates, which, as their name denotes, resembled those of the Royal Navy, were beautifully built of the finest Malabar teak.

Now the famous Dicky Green, the head of the firm of R. and H. Green, was one of the old hard-shell Conservatives, and clung to old methods, old customs and old habits with a strenuous fierceness which was curious in so gentle a nature. As long as he was alive no man dared to suggest his abandoning his wooden frigates and following the growing fashion for iron ships.

But when Dicky Green died in 1863 the firm hastened to make up for lost time, and launched their first iron ship, the *Superb*, in 1866, and their second, the *Carlisle Castle*, in 1868. Finally, they built the *Melbourne* for their growing passenger trade to Australia.

It so happened that they found themselves with a quantity of surplus plates after building a man-of-war. They thereupon decided to use these plates with the object of producing the finest iron passenger ship which could possibly be built. This, the last ship of a line which was considered to have no equal in our Mercantile Marine, was called the *Melbourne*, and registered 1,857 tons, 269 feet 8 inches long, 40 feet 1 inch beam, and 23 feet 7 inches depth. She cost when ready for sea as much as £42,000—a little over £22 10s. per ton.

For an iron ship she was most lavishly ornamented with gilding and scroll-work, whilst her figure-head was a beautifully carved portrait of Queen Victoria. Under a 69-foot poop she carried a first-class accommodation which was considered a great advance on that of any previous ship. The cabins were larger and better ventilated, whilst, what was hardly yet the custom, they were completely furnished. In retaining a stern cabin with large stern windows she formed the very last link with the old East Indiamen of John Company days.

This magnificent vessel was launched in June, 1875, and on August 16th, 1875, she left the East India Docks under Captain R. Marsden, late of Green's *Agamemnon*, with sixty passengers for the great Australian port after which she was named.

The firm of R. and H. Green were never ready to sacrifice the safety and comfort of their passengers for the sake of being able to advertise record passages. Thus the *Melbourne*, though a magnificent sea-boat specially noted for her dryness, was no record breaker. Her passages were good without being in any way above the average.

On her maiden trip she arrived in Hobson's Bay on November 16th, 86 days from the Start.   This was not a bad performance considering that she lost her foretop mast and main topgallant mast in a squall on the edge of the N.E. trades when only 25 days out.   Her run home was made in 104 days.

On her second voyage she went out to Melbourne in 77 days, and this was about as good as she could do.

Captain Norwood Harrison followed Captain Marsden in the command, and the following Australian shipping notice of the ship's Melbourne period is of interest :

FIRST SHIP
For the February Sales :
Messrs. Green's Blackwall Line of Passenger Ships.

For LONDON DIRECT.
To be despatched from the Williamstown Railway Pier about the middle of October.

The magnificent new passenger ship " MELBOURNE."

Norwood Harrison, R.N.R., Commander.

The SALOON CABINS are specially suited for families, and fitted with cabin furniture ; are also unusually roomy, well-lighted, and thoroughly ventilated.

Bedding and all cabin requisites are provided.

Ladies' and gentlemen's bathrooms.

The ship is accompanied by a surgeon.

For freight or passage, circulars, plans, etc., apply to J. H. White & Co., 49 William Street.

*   *   *

SPECIAL NOTICE TO SHIPPERS OF WOOL.

As a large portion of the *Melbourne's* cargo consists of flour and wheat the space for wool is sufficiently reduced to permit of the ship sailing earlier than usual.

———

The date of this notice is September 20th, 1880, and it is very interesting when compared with those of the great passenger lines of the present day, 47 years later.

The *Melbourne* was a regular first-class passenger ship to Hobson's Bay until 1887, when Messrs. Devitt & Moore bought her from the Greens in order to replace their old *Parramatta* in the Sydney trade.   On her first passage to Sydney she took out fifty passengers under Captain Goddard, who transferred to the *Melbourne* from the *Parramatta*.   Sydney was reached on December 27th, when the ship was 94 days out.

It was in 1888, on her second voyage to Sydney, that her name was changed to *Macquarie*, the name by which she is best remembered.   Captain Goddard commanded the *Macquarie* until 1896 ; then the veteran Captain Corvasso, of *La Hogue* and *Dunbar Castle* fame, took her for a voyage, bringing home 5,555 bales of wool from Sydney in 95 days.

In 1897 Messrs. Devitt & Moore sold their famous cadet ship *Harbinger*, having decided to replace her by the *Macquarie*, which, now that a full passenger list was a thing of the past, was very well adapted to the carrying of a large number of cadets.   The command was given to Captain Corner, who had been mate under Barrett in the cadet ship *Hesperus*.

Corner, to whose skill as a photographer we owe the many delightful views of the *Macquarie*, had a great success with the beautiful ship.   On his first cadet passage he took

"Macquarie"
Built 1875 Blackwall Passenger Ship.

her out to Sydney in 86 days, leaving London September 3rd, 1897, and arriving at Port Jackson on November 28th.

The *Macquarie*, after six successful voyages as a cadet ship, was sold by Messrs. Devitt & Moore to the Norwegians for the sum of £4,500. Her new owners at once disguised the stately Blackwaller by stripping the yards off her mizen-mast and changing her name to *Fortuna*. Instead of passengers or premium cadets she henceforth carried timber. On January 13th, 1906, she once more visited Melbourne after a long absence, having come out from Frederikstadt in 100 days.

Three years later the Norwegians sold her to Lund for £3,500, the latter fitting her as a coal hulk in Sydney. Let me finish this account by quoting a letter from Sydney, written on June 10th, 1920 :

" The one-time clipper ship *Melbourne* has struck her last job. She has been converted into a coal elevator capable of bunkering steamers at the rate of 200 tons an hour. As she lies at Darling Island with her upper works demolished, coal-grabs fitted to her starboard deck, and a couple of 60-foot elevators towering over her port side, it is hard to realize that she was once a famous flyer."

THE "LOCH ETIVE."

SHIPS, like men, are remembered for many reasons. Some have made history—others ghastly tragedy. Some have been celebrated, like the *Cutty Sark*, and *Thermopylæ*, for the quality of speed; others, like the *Patriarch* and the *Harbinger*, for their splendid seaworthiness; others, again, like the *Golden Fleece* and the *Glengarry*, for their outstanding beauty. A few, however, have gained distinction through their connection with some well-known man. Of these, the *Torrens* and *Loch Etive* are examples, owing to the fact that the late Joseph Conrad served in them—in the *Torrens* as mate, and in the *Loch Etive*, at an earlier period of his sea career, as 3rd mate.

Probably the most popular of all Conrad's books amongst seamen is his " Mirror of the Seas." In this brilliant collection of essays he thus refers to the *Loch Etive* :

" The ship was one of those iron wool clippers that the Clyde had floated out in swarms upon the world during the seventh decade of the last century. It was a fine period in shipbuilding, and also, I might say, a period of overmasting. The spars rigged up on the narrow hulls were indeed tall then, and the ship of which I think, with her coloured-glass skylight-ends bearing the motto, ' Let Glasgow Flourish,' was certainly one of the most heavily-sparred specimens. She was built for hard driving, and unquestionably she got all the driving she could stand."

Loch Etive was the fifteenth vessel built for the famous Loch Line of Glasgow, which was managed by Messrs. Aitken, Lilburn & Co., and she was their first contract with Messrs. J. and A. Inglis, the builders of the beautiful tea clipper *Normancourt*. The new Loch liner registered 1,235 tons, and measured 226 feet 9 inches in length, 35 feet 9 inches breadth and 21 feet 6 inches depth of hold.

She was heavily rigged, as Conrad states, with a skysail yard at the main, but it would not be fair to conclude from his description that she was overmasted, for she carried her canvas well and, so far as I know, never lost a spar of any consequence. In her later years, along with all Aitken, Lilburn's 1,200-ton ships, she was cut down to a barque to save expense.

The *Loch Etive* was launched in November, 1877, at a time when extreme clipper hulls were giving way to a slightly fuller model, with a greater carrying capacity. Nevertheless, that *Loch Etive* was intended to be a flyer is evident from Aitken, Lilburn's choice of a commander.

Captain William Stuart of Peterhead, who commanded her from her launch until 1894, was at the top of his profession. Since 1863 he had had *The Tweed*, a vessel, as Conrad remarks, "famous the world over for her speed." By 1877 the old wonder, which had been sent afloat as far back as April, 1854, was becoming a bit leaky and loose in her fastenings, otherwise it is probable that Captain Stuart would not have been tempted to exchange Willis's flagship for the modern iron clipper. Captain Stuart naturally had a very high standard as regards speed, and though he drove the *Loch Etive* to the limit of her strength, she was rather a disappointment to him after *The Tweed*.

That Conrad was somewhat in awe of the great man, and at the same time looked upon him as the beau ideal of a sailor, is clear from the following :

" Captain S—— had a great name for sailor-like qualities—the sort of name that compelled my youthful admiration. To this day I preserve his memory, for, indeed, it was he, in a sense, who completed my training. It was often a stormy process, but let that pass. I am sure he meant well, and I am certain that never, not even at the time, could I bear him malice for his extraordinary gift of incisive criticism. And to hear him make a fuss about too much sail on the ship seemed one of those incredible experiences that take place only in one's dreams."

This last sentence requires explaining. Whilst the great author was serving in the *Loch Etive* she had a mate who was " that deaf he could not tell how much wind there was " and who therefore carried on in a manner which worried even such a driver as Stuart ; and the best of it was, that the captain " seemed constitutionally incapable of giving his officers a definite order to shorten sail."

Thus it came about that the combination of old Stuart and his deaf mate gave Conrad an example in sail-carrying which he hastened to follow as soon as he was given charge of the deck on the 2nd mate falling ill. When this occurred, Stuart's only instructions to his young officer were characteristic of the man. He would leave the deck with the words : " Don't take any sail off her." Then, just as he was going down the companion-way, would add curtly : " Don't carry anything away."

Conrad was evidently no mean follower of his chief ; and one night, when he had to shorten sail in a hurry through a sudden shift of wind, Stuart sent for him at the end of the watch, and Conrad received a wigging. Let me give it in his own words :

" ' What was the matter with you up there just now ? ' he asked.

" ' Wind flew round on the lee quarter, sir,' I said.

" ' Couldn't you see the shift coming ? '

" ' Yes, sir, I thought it wasn't very far off.'

" ' Why didn't you have your courses hauled up at once, then ? ' he asked, in a tone that ought to have made my blood run cold.

" But this was my chance, and I did not let it slip.

" ' Well, sir,' I said, in an apologetic tone, ' she was going 11 knots very nicely, and I thought she would do for another half-hour or so.'

" He gazed at me darkly out of his head, lying very still on the white pillow, for a time.

" ' Ah, yes, another half-hour. That's the way ships get dismasted.'

" And that was all I got in the way of a wigging."

*   *   *

The *Loch Etive* was put into the Sydney trade to start with. On her maiden passage she left Glasgow on January 9th, 1878, took her departure from the Scillies at 6 p.m. on January 17th, and crossed the Equator on February 6th. Up to this date she had not been favoured in her winds, but with the help of Captain Stuart's hard driving she now began to make up time. The Meridian of Greenwich was crossed on March 1st, 23 days from the Line. Stuart ran down his easting in 46° S. and had light winds for the most part, nevertheless, he passed the South Cape, Tasmania, on March 28th, and anchored in Sydney Harbour at 8 p.m. on April 3rd, 76 days out from the mouth of the Channel.

"Loch Etive"

Built 1877 Wool Clipper

The *Loch Etive* did not load wool on her first voyage. Captain Stuart, who was used to a free hand with his owners in regard to charters, for he was a noted money-maker, took her up to Calcutta and loaded a jute cargo home. Nor did he load regularly for Sydney, sometimes he went to Melbourne from the Clyde, though he usually came home with wool or wheat.

The *Loch Etive's* passages, both outwards and homewards, seem to have averaged about 90 days, until she suddenly made two outstanding voyages in 1892-3—the last two voyages, as it happened, that Captain Stuart was to make in this world.

On October 15th, 1892, she left Glasgow and arrived in Hobson's Bay on Christmas Day, 70 days out from the Tail of the Bank. Then leaving Melbourne with a wool cargo on January 26th, 1893, she arrived in the Thames on April 29th, 93 days out, being under 6½ months for the round voyage.

At 8 p.m. on September 23rd, 1893, she sailed from the Clyde for Adelaide, which she reached at 10 a.m. on December 12th, 80 days out. That old Stuart was still a hustler is evident, for she towed to the powder ground, discharged 20 tons of gunpowder, and berthed at the wharf for discharging on the same afternoon. On the 13th she began discharging 800 tons of cargo; she then took on board 300 tons of lead spelter, towed down the river, and on the 16th dropped her anchor off the Semaphore; sailed on the 17th, and arrived at Melbourne on the 19th. Here she discharged the remainder, some 750 tons, of her outward cargo and took in wool for Antwerp.

On his homeward passage, Captain Stuart took his departure from Melbourne Heads on January 18th, 1894, but was held up in Bass Straits by light head winds for a week. The Horn was passed, 3 miles off, at noon on February 15th, the Equator crossed at noon on March 15th, the Lizard signalled at noon on April 12th, and the ship docked in Antwerp on April 15th, 87 days out.

Though Captain Stuart was far from well he refused to stay ashore, and sailed again from Glasgow on September 16th. When the *Loch Etive* was five days out the famous master mariner passed away, on his 63rd birthday, and was buried at sea, about 300 miles S.W. of Queenstown. He had been 43 years a shipmaster, with the proud record of never having lost a man or a mast overboard. Though many enticing offers had been made, inviting him to command big steamships, he remained faithful to his old windjammer. Many of his men had sailed with him voyage after voyage, and more than one of them had reached command after having been not only sea trained, but educated by Captain Stuart.

Mr. Wade, the mate (who afterwards had command of the *Loch Sloy*), took the ship out to Adelaide in 98 days. The *Loch Garry* happened to be at Melbourne, and her chief officer, A. T. Fishwick, was sent down to take command of the *Loch Etive*.

Captain Fishwick commanded the *Loch Etive* from 1895 until 1909, when he was called upon to take over the *Loch Torridon* from Captain Pattman, who had decided to give up sail for steam.

It was not until 1904 that the *Loch Etive* had her after-yards and main skysail removed.

On November 13th, 1904, she left Glasgow as a barque; passed the Tuskar on the 19th, and crossed the Line on December 12th in 26° W. The Prime Meridian was crossed on January 2nd, 1905, and the Cape Meridian on January 7th in 40° S. The Leeuwin Meridian was crossed on January 27th, and the ship arrived in Port Jackson, only 80 days out. This was a very smart passage to make after being cut down, and the shippers at once decided that her sailing powers had not been spoilt.

Right up to 1911 the *Loch Etive* continued to load cargoes for Adelaide, Melbourne and Sydney. Captain Anderson, late of *Loch Katrine*, had succeeded Captain Fishwick. Anderson was notorious for his interest in the lonely inhabitants of Tristan d'Acunha. On his outward passages he always endeavoured to communicate with the islanders, and present them with clothes, books, comforts and small stores. On his last voyage in the *Loch Etive*, however, though he arrived off the island as usual, the weather was so bad that the hardy boatmen could not put off to the ship, and he was obliged to proceed without delivering his gifts. This was in 1910; in the following year the old Loch liner was sold to the French for the paltry sum of £1,350, and by 1914 she had disappeared from the register.

THE "MOUNT STEWART."

IN Lloyd's Register of 1923–4 only 28 British-owned sailing ships of over 1,000 tons are listed; and, of these the only vessel which was still under her original house flag was the *Mount Stewart*, owned by Donaldson, Rose & Co. Shipowners are credited by most seafarers with stony hearts and hard business heads; yet the fact that sailing ships are still making voyages proves that there is a strong dash of sentiment in the make-up of the man who earns a livelihood through his ships. And this has always been so.

Owners have always had their pet ships, vessels upon which they have lavished money, often without any hope of a return. Of all man-made creations, the ship has always possessed a curious power of gaining a place in the inmost recesses of the human heart. This is easy to understand in the case of a captain or even a foremast-hand, who from long association has come to love his vessel like a home; who has learnt to appreciate her character, delight in her beauty and glory in her brave seaworthiness. But, with owners, who have little opportunity of really knowing their ships, who rarely see them except when alongside a wharf, loading or discharging or in the grip of a tug, inward or outward bound, this affection, which very often makes a heavy inroad on the bank account, is a tribute both to man and ship.

Of these ships of sentiment *Mount Stewart* was probably one of the finest still afloat in 1925.

She and her sister ship *Cromdale* were the last two ships to be specially built for the Australian wool trade. Though not so fine lined as their predecessors and designed to carry large cargoes, they were yet vessels of a very fair speed, capable of running up to 300 miles in the 24 hours. Without the necessary speed in light and moderate winds to break records, they could be depended upon to catch the wool sales, and their names were rarely seen in the overdue list.

Mount Stewart was launched from the yard of Barclay, Curle & Co. in May, 1891. In this year, besides her sister ship *Cromdale*, Barclay, Curle built the well-known full-rig ship, *Talus*, 1,954 tons, for Carmichael's Golden Fleece Line.

It would be hard to name a more sightly trio than these three ships or to give finer examples of the very last phase of the full-rig ship. Built of steel, finely proportioned, perfectly sparred, with the dainty skysail yard at the main, they were a delight to the sailor's eye and received the admiration of the shipping fraternity wherever they went.

Mount Stewart registered 1,903 tons. She measured 271 feet 6 inches in length; 40 feet 1 inch breadth; 23 feet 4 inches depth; moulded depth, 25 feet 1 inch, with a freeboard amidships of 5 feet 3 inches. Her poop was the short one of the cargo carrier, not the long one of the passenger sailing ship, and barely reached to the mizen mast, being just 41 feet in length.

There is one aspect of sea life which is rarely to be found on board a steamship, and that is the homelike aspect. In many a square-rigged, "deep waterman," captains took their wives and children to sea for voyage after voyage. Such vessels were floating homes, and provided the wives were women of the right sort, were invariably happy, peaceful ships. One has, of course, met old shell-backs who shuddered at the very idea of a woman aboard ship, but these men are the rare exceptions who had been unlucky enough to be shipmates with one of those captain's wives who, having subdued her own husband, followed this conquest up by subjecting the whole ship's company to a rule of either the meanest type of economy or the bitterest kind of virulent terrorism. A few cases of such women could be recalled, but as a general rule the skipper's wife helped to make a peaceful, happy ship and most seamen will agree that the hardness of the life is very appreciably softened by the feminine presence aboard.

Of these homes on deep water the old *Mount Stewart* was a fine example. Her commander, Captain M. C. McColm, took charge of her in 1908 and remained in her until 1925, a period of 17 years. He never was in steam. His wife, an Australian lady, was at sea with him for a little over 13 years. But a still greater testimony to the peaceful, homelike life of the ship is the fact that the *Mount Stewart's* sailmaker was in her for 16 years, and her cook for 11 years.

In August, 1913, an interesting letter to his father from one of the *Mount Stewart's* apprentices appeared in a Sydney newspaper. This letter, describing his passage home, is of value as showing the life and training experienced by an apprentice in a first-class sailing ship during the last days of sail, and I therefore take the liberty of giving a few extracts. The boy, who was 16 years of age, was making his first deep-water trip, after an early training in the old *John Murray*. He writes from Queenstown as follows :

" We have had a fairly decent trip, though a long one. I liked it all right and have learnt a good bit, including decent steering. I have had plenty of practice in Morse and Semaphore, as there is a fairly decent crew, mostly young. . . . On the 25th the ' Old Man ' gave all the boys each a turn at furling the mizen royal, but out of 12 of us none could beat me. . . ."

And here are two samples of the windjammer virile methods of discipline :

" Tuesday we were running under fore and main topsails, mizen lower and fore and afters. The next day a dollop sent me gasping into the lee scuppers. Do you remember Chips ? Well, the same morning the 2nd mate wanted him to chock off the fore topgallant mast. The ship was rolling a good bit and Chips would not go. The 2nd mate promptly gave him a lesson on how to fight, and both were rolling about on the wet deck ; then the ' Old Man ' came forward, and on learning the cause of the fight, gave Chips a gentle reminder in his port sidelight, and poor old Chips went up like a lamb. . . Sunday, 23rd of March, I had a fight with a seaman for ordering me about, and lashed into him while the watch were squaring in the cross-jack yards. The mate, who is really a decent chap, saw us from where he was slacking the lee cross-jack braces. He made one rush at both of us, and a minute later I was rolling in the lee scuppers with a lift under my left flying-jib and a severe pain in my stern sheets. When I picked myself up from the scupper he was severely chastising the seaman, and both of us ran to the braces a little sadder, but also a little wiser. . . ."

He next gives a very vivid account of a squall, experienced when the ship was nearing the Horn :

" This Sunday the boys were keeping day look-outs, and it was mine from two o'clock till four o'clock in the afternoon. The weather was nice and fine, and I went up in pants

"Mount Stewart"
Built 1891 Wool Clipper.

and singlet and sea boots, with my oilskins over my arm. It had just gone seven bells, and I was thinking that I would have a sleep in the dog watch, when the mate came forrard to pull on the jib sheets. Mind you, there was a fair breeze blowing, but he had only just got into the forecastle head with a couple of hands when it fell a dead calm. The ' Old Man ' had just gone on to the poop and was looking up aloft. He walked to the wheel, and as I heard afterwards, told the helmsman that he expected a bit of a blow. The ship was then under topsails and staysails. He next turned to the lee side and I happened to look the same way. On the horizon I could see nothing but one mass of froth and tremendous waves. The ' Old Man ' turned, ' Stand by topsail halyards, lower the yards half down,' he shouted, at the same time motioning the wheel hard over. In three seconds the storm had struck us. Talk about hail and spray storms, you could not beat it, and we were very nearly caught aback, when it would have been time to say our prayers. The fore-topsails blew away at once, making a noise like guns firing, and I can tell you I didn't feel exactly at my ease. After the fore-topsails had gone the ' Old Man ' got the mizen topsails in safe, when the main upper blew away. The wind and seas were something terrific. Every time she rolled, under went the lee rail, taking huge dollops, which swept the ship from rail to rail. I was shivering on the forecastle head ; the weather was as cold as ice— absolutely freezing—and I had hail and spray dashing into my face all the time for seven and a half hours, while all hands were aft on the poop.

" Something had gone wrong with the mizen staysail sheet, and two hands were sent on deck to attend to it. The first on deck, a seaman named Reginald Ick, an Australian and a nice young fellow, jumped on to the spar at the weather main-braces to see to it, and in doing so, got a weather sea on top of him, and before he had hime to get off the spar, the weather rail went under and a big lee sea sent him head first overboard. The other seaman yelled to the mate, who flung a couple of life-belts, but of no avail. The mountainous seas prevented a boat from being launched, and we had to loop ahead. The ' Old Man ' did his best to put the ship round, but all hands could hardly move the yards. At midnight the wind died down gradually, but the sea was still big. . . ."

Three days later the ship passed within sight of the Diego Ramirez Rocks and headed up to the nor'ard. Then came the time of holystoning, tarring down, cleaning, chipping, scraping, and painting ; and every night in the second dog watch the " Old Man " had the boys aft on the poop and taught them to box. One Saturday in the doldrums, the Line was crossed, " and several of us were put through by Neptune, and after being tarred all over, shaved, dosed with salts by the glassful, and swallowing some curious-looking things they called pills, we were photographed and got our certificate."

The rest of the passage was uneventful, and after getting her orders at Queenstown, the *Mount Stewart* arrived at Barry Dock, after 120 days at sea. This was a long passage and by no means worthy of the old ship. One of her best homeward passages was made in 1893, under Captain G. E. Pryde, when she came home from Sydney in 88 days.

Captain McColm, who succeeded Captain C. Green in 1908, brought the old ship safely through the many dangers of the war, and finally hauled down his flag at Nantes in the summer of 1925. A very young man when he took command, Captain McColm was always a sail-carrier, and in June–July, 1921, drove the *Mount Stewart* from Delagoa Bay to Sydney in 38 days.

As long as it was possible for the sailing ship to get a homeward cargo of wool or wheat, *Mount Stewart* was kept in the London and Sydney trade, but in 1922–3 the ship was laid up for over a year in Milford Haven. Then she was ordered to load salt at Gracie, Beazley's berth in Liverpool. Her presence in the famous sailing ship port of old times raised quite an excitement amongst the many windjammer men living in retirement along the shores of the Mersey, especially as she was one of the last half-dozen deep-water sailing ships still flying the Red Ensign.

Alas ! it was to be her last voyage. She jogged out to Sydney in 125 days ; crossed to Iquique from Newcastle, N.S.W., and then on her arrival at Nantes from the West Coast of South America, was sold to the ship-breakers. This was a heart-breaking affair for many of the old seamen, who had been a long time in the ship, and one of her hands, who had no home except the *Mount Stewart*, prophesied that he would not survive her long. Sure enough, a few days before the crew were paid off, he fell down the hold, broke his back and died in hospital

Captain McColm, on giving up command of the *Mount Stewart*, retired with his wife and two young sons, who had never lived in a house ashore, to a dairy farm in New South Wales.

THE "HESPERUS."

ON March 27th, 1872, the *Yatala*, the finest passenger ship in the Orient Line, went ashore near Cape Gris Nez, when homeward bound from Adelaide, and became a total loss. This was a very serious loss to the firm, coming, as it did, at a time when the rush of emigrants to South Australia was at its height.

The *Yatala* was a composite ship of 1,127 tons, and under the famous Captain Legoe was noted for her passages, her best being 66 days to Adelaide in 1867. But, by 1872 the day of the composite clipper was already on the wane, and iron clippers were being built as fast as the North Country yards could lay them down. With their teak-built frigates and small composite clippers the great London shipping firms were already finding the competition of the new iron clippers from the Clyde and the Mersey more than serious, and it was quite evident that unless they abandoned teak for iron, they would lose their hardly-won position at the head of the British Merchant Service.

Thus it was that Messrs. Anderson, Anderson & Co. decided to replace their lost ship by the two finest iron clippers that could be built. Robert Steele, of Greenock, the foremost designer and builder of clipper ships in the world, was given the order for the two new Orient liners, and both in design and workmanship he gave of his very best. The new ships were named *Hesperus* and *Aurora*. *Hesperus* was launched in November, 1873. She registered 1,777 tons ; was 262 feet 2 inches in length with 39 feet 7 inches beam and 23 feet 5 inches depth, whilst her poop was 74 feet long, and her fo'c'sle head 40 feet. Her sail plan was a large one, with double topgallant yards on all three masts. She had very long poles above her royals, so that skysail yards could be sent up and crossed in the tropics, and her jib-boom was noted as the longest belonging to any ship sailing out of the Port of London.

On February 14th, 1874, the veteran Captain Legoe was appointed to the command of the new clipper, and she was put on the berth for Adelaide. Previous to commanding the *Yatala* from 1865 to 1872, Captain Legoe had had the *Murray* for four voyages, and before that the little tea clipper, *Celestial*.

The year 1874 was a boom year in the passenger trade to the Colonies, and nearly every ship sailing for Australia or New Zealand had her 'tween-decks full of emigrants. That spring the following ships left the United Kingdom for the Land of Promise :

Hesperus	with	416	emigrants for	Adelaide.
Lady Douglas	,,	300	,, ,,	Rockhampton.
Great Queensland	,,	644	,, ,,	Maryborough.
La Hogue	,,	443	,, ,,	Wellington.
Rooparell	,,	361	,, ,,	Auckland.
Ballochmyle	,,	484	,, ,,	Canterbury.
James Nichol Fleming	,,	367	,, ,,	Port Chalmers.

With a full complement of passengers, Captain Legoe made no attempt to beat records, but relied on the natural speed of his ship. Many a captain, in those early days of iron, made the lives of his passengers into a sort of inferno, in his effort to make a good passage.

Small heed was taken of the fact that iron has not the buoyancy of wood, and many a ship was driven through the " roaring forties " like a submarine, with her passengers battened down below and her crew standing by on the poop. Of such was the *Loch Awe*, Captain Weir, which arrived in Auckland with her decks swept clean, her boats gone, and her passengers half-crazed with fright and half-dead with fatigue, from being hurled about below, whilst the ship crashed from sea to sea.

But this hard driving was not encouraged in the Orient Line, nor was it necessary in the case of a ship like the *Hesperus*, for not only did she prove to be a fine sea boat, stiff under canvas and easy to handle, but also a vessel of very exceptional speed. Though her passages under the Orient flag were always good, she was never raced, and always came home via the Cape and St. Helena in preference to the more strenuous route round the Horn.

Her sister ship, *Aurora*, was unfortunately lost on her maiden voyage, being abandoned in flames with fore and main masts gone in 40° N. 35° W. on August 9th, 1875, her homeward cargo of wool having caught fire by spontaneous combustion. Her place was filled by the famous *Harbinger*. *Hesperus* and *Harbinger* were favourite passenger ships in the Adelaide and Melbourne trade right up to 1890, when they were bought by Lord Brassey and Messrs. Devitt & Moore for their new cadet-training scheme.

Legoe retired from the sea at the end of the 'seventies, and set up as a stevedore at the Semaphore. He was succeeded by Captain T. R. Harry, who remained in command of the *Hesperus* until the Orient Line sold her.

On taking over the *Hesperus*, Messrs. Devitt & Moore transferred their crack skipper, Barrett, and his chief officer, F. W. Corner, from the *Rodney*. It was under these two officers that the *Hesperus* made her best passages. Captain Barrett, who had a strong objection to skysails, did away with the clipper's skysail yards ; he also removed her standing gaff and spanker-boom, and contented himself with a leg-of-mutton spanker.

On September 11th, 1891, *Hesperus* left London with a full complement of cadets. She reached Sydney on December 8th, 88 days out. Here her crew cleared out in order to follow a gold stampede up-country, leaving the cadets to do everything during the ship's four months' wait for a wool cargo. No history of Sydney would be complete without some mention of the sailing ship brassbounders ; the cadets of the *Hesperus* proved only too true to type, and when the vessel sailed for home, the three brass balls of a well-known pawnbroker in Argyle Cut hung conspicuous in their golden splendour from the end of the clipper's jib-boom. The run home was made in the good time of 85 days. In 1892 and 1893 the *Hesperus* made the two best passages of her career.

On October 11th, 1892, she left London and took her departure from the Lizard on the 13th ; the Equator was crossed on November 8th in 30° W. and the Greenwich Meridian on November 29th in 42° S. Her best runs in the 'forties were 300, 302, 319, 326 and 328 miles, and on December 23rd she arrived in Hobson's Bay, 71 days from the Lizard.

In 1893 she took her departure from the Lizard on October 18th ; crossed the Equator in 25° W. on November 8th, and the Cape Meridian on the 30th. On December 10th she made her best 24-hour run, 363 miles, with a strong North wind and smooth water. This was under all plain sail except the mainsail, which had to be furled, as it was badly torn whilst all hands were attempting to reef it at 4 a.m. The Otway was sighted at 6 p.m. on December 28th, but a strong southerly gale was blowing and the ship had to be hove to for some hours, and could not get inside until the following day, when she anchored in Hobson's Bay, 72 days from the Lizard.

J. Spurling
1923

"Hesperus"
Built 1873 Blackwall Passenger Ship.

Throughout the 'nineties the *Hesperus* sailed to Melbourne with cadets and brought home a cargo of wool or grain. Her passages were nearly always above the average, which is not to be wondered at with picked officers and double watches.

In 1895 she arrived in Hobson's Bay, 81 days out from the Start. This year she lost Fred Corner as chief officer; he left the *Hesperus* to take command of the *Rodney*. The former's worst passage appears to have been her homeward one in 1897, when she signalled the Lizard on July 18th, 138 days from Port Phillip. On her next passage out, in 1898, she soon showed that she had not lost her speed, by making the run in 76 days from the Wight.

At the end of this voyage Captain Barrett had to give up his command owing to ill-health, and so it came about that Captain Maitland had the old ship during her last voyage under Devitt & Moore's house flag. He drove the *Hesperus* from the Lizard to Melbourne in 84 days. On her arrival home in 1899 Devitt & Moore sold their beautiful cadet ship to the Russian Government for £9,000. She was renamed *Grand Duchess Maria Nikolaevna*, and stationed in the Black Sea as a training ship.

When the war broke out she happened to be refitting at Wallsend. The famous cadet ship was not allowed to play any part in the gigantic struggle, but was taken across to Frederikshavn, Denmark, where she lay moored bow and stern throughout the war.

Soon after the armistice she was claimed by the Russian Republic, and the officials of the Russian Volunteer Fleet, who had headquarters in London, took her over and had her fitted for sea at Newcastle, with the intention of sending her into general trading. Her first charter under the Republican flag was to fetch a cargo of bass-wood logs from Montreal, where the lumber had been lying piled on the wharf, waiting to be taken to England to be manufactured into matches.

The *Grand Duchess* sailed from Newcastle in water ballast and made the run across to Montreal in 30 days. This was before the days of the Soviet, and her officers were Russians of the old regime. Both her captain and chief officer were gentlemen, and quite young. The skipper was a very clever navigator, and he showed his skill by sailing his ship through Belle Isle Strait and past Anticosti, by the North Channel. The mate was also very capable. He had been a cadet in her when she was the Odessa training ship before the war.

On her arrival at Montreal the crew deserted as soon as they saw what kind of a deck cargo the poor old ship had to load. This consisted of round, unbarked tree-trunks of bass-wood which, lashed down with chains, so blocked the main-deck, that one could hardly get at the gear, much less pull on it. The author and journalist, Frederick William Wallace, made the passage back to England in the ship, and in a letter written in January, 1922, he thus describes the ex-cadet ship :

" The old packet was in splendid shape—sails all new, gear rove off anew, and everything spick and span. The brass-work, teak and carving about her would have served a yacht and delighted the heart of a ' Blue Nose ' mate. Her figure-head and lines were beautiful and her iron hull was as good now as the day she was built. I have been down in her run and fore-peak, and there was no sign of corrosion. We had wireless and got all the news of the day, also the weather forecasts, and rated chronometers from Eiffel Tower. She was fitted with two donkey-boilers, steam heat and electric light—needless to say we had neither heat nor light as a common timber-drogher. Her original standing rigging was set up by lanyards and dead eyes—she now has rigging-screws and shear-pole ratlins. The teak forward-house was rebuilt of steel; fo'c'sle bunks are of the sanitary steel kind and steam heat and electric light were also fitted, though not used on our trip. There was enough spare gear in her peak to fit her out twice over. I never was aboard such a ship for fine fittings."

The difficulty, once the cargo was loaded, was to ship a crew. The mate made a trip to New York, and came back with nine men, but when the ship left Montreal, out of twenty hands in her fo'c'sle, only six could be called sailormen; the rest were steamboat roustabouts, stiffs and hoboes. And when the old ship got clear of the Gulf, the officers soon discovered that there was no hope of making a passage, owing to her poor crew. Half the crowd were shirkers, who, when there was work to do aloft, loitered on the shear-poles or hid in the tops. One man, according to Wallace, hid behind the donkey-boiler and never went above the rail the whole passage. Other men actually went aloft up the inside of the lee rigging and crawled through the lubber's hole. And when it breezed up a bit, it took eighteen men a hard struggle to make the main upper topsail fast.

The *Grand Duchess* towed away from Montreal behind a Diesel-engined tug on October 2nd, 1920. It was a 240-mile tow down to Father Point. In the traverses there was something of a mix-up. It was raining hard and pitch dark. The tide took charge of the tug-boat; the tow-rope fouled the ship's martingale, broke off the arm of the figure-head, carried away the back-ropes, and took a turn round the fluke of the anchor, which was hanging from the hawse-pipe. For some minutes it looked as if the ship might go ashore before the tug got straightened out.

On her passage to Liverpool the best 24-hour run was 240 miles, but what with light winds and an indifferent crew, she never had a chance. Cape Clear was abeam on the 29th day out, but the ship was then held up by head winds. Finally, after a pluck from the Bar lightship, which cost £300, the *Grand Duchess* dropped her anchor in the Mersey on November 5th.

Since her sale to the Russians the old ship's bowsprit and long jib-boom had been replaced by an unusually long spike bowsprit of steel. Whilst she was warping into the basin of the North Carrier's Dock the following evening, this steel bowsprit raked the side of a steamer, sweeping away 22 feet of her rail and her port topmast backstay.

The next event in the life of the *Grand Duchess* was the eclipse of the Russian Republic by the Soviet; the day after she had docked, General Wrangell's defeat was in the papers. Uncertain what to do, the skipper of this aristocratic vessel put the *Grand Duchess* under the protection of France and hoisted the Tricolour. Then, after lying discharged for some time in the Wallasey Dock, the old ship once more came under the Red Ensign, her new owners being the London Steamship and Trading Corporation.

For some reason or other she was not given back her old name, but disguised under that of *Silvana*. Captain P. Balk handed over to Captain C. J. Soutar, and in September, 1921, the *Silvana* sailed for Santa Pola, Spain. Here she loaded salt and sailed for Buenos Ayres on July 12th, 1922. This last voyage of the famous passenger clipper seems to have been the most leisurely of her existence. She was no less than 88 days from Spain to the River Plate. Then on January 9th, 1923, she left Buenos Ayres and turned up at St. Michael's, Azores, 117 days later. Lastly we find her in sad straits, lying at Bordeaux, held up for want of money to meet the claims of various creditors, including her officers and crew.

With her owners unable to meet their liabilities, the civil tribunal at Bordeaux awarded the ship to the firm which had supplied her with 50,000 francs' worth of provisions. Then the Imperial Merchant Service Guild intervened on behalf of the ship's officers. Upon which the legal dispute raged round a very interesting object—this was a valuable icon, in the shape of a gold statue, set with precious stones, which, rumour stated, had been presented to the ship either by the late Czar himself or by one of the royal princesses of Russia. This icon was valued at £1,000. Suddenly it disappeared, but after being missing for some months, was at last discovered in the possession of a money-lender, who had advanced a small sum upon it. On being recovered it was deposited with the Finnish Consul at Bordeaux until the legal dispute over wages and claims was settled.

Finally the financial difficulties were cleared up, and an Italian captain was appointed, who sailed the famous old ship to Genoa, where she was broken up during the summer of 1923.

THE "TAEPING."

THE famous tea clipper *Taeping* was launched from Robert Steele's yard at Greenock on December 24th, 1863. She was built for Captain Rodger, with the special object of beating the flying *Fiery Cross*, which had won the premium given to the first arrival in both the previous seasons, 1861 and 1862. Nor was she the only vessel launched that year with the express purpose of lowering the colours of the *Fiery Cross*. During the summer Steele had produced the *Serica* for James Findlay and the *Young Lochinvar* for Messrs. McDiarmid & Greenshields, whilst the Aberdeen clipper of the year was the *Black Prince*, designed by John Rennie, and built by Hall. Then there was the Workington crack, *Belted Will*, belonging to Bushby.

It may be of interest to compare the measurements of these five beautiful tea ships :

	Tons reg.	Length.		Breadth.		Depth.	
		ft.	in.	ft.	in.	ft.	in.
Taeping	767	183	7	31	1	19	9
Serica	708	185	9	31	1	19	6
Young Lochinvar	724	186	1	31	1	19	8
Black Prince ..	750	183		35		19	6
Belted Will ..	812	186	4	32	4	20	8

Steele's ships were celebrated not only for beauty of model and perfection of build, but for their superb finish, the figure-heads, gingerbread work, and deck fittings of picked teak, with brass inlay, being specially notable. All who saw them declared that the skill and care used on the 1863 ships had never been surpassed, even by the famous yard of Robert Steele & Co.

It is less easy to say which of the five ships was the fastest. The *Young Lochinvar* was wrecked during a fog at the entrance to the Min River, in 1866, before she had found her form. *Black Prince* undoubtedly was very fast indeed, but she had a careful skipper, who could never be induced to drive his vessel. *Belted Will* was in the Canton trade, loading at Whampoa and Macao, and never joined the " full bloods," as they were called, at the Pagoda anchorage in the Min River. But the wood *Serica* and composite *Taeping* had many a hard tussle, and, on the whole, the Rodger crack had a bit the best of it. Both ships were superbly sailed. Captain Innes, of the *Serica*, had been in the tea trade since as far back as 1851, when he was with old man Findlay in the *Foam*. Captain McKinnon gave up the *Ellen Rodger* in order to take over the *Taeping*.

Like another very famous ship (*Sir Lancelot*), the *Taeping* was kept out of the first flight for two years, owing to mischance. *Serica*, on the other hand, had the luck to win her first tea race, beating the *Fiery Cross* from Foochow by five days.

The *Taeping* made a good passage out to China on her maiden trip, showing unusual speed in light winds. Being too late for the first teas from Foochow, she cleared for Shanghai. When she was running her easting down, a small Liverpool clipper, the *Vigil*, of 550 tons, which had been built by Vernon in 1862, hung on to the new tea ship for several days in the

" roaring forties," and this encouraged her to think that she would make a good race of it to Shanghai. However, directly the wind lightened *Taeping* went clean away, and had discharged, and was nearly full of tea by the time the *Vigil* reached port.

The *Taeping* was loaded in the Shanghai river, alongside the pretty little Aberdeen flyer, *Coulnakyle*, of 579 tons, which had been built in 1862, by Hall, for Jamieson. In 1863 *Coulnakyle* had taken 131 days from Woosung, being beaten by the old *Challenger* and the Clyde-built *Guinevere*. However, Captain Morrison, of the bottle-green clipper, was quite ready to bet the usual hat with McKinnon. Both ships sailed on July 1st, 1864.

On July 20th *Coulnakyle* came limping into Hong Kong harbour under her courses and jury topsails, having narrowly escaped from a severe typhoon off the south end of Formosa. With all her canvas blown to ribbons, the *Coulnakyle* lay down on her beam ends, and the topmasts had to be cut away to save the ship. It was the usual strenuous business. The fore-topmast took the lower masthead with it in falling ; the main topmast refused to go clear, and the gallant old Aberdonian carpenter risked his life in cutting the wreck adrift. *Taeping* turned up at Amoy on July 23rd, having had an even worse time. Her foremast was gone, together with the bowsprit and main and mizen topmasts.

These dismastings effectually ended the race between *Taeping* and *Coulnakyle*. It took Captain McKinnon three months to refit the *Taeping*, and she did not arrive in the London river until January, 1865, having made the passage from Amoy in the splendid time of 88 days. This mishap again threw *Taeping* out of the first flight from Foochow in 1865. In that year *Serica* (Captain Innes) and *Fiery Cross* towed down the Min River behind the same tug on May 28th, and, after being constantly in company during the passage, made the Wight together on September 11th, 106 days out. Off Beachy Head *Serica* was leading by two miles. Unfortunately for Innes, whilst he was keeping well out in the Channel, in order to get the strength of the flood, the *Fiery Cross* picked up a tug in under the land, and thus docked a tide ahead, and won the premium.

Taeping did not leave Foochow until June 29th. She reached the Downs on October 9th, her 102 days being the best passage made that season. Though the *Taeping* was recognized as a full blood, she had never been tried out against any of the cracks, but her chance came in 1866, and she made history. This famous race is fully described in the account of *Taeping's* rival, *Ariel* (pages 61–64). Nothing, however, was said about the strain of such a race on the captains of the racing clippers. Only those who have gone through a hard yacht-racing season can properly sympathize with Keay (*Ariel*), McKinnon, and Innes. It is said that Captain Innes, at the end of the race, could not lift a cup of tea to his lips without spilling it. McKinnon died on his next outward passage, and only the imperturbable Keay seemed to suffer no ill-effects from the 99 days of strain and stress.

The *Taeping* was lucky to have a very good man in Captain Dowdy as successor to Captain McKinnon. In the 1867 race Captain Dowdy brought the *Taeping* home a week ahead of any other tea ship, his time being 102 days 5 hours. Her great rival, the *Ariel*, was late in loading, owing to long intermediate passages, but as the extra premium for the first ship in had been discontinued, there was not the same financial interest as in previous years, though the clippers were just as keenly raced. *Taeping* arrived in the Thames on September 14th ; *Ariel* arrived on September 23rd, exactly 102 days out, but both *Ariel* and *Taeping* had to lower their colours to *Ariel's* sister ship, *Sir Lancelot*, which arrived on September 22nd, only 99 days out from Shanghai.

In many ways the tea race of 1868 was the most interesting of the whole series. This year *Taeping*, *Ariel*, and *Sir Lancelot* found themselves pitted against three new cracks— *Spindrift*, *Lahloo*, and *Undine*.

"Taeping"
Built 1863 Tea Clipper.

The table below gives the starters from Foochow, and their times :

Ship.	Cargo.	Date Sailed.		Date Arrived.		Days Out.
Ariel	1,221,508 lbs.	May 28.	3.45 p.m.	Sept. 2.	1 p.m.	97
Sir Lancelot ..	1,250,057 lbs.	,, 28.		,, 2.	midnight.	98
Taeping	1,165,508 lbs.	,, 28.		,, 7.	2 a.m.	102
Spindrift	1,306,836 lbs.	,, 29.	5 p.m.	,, 2.	midnight	97
Lahloo	1,231,397 lbs.	,, 30.		,, 7.	7.30 p.m.	101
Black Prince ..	1,051,300 lbs.	,, 31.		,, 30.		122
Serica	967,500 lbs.	June 1.		,, 21.		113
Fiery Cross ..	867,600 lbs.	,, 2.		,, 30.		120

It will be noticed that the ships which had already proved themselves were favoured by the shippers before the new clippers ; *Ariel*, *Sir Lancelot*, and *Taeping* getting the first tea chops, as the lighters, laden with tea-chests, were called. The Pagoda anchorage must have been a wonderful sight that year, for there was nothing more beautiful afloat than a tea ship when she was ready to load. The competition in seaman-like smartness was tremendous. The black hulls of the clippers, with their golden scroll-work, shone like satin, whilst the copper above the water-line, which was oiled and burnished by hand, sparkled dazzlingly in the sun. Aloft each ship was spick and span to the smallest detail, with standing rigging freshly tarred and rattled down, masts and yards under new coats of paint, and the newly-rove running gear either flemished down, or neatly turned up with stops of canvas.

It was soon recognized, in May, 1868, that the first three ships would finish loading within a few hours of each other, and at 4 a.m. on Wednesday, May 27th, a tremendous sail-bending competition began. The gantlines had been rove the previous evening, with the sails bent on ready to sway away aloft, and directly the order : " Turn to ! Bend sail ! " was given (at the same moment on each ship), the stamp of bare feet and the quick rhythm of running choruses awoke all sleepers at the Pagoda anchorage.

By eight bells, breakfast time, *Ariel*, *Sir Lancelot* and *Taeping* were each ready for sea, with every roband passed, square sails harbour stowed, and staysails snugly furled inside painted sail covers.

Captain Keay was the first man to trip his anchor, the *Ariel*, with the tug *Woosung* alongside and coolies still tapping the chests into place below, proceeding at 3.45 p.m., amidst the cheers of the assembled fleet. But she was not able to get clear away, having to anchor between Temple Point and Sharp Peak at 6.30 p.m. whilst the tug went back to fetch down the *Taeping*.

At 9 a.m. on May 28th *Taeping* anchored close to *Ariel*, off Temple Point, and at 10 o'clock *Sir Lancelot* came along in tow of the steamer *Island Queen*, and brought up below the *Taeping*. At 12.30 p.m. the tide served and *Ariel*, having a prior claim on the *Woosung*, hove up and proceeded with the tug ahead. At 2 p.m. *Sir Lancelot*, having the best tug, towed past the *Ariel* and thus was first across the bar by a few minutes, both ships discharging their tugs at 2.25 p.m., and making all plain sail on a wind. *Taeping* was quite half an hour behind at the bar, which she logged as being crossed at 3 p.m.

The three racing ships were soon covered with every kind of flying kite, the wind being very light in the N.E. quarter. For the first three days of the passage, whilst *Ariel* and *Sir Lancelot* were having a ding-dong struggle, *Taeping* pursued her way alone, being just under the horizon. Then on June 2nd, 3rd and 4th *Ariel* had a clear horizon, whilst *Taeping* and *Sir Lancelot* tried conclusions.

On June 9th Captain Keay, who thought he was leading, after running *Sir Lancelot* under astern, was much disgusted to discover three tea ships on his weather-bow at daybreak, the wind being fresh and squally from the sou'-west. Two of these ships were *Taeping* and *Spindrift*, the other being *Undine*, which had sailed from Whampoa on May 30th. *Taeping* had *Sir Lancelot* in sight, whilst *Lahloo* was only just below the horizon.   For the next three days strenuous times reigned in the competing ships, which were close-hauled on a wind in very squally weather, with fierce bursts of wind and torrents of rain.   At one moment the sky was black, at the next the sun was shining.   There was no rest for officers or men, for after every squall split sails had to be unbent and replaced.   In one furious gust of wind the *Ariel* was caught aback whilst in stays, and her royals, fore and main topgallant sails, flying jib and mizen staysail, were all blown away.   To add to the overwrought feelings of her crew, the new *Spindrift* seized the opportunity to pass her to windward.

For five days first one ship was ahead and then another.   On June 9th, 10th and 11th, *Taeping*, *Sir Lancelot*, *Ariel*, *Spindrift*, and *Undine* were fighting a battle royal.   Then on June 12th *Taeping*, *Sir Lancelot* and *Spindrift* parted company with *Ariel* and *Undine*.   On the 13th *Taeping* saw the last of *Sir Lancelot* and *Spindrift* for a few days, whilst *Ariel* found herself sailing tack and tack with the new Rodger clipper *Lahloo*, which, it was hoped, would prove herself an improved *Taeping*.

By sheer daring in running through the Thousand Island Group on a dark night, Captain Keay had the honour of being first past Anjer : he sent his letters ashore at 11 a.m. on June 22nd.   But *Taeping* and *Sir Lancelot* were both in sight astern.   *Spindrift*, which had been in company with *Ariel* off Api Point on June 18th, did not pass Anjer until 6 a.m. on the 23rd, and *Lahloo* went through at 10 a.m. on the same day.

All five Foochow ships rounded the Cape within 30 hours of each other, after having experienced a severe dusting off Agulhas.   On July 19th, when *Lahloo* and *Sir Lancelot* were in 35° 27′ S. 21° 20′ E. head reaching in sight of each other in the worst of the sou'-wester, *Ariel* was in 35° 26′ S. 18° 37′ E., leading the fleet by a day.   *Taeping* was fourth ship, and the *Spindrift* last.   But this order did not last long.

On July 29th *Taeping* and *Spindrift* were together in 18° 55′ S. 4° 5′ W., *Ariel* being a day ahead still in 16° 58′ S. 5° 15′ W.   On August 5th *Spindrift* crossed the Equator in 22° W., *Ariel* being in 2° 4′ S., and *Taeping* and *Lahloo* in company in 3° 36′ S. 19° 3′ W.

On August 9th *Ariel* had regained her lead, being in 8° N. 26° 5′ W., whilst *Taeping*, *Lahloo* and *Spindrift* were in sight of each other in 6° 40′ N. 24° 52′ W.   Three days later all four ships were in company in 14° 24′ N. 26° 5′ W., whilst *Sir Lancelot* was close by, though under the horizon.

The following extracts from Captain Keay's private log-book are worth recording, as showing the closeness of the sailing :

" Aug. 12th.   Wind S.S.W., hauling to West and falling very light.   Two homeward bound clippers in sight—*Taeping* and *Lahloo*—former signalized that *Spindrift* was in sight this morning, bearing from them E.S.E. ; so here we are, four in a group.   Where is *Sir Lancelot ?* Lat. 14° 17′ N., Long. 26° 32′ W.

" Aug. 13th.   At daylight *Taeping* about four miles dead to windward and *Lahloo* hull and lower yards down on weather beam.   Moderate N.E. wind, the Trades, we hope.

" Aug. 14th.   Lat. 18° 47′ N., Long. 30° 18′ W., Distance 250 miles.   *Taeping* gradually dropped astern and to leeward, is now nearly hull down on lee quarter.   We have more advantage of her in this fine breeze than in light winds.   *Lahloo* reached and weathered on us.

" Aug. 15th.   *Taeping* lower yards down on lee quarter.   Moderate trade wind.

" Aug. 16th.—7 a.m. *Taeping* S.W. ½ S. main topsail yard dipping. 11 a.m. light shower, wind broke off to West and W. by S. for short time. *Taeping* carried the true wind throughout and neared us about 3 miles.

" P.M. Wind freshening. Leaving the *Taeping* again.

" Aug. 17th.—6 a.m. *Taeping* seen from mizen cross trees, hull down. 10 a.m. *Taeping* not visible from cross trees, having dropped astern."

Ariel passed to the westward of the Azores on August 21st, leading from *Spindrift*, which sighted Corvo on the 22nd. It was anybody's race as far as the Scilly Isles, where *Ariel* was still half a day ahead.

On August 26th *Taeping*, *Sir Lancelot* and *Lahloo* were in sight of each other in 45° 25′ N. 20° 53′ W. *Spindrift* was only just under the horizon, whilst *Ariel's* noon position was 46° 15′ N. 19° 31′ W.

On August 28th *Ariel* was in 47° 48′ N. 13° 28′ W., the other four being in company just out of sight astern. August 30th was the decisive day of the race. At 11 p.m. *Ariel* sighted the Scilly Lights from aloft, bearing N. by E. At noon that day Captain Dowdy's sights put *Taeping* 60 miles S.W. of the Scillies. The wind was barely ruffling the surface of the water, and the lucky ones just had steerage way, whilst the unlucky drifted helplessly on the tide. And whilst *Ariel* went ghosting up-channel with a six-hour lead of *Spindrift* and *Sir Lancelot*, *Taeping* and *Lahloo* lay becalmed off the Scillies.

The positions of the five racers at noon on September 2nd showed how much the element of luck had spoilt what promised to be the finest finish of an ocean race ever known. Whilst *Ariel* was passing through the dock gates, *Spindrift* and *Sir Lancelot* were towing through the Downs, *Taeping* was only 20 miles east of the Lizard, and the *Lahloo* had barely run the Scillies out of sight. It must have been a very unusual spell of calm weather, for *Taeping* and *Lahloo* continued to make little progress, the latter actually being becalmed for 30 hours off the Eddystone.

The race was awarded to *Spindrift*, which had beaten *Ariel* by some 6 hours on time.

This was *Taeping's* last race in the first flight from Foochow. In 1869 the market opened very late. *Ariel*, with a new jockey in Captain Courtenay, was the first away, sailing on June 30th. *Taeping* did not leave the Pagoda anchorage until July 9th ; the two old rivals made passages of 104 and 108 days respectively, but all records were broken this year by *Sir Lancelot's* 89 days and *Thermopylæ's* 91 days.

In 1870 *Taeping* went out to Shanghai in 102 days, and loading at Whampoa and Macao, took 112 days coming home.

On her last voyage the *Taeping* was commanded by Captain Gissing. She sailed from Amoy for New York and was wrecked on Ladd's Reef, her mate's boat, containing six men, being picked up three days later.

THE "ARIEL."

IN the days of our grandfathers the annual clipper ship race from China with the first teas of the season caused almost as much interest amongst the general public as the Derby. Just sixty-one years ago the greatest and most exciting of all the tea races started from the Pagoda anchorage in the Min River, and ended on the inside of the London Dock gates. The struggle, however, began long before the ships hove up their anchors in the Min River. It began in the offices of the ships' agents and in the hongs of the Chinese merchants, fortunes in money being dependent on the winning ship. Thus the favourites for the race got the first chests, and were, therefore, the first to finish loading.

The tea came down the Min River from Foochow to the anchorage in large sampans, and was slung aboard the ships, and stowed into every nook and cranny—even to the captain's cabin—by clever Chinese stevedores, who worked in shifts, day and night. And whilst the tea-chests were being stowed, the crews of the ships were getting the clippers ready for the fray. The most elaborate chafing gear was sent aloft. Every rope and wire was carefully examined and replaced by new if it showed the least sign of wear. The stunsail gear was overhauled, and the stunsail-booms sent aloft. The carpenter sheathed over all chain plates with 2 to 3-inch pine planks, so that they should not drag in the water when the ship was well heeled. Stores, too, had to be shifted to make way for tea, which found its way into the lazarette, into the forepeak, and even into the paint locker. As each ship began to fill up, the excitement became greater and greater, and the ships resounded with a variety of noises—the pidgin-English of the Chinese stevedores contrasting weirdly with the stronger seafaring English of the mates and bos'ns.

In May, 1866, there were loading at the Pagoda anchorage the following first-class tea clippers, beautiful little ships, built of oak and teak specially for the trade :

Ariel, 852 tons, Captain Keay, built by Steele of Greenock, owners Shaw, Maxton.
Fiery Cross, 695 tons, Captain Robinson, built by Chaloner of Liverpool, owners J. Campbell.
Serica, 708 tons, Captain Innes, built by Steele of Greenock, owners Findlay.
Taeping, 767 tons, Captain McKinnon, built by Steele of Greenock, owners Rodger.
Taitsing, 815 tons, Captain Nutsford, built by Connell of Glasgow, owners Findlay.
Ziba, 497 tons, Captain Tomlinson, built by Hall of Aberdeen, owners J. Wade.
Black Prince, 750 tons, Captain Inglis, built by Hall of Aberdeen, owners Baring Bros.
Chinaman, 668 tons, Captain Downie, built by Steele of Greenock, owners Park Bros.
Flying Spur, 735 tons, Captain Ryrie, built by Hall of Aberdeen, owners Jardine & Co.
Ada, 687 tons, Captain Jones, built by Hall of Aberdeen, owners J. Wade.
Falcon, 794 tons, Captain Gunn, built by Steele of Greenock, owners Shaw, Maxton.

I have put down the ships in the order in which they sailed from the anchorage. *Ariel* and *Taitsing* were new ships, and of the two, *Ariel* was made the favourite in the betting on the race. *Taeping* had made the fastest passage in 1865, and the first ships in that year were *Serica* and *Fiery Cross*, the latter having the luck to fall in with a tug-boat off Beachy Head, when *Serica* was leading her by two miles. But, as regards speed, there was only a slight difference between the first and last, and the race depended quite as much on the skill and nerve of their captains as upon the ships themselves. In this the new clipper *Ariel* was particularly fortunate, for she was commanded by Captain John Keay, one of the most experienced masters in the China trade, who had previously sailed the *Ellen Rodger* and the *Falcon* with great success.

Captain Keay took the *Ariel* from the stocks, and in the maiden passage out to Hong Kong, accomplished in 103 days from the Tuskar, had satisfied himself that his new command was a knot faster all round than the famous *Falcon*. From the first he fell in love with the beautiful little vessel, as may be seen from the following eulogy which he penned to me some years ago :

" *Ariel* was a perfect beauty to every nautical man who saw her : in symmetrical grace and proportion of hull, spars, sails, rigging and finish, she satisfied the eye, and put all in love with her without exception. The curve of stem, figure-head and entrance, the easy sheer and graceful lines of the hull, seem grown and finished as life takes shape and beauty : the proportion and stand of her masts and yards were all perfect. On deck there was the same complete good taste : roomy flush decks with pure white bulwark panels, delicately bordered with green and minutely touched in the centre with azure and vermilion. She had no topgallant bulwarks (her main rail was only 3 feet high), but stanchions of polished teak, protected by brass tubing let in flush."

And here is his testimony to her sailing qualities :

" It was a pleasure to coach her. Very light airs gave her headway and I could trust her like a thing alive in all evolutions : in fact, she could do anything short of speaking. *Ariel* often went 11 and 12 knots sharp on a bowline, and in fair winds 14, 15 and 16 knots for hours together. We could tack or wear with the watch, but never hesitated to call all hands, night or day, tacking, reefing, etc., in strong winds. The best day's work in South latitude, running East, was 340 nautical miles by observation, and that was done carrying all plain sail except mizen royal, the wind being 3 or 4 points on the quarter."

The *Ariel*, like all the fairy-like Steele clippers, was a ticklish jade to handle, and it took a master to get the best out of her. If over-pressed, she had a habit of settling down aft, and had to be quickly relieved of her mizen canvas, or she would drown her helmsman. This fault was due to a want of bearing aft, which was practically the only flaw in Robert Steele's tea ship designs.

The *Ariel* was built for Shaw, Maxton & Co., and launched on June 29th, 1865. Her dimensions by builder's measurement were as follows :—Length of keel and fore-rake 195 feet ; breadth of beam, 33 feet 9 inches ; depth of hold, 21 feet ; tonnage 1,058 73/100. Her registered tonnage was 852 tons. She was ballasted with 100 tons of fixed kentledge, fitted into the limbers along the keelson, besides 20 tons of movable iron pegs for shifting ballast. But for a tea cargo she also required some 200 tons of washed shingle in addition to her permanent ballast.

Here are a few of her spar measurements :—Bowsprit and jib-boom, extreme length, 62 feet ; mainmast, deck to truck, 143 feet ; main lower mast, deck to cap, 65 feet ; mainyard, 73 feet ; main skysail yard, 27 feet ; spanker-boom, 47 feet ; outer end of flying jib-boom to end of spanker-boom, 267 feet.

The most remarkable feature of her sail plan was the depth of her courses and the length of her lower masts. These big courses, with their tacks coming right down to the deck, were grand pulling sails in light and moderate winds. The new clipper was of composite construction with teak planking to bilge and elm bottom.

"Ariel"
Built 1865. Tea Clipper.

The *Ariel* was the first ship to finish loading, but she made an unfortunate start, as will be seen from the following quotations from Captain Keay's private log :

Monday, May 28th.—8 a.m., found we required one more boat (of tea), tide averse and blowing hard with rain from N.E.   Could not get her alongside till noon.   2 p.m., finished.   5 p.m., unmoored. 6.30 p.m., dropped below the shipping with *Island Queen* steamer alongside.   7 p.m., anchored.

Tuesday, May 29th.—5 a.m., hove up.   5.30, proceeded towing alongside down the river.   8.30, nearing Sharp Rock ; discharged China pilot.   9 a.m., tried to get steamer ahead to tow, but very soon sheered wide to port and could not recover command of the helm, obliged us to anchor.   Again tried to tow alongside and proceeded outside the wreck of the *Childers*, but were damaging steamer's sponsons and our side so much that we had to cast off, and pilot would not risk going on as steamer could not be relied on to get ahead in time, tide already having fallen, therefore anchored in hopes of getting on to-night.   The *Fiery Cross* towed past us and went to sea all safe, drawing less water. [*Fiery Cross* left Pagoda anchorage, May 29th.]   8.10 p.m., had the night been clear, would have gone to sea, but showery, thick weather, pilot would not venture.   Wind N.E. moderate.

Wednesday, May 30th.—8.30 a.m., hove short and got the steamer ahead, tow ropes fast, one from each bow to his quarters.   9 a.m., proceeded under tow, the *Taeping* and *Serica* following us. [*Serica* had left the anchorage on May 29th, and *Taeping* on the 30th.]   10.30 a.m., were well outside the outer knoll, cast off the tug, and hove to for his boat to fetch away our pilot, Smidt.   They lowered the boat, steamer going ahead, she filled, men were saved, but so long picking up the men and boat, we signalled for a pilot boat to take away our pilot.

At 11.10 a.m. filled the mainyard and steered S. by E. ½ E. for Turnabout Island.   Made sail and set fore-topmast and lower stunsail and main skysail.   Rain and moderate N.E. wind.   We left the *Taeping* and *Serica* a little.

It will be seen from the above that the *Fiery Cross*, owing to *Ariel's* troubles with her tug, got a day's lead, whilst *Ariel*, *Taeping*, and *Serica* crossed the bar of the Min River together.

The other ships left the anchorage on the following dates :—May 31st, *Taitsing ;* June 2nd, *Ziba* (for Liverpool) ;   June 3rd, *Black Prince ;*   June 5th, *Chinaman* and *Flying Spur ;*   June 6th, *Ada ;*   and June 7th, *Falcon.*

In a race of 100 days across three-quarters of the globe, one would imagine that a few days' start would have made little or no difference in the result, but, as a matter of fact, these racing tea ships were as closely matched as a one-design class of racing yachts, and every hour was of value.   It so happened in this race that none of the ships were in company for any length of time, but in later races they were often together for days. Captain Keay, of the *Ariel*, considered that in light winds single topsails paid, and gave the older ships, such as *Fiery Cross*, *Serica*, and *Taeping*, an advantage over the new *Ariel* and *Taitsing*—especially when on a wind—and this was the reason why skippers laced the foot of the upper topsail to the jackyard of the lower topsail when the double yards first came out.

Each of the tea ships carried a picked crew—*Ariel's* numbered 32 all told, all A.Bs., no boys or O.Ss.—but there was no doubling of crews as has often been stated in print ; when racing the skipper signed on two extra hands, that was all.   *Ariel's* normal complement was 30 men.

We have left *Ariel*, *Taeping*, and *Serica* making the best of the N.E. monsoon, with *Fiery Cross* a day ahead.   They carried the fair wind as far as the Paracels, *Ariel* making runs of 190, 195, and 240 miles on May 31st, June 1st, and June 2nd.   On the 2nd *Taeping* and *Ariel* were in sight of each other.   A week later they were again in company in 7° N. 110° E., and *Taeping* signalled that she had passed the *Fiery Cross* the day before. Both captains congratulated themselves on the supposition that they were ahead of Captain Robinson, but he was a hard man to beat in the tricky China seas, and he very soon regained his lead.

The times at Anjer were as follows :

Fiery Cross	at	noon	on	June 18	20 days out	
Ariel	„	7 a.m.	„	June 20	21	„ „
Taeping	„	1 p.m.	„	June 20	21	„ „
Serica	„	6 p.m.	„	June 22	23	„ „
Taitsing	„	10 p.m.	„	June 26	26	„ „

With the steady S.E. trade of the Indian Ocean the racing tea ships hung out every kind of flying kite. The Jamie Green was spread under the jib-boom. (This sail was made of No. 4 canvas, and was the same shape and size as a topgallant stunsail, with some 3 feet more hoist.) Outside the spanker there came the ringtail, with a watersail underneath the boom. This sail consisted of 76 yards or more of No. 4 canvas. A bonnet was laced underneath the foresail, and watersails were hauled out under the passeree booms, which spread the lower stunsails.

But the tea ships were not content with an immense lower stunsail on either side of the courses, but laced spare mizen staysails on to the leech of these lower stunsails, lashing another boom on to the end of the passeree. Every stay had its sail, the fore and main topmast staysails reaching to the collars of their respective stays. And up the fore royal stay a spare flying jib was hoisted. Some ships even set three-cornered sails above their royal yards, using the lead of the signal halliards through the truck for hoisting these skyscrapers.

The trades in the Indian Ocean often piped up good and strong, and broken stunsail yards and booms were common. In 1866 *Ariel* carried away two topmasts, one topgallant and one royal stunsail yard ; but her daily runs, from June 22nd, when she passed Keeling Island, to June 30th, were as follows :—215, 290, 280, 317, 330, 270, 230, 255, 270 miles. And each ship was doing as well. *Fiery Cross*, still a day ahead at Mauritius, ran 328 miles on June 24th, *Taeping* made 319 on the 25th, and *Taitsing* 318 on July 2nd. But by the time the Cape was reached *Ariel* had nearly wiped off her lost 24 hours, being only two or three hours behind *Fiery Cross* on July 15th, when both ships rounded. *Taeping* was 12 hours astern, whilst *Serica* and *Taitsing* still lagged behind.

In the passage up the Atlantic all five ships got closer and closer to each other without knowing it. At St. Helena two and a half days covered the first four ships, the order being, *Taeping*, *Fiery Cross*, *Serica*, *Ariel*, *Taitsing*. *Taeping*, *Fiery Cross*, and *Ariel* all crossed the Line on the same day, August 4th. *Serica* had dropped a couple of days, and *Taitsing* was still over a week astern.

From August 9th to 17th, 12° 29′ N. to 27° 53′ N., *Taeping* and *Fiery Cross* were within sight of each other in doldrum weather ; *Ariel* further to the westward having better winds and running into the lead. On August 17th *Fiery Cross* saw *Taeping* pick up the breeze, and run out of sight ahead in a few hours, the Liverpool crack being left becalmed for 24 hours. This Robinson always declared cost him the race. Nevertheless, he was up in the van again at the Western Isles. Here the times were truly remarkable, the order at Flores being :

1. *Ariel*	passed	on	Aug. 29	91 days out		
2. *Fiery Cross*	„	„	Aug. 29	92	„ „	
3. *Taeping*	„	„	Aug. 29	91	„ „	
4. *Serica*	„	„	Aug. 29	91	„ „	
5. *Taitsing*	„	„	Sept. 1	93	„ „	

With fresh westerly winds all five ships made the run to soundings in six days. At 1.30 a.m., September 5th, *Ariel*, the leading ship, picked up the Bishop and St. Agnes

Lights. At 5.30 a.m., with the sky clearing and wind fresh at about W.S.W., Captain Keay set all possible sail. In the skipper's private log there is this entry :—" A ship, since daylight, has been in company on starboard quarter—*Taeping*, probably."

Ariel's times past the various lights were as follows :

Sept. 5.	2.50 a.m.	St. Agnes North distant about 10 miles.
	8.25 a.m.	Lizard Lights about W.N.W. 11 miles.
	0.30 p.m.	Start Point Lighthouse North 3 miles.
	4.15 p.m.	Portland Lights North about 6 miles.
	7.25 p.m.	St. Catherine's North 1 mile.
	9.45 p.m.	Owers Light North 4 miles.
Sept. 6.	12.30 a.m.	Beachy Head Light North 5 miles.
	3 a.m.	Dungeness Light N.E. 8 miles.
	4 a.m.	Hove to abreast of Dungeness Light, distant 1½ miles.

All this time the two ships had been tearing up-Channel, with *Ariel* slightly in the lead. Captain Keay remarks in his log :—" Going 14 knots, royal stunsails and flying kites set, wind strong from W.S.W."

At 6 p.m. *Ariel* got her anchors over, and was compelled to take in her jib-topsail and Jamie Green so as to have all clear forward. Then, when off St. Catherine's, all small sails had to come in, except the fore-topmast stunsail. Off Beachy Head *Ariel* had about an hour's lead of *Taeping*, and as she neared Dungeness she began to burn blue lights and send up rockets for a pilot.

One may imagine the excitement, both aboard the two ships and ashore, where the news that two tea ships were racing up-Channel spread like wildfire. From each headland the report of their positions was rushed to the nearest post-office, and, though they had not our facilities in those days, the owners of both ships and their agents in London soon learnt that the two vessels were neck-and-neck. But it was aboard the ships that the excitement must have been greatest, and also the anxiety, for the prize-money ran into hundreds of pounds.

Let me now quote from Captain Keay's log ; behind his words one can feel the thrill, the tension, and the suppressed agitation, which must have almost kept his heart from beating. Captain Keay was an experienced hand in the China trade, and up to every move in the game—a calm, confident, level-headed skipper—yet that night must have tried his nerves. He missed nothing, however, and the time of every move in the contest was jotted down in his log :

Sept. 6, 5 a.m. Saw the *Taeping* running and also signalling ; bore up lest they should run Eastward of us and get pilot first ; seeing us keep away, they hove to, we again hove to.

5.30. Saw two cutters coming out of Dungeness Roads.

5.40. Kept away so as to get between *Taeping* and the cutters.

5.55. Rounded to close to the pilot cutter and got first pilot. Were saluted as first ship from China this season. I replied : " Yes, and what is that to the westward ?—we have not room to boast yet. Thank God we are first up-Channel and hove to for a pilot an hour before him."

6 a.m. Kept away for South Foreland ; set all plain sail ; were immediately followed by the *Taeping*. They set, also, topmast, topgallant, and lower stunsails one side—wind slightly quartering. We kept ahead without the stunsails or would also have set them. *Taeping* neared us a mile or two, but was a mile astern when he had to take stunsails in (had shifted them to port side when hauling up through the Downs).

Hoisted our number abreast of Deal, we were then fully a mile ahead of *Taeping*, and kept so until obliged to take in all sail and take steamer ahead.

The times of the five ships in the Downs were as follows :

Ariel, at 8 a.m., Sept. 6	..	..	..	99 days out
Taeping, at 8.10 a.m., Sept. 6	..	..	99	,, ,,
Serica, at noon, Sept. 6	..	..	..	99 ,, ,,
Fiery Cross, during the night, Sept. 7	..	..	101	,, ,,
Taitsing, at forenoon, Sept. 9	..	..	101	,, ,,

None of the other ships made a race of it with these five. The *Serica* had come up-Channel on the French side. *Fiery Cross* was off St. Catherine's at 10 a.m. on September 7th, but she was compelled to bring up in the Downs owing to a severe W.S.W. gale.

The race was not finished until the sample boxes of tea were hurled ashore in the London Docks ; but, so scared were the owners of *Ariel* and *Taeping* of losing the 10s. extra per ton on a quibble as to which ship really won, that they agreed privately to divide the premium, the first ship in dock claiming. But the captains did not know of this arrangement, and the excitement aboard both ships was still at fever-heat. Let me again quote Captain Keay :

Taeping's tug proved much better than ours, and soon towed past us. I thought of taking another boat, but found there would be no need as far as docking was concerned, as we could reach Gravesend two or three hours before it would be possible to go on, till tide made, therefore saved the £10 or £12 asked by boats.

Taeping reached Gravesend 55 minutes before us. We avoided anchoring by getting a tug alongside to keep us astern. Proceeded with first tug ahead, as the flowing tide gave us sufficient water to float, thus reached Blackwall and East India Dock entrance at 9 p.m. Could not open the gates till tide rose higher. 10.23 p.m., hove the ship inside dock gates. *Taeping* had preceded us up the river, but having further to go, did not reach the entrance of London Docks till 10 p.m. ; and, drawing less water than we, also dock having two gates, they got her inside outer gate, shut it, and allowed the lock to fill from the dock, then opened the inner gate, so she docked some 20 minutes before us—the papers have it half an hour, for the sake of precision.

One can hardly imagine a more harrowing, gruelling finish to a race, with the tension kept at boiling-point. Since 8 p.m. a strong westerly gale had been blowing, and we may imagine the language flying between the tug-men and the officers of the two clippers. The air must have been blue all round *Ariel* when it was realized that her tug could not keep her ahead of *Taeping*. *Ariel's* first officer, Duncan, considered the smartest racing mate in the whole tea fleet, had a flow of language justly celebrated for its richness and variety of expression, but the things he said to that tug-skipper beat all records. The yarn goes, also, that half a dozen great burly seamen, headed by the *Ariel's* bo'sun, offered to board the tug, by way of the tow rope, in order to supplement the stokers and sit on the safety-valve. However, there was no help for it. A more extraordinary, and yet more unsatisfactory, finish could hardly be imagined. After such a magnificent exhibition of racing seamanship it was no consolation to divide the stakes, and all shipping people agreed that the race should have finished when the leading ship took her pilot.

Serica managed to haul inside the West India Dock at 11.30 p.m., just as the gates were being closed ; thus *Ariel*, *Taeping*, and *Serica*, after crossing the bar of the Min River on the same tide, all docked in the Thames on the same tide.

On her second voyage the *Ariel* still further distinguished herself by breaking the record for the run out to Hong Kong. Leaving the London Docks on October 13th, 1866, Captain Keay cast off the tug and set all plain sail to a light northerly wind at noon on the 14th, and the pilot was dropped off the Start at noon on the 15th. Without being in any way favoured by the winds, *Ariel* crossed the Equator in 25° 30' W. on November 3rd, only 19 days out ; and another 16 days were all that she needed to cross the Greenwich

Meridian in 43° 30′ S. A month later, on December 18th, to be exact, the *Ariel* was in the Ombay Passage, Captain Keay going "East about," as this course through the islands was called. The Hong Kong anchorage was reached on the morning of Sunday, January 6th, 1867, after a hard thrash to windward of a week's duration against the N.E. monsoon.

Captain Keay's remarks on his passage are worth quoting :—" Our 80 days (79 days 21 hours) from pilot to pilot and 83 from Gravesend to Hong Kong, made quite a sensation in Hong Kong, and at home, when the telegram reached, 'twas scarce believed. There were many reports of quicker passages than ours talked of by lovers of the marvellous, but on best authority in Hong Kong there was found to be no foundation for the mythical things said to have been done by some gun brig or some clipper : several naval officers visited us for a look at our chart and track out, also surveyors of long experience in China, and all agreed as to its being the fastest on record by some five or six days in any season, hence very difficult to beat in N.E. monsoon."

Owing to long intermediate passages, first to Yokohama with a number of Japanese passengers, and then to Saigon for the usual rice cargo, *Ariel* was not in time to load amongst the first flight from Foochow in 1867, and no less than eleven first-class clippers were in front of her when she left the Pagoda anchorage on June 13th. However, Captain Keay managed to pass every one of his rivals, except the *Taeping*, which arrived in the Thames, the first tea ship of the season, on September 14th. *Ariel* arrived on September 23rd, 102 days out, her passage being reckoned as five hours better than *Taeping's*, though both ships were overshadowed by *Ariel's* sister ship, *Sir Lancelot*, which docked on September 22nd, only 99 days out from Shanghai.

On her third voyage, *Ariel* went out to Shanghai in 103 days, beating her rival, *Taeping*, by five days.

In the 'sixties the English Channel was such a sight of fair ships as can hardly be realized in these days. Here is a quotation from Captain Keay's journal which should stir the imagination of the ship-lover :

October 25, a.m. At daylight many vessels bound same way. Wind South-East, set fore-topmast and lower stunsails.

Noon. Lat. 48° 37′ N., Long. 5° 51′ W.

P.m. Have passed in some 10 hours not less than 100 vessels, 5 or 6 miles each side of us. From 25 to 30 in sight when counted several times, passing them all from 2 to 3 miles an hour and weathering same time ; rainy weather, many more would have been in sight in clear weather. About 5 p.m. approached a line of brigs, barques, ships and schooners, 10 to windward and 7 to leeward.

The 1868 tea race is fully described in the account of *Taeping*. It was Captain Keay's last race, and he must have been pleased at being first ship home. He left the *Ariel* to take over Shaw, Maxton's new auxiliary clipper *Oberon*, and the former's chief officer, Courtenay, was appointed in his place.

Captain Courtenay did not do badly in his first tea race. *Ariel*, as usual, was favoured by the shippers and led the tea fleet out of the Min River. This (1869) was the year that *Sir Lancelot* and *Thermopylæ* spread-eagled the fleet with runs of 89 and 91 days, but the first three ships away made a great race of it between themselves, their times being :

Ariel	sailed	June 30	Arrived	October 12	104 days.
Leander	,,	July 1	,,	October 12	103 ,,
Lahloo	,,	July 2	,,	October 12	102 ,,

In 1870, after a passage out to Shanghai of 108 days, Captain Courtenay took his vessel up to Yokohama. On his return South, when only a few days out, he was unfortunate enough to encounter a typhoon on April 26th. The tender *Ariel* went over on her beam ends, and the topmasts had to be cut away to save her, after which Courtenay put back to Yokohama. Here the refit took up so much time that the *Ariel* lost her chance of sailing in the first flight, and rather than load amongst the second division in the N.E. monsoon, Captain Courtenay took a Japanese charter to New York, where he arrived on January 16th, 1871.

When the *Ariel* finally arrived in the London river in March, Captain Courtenay was replaced by a Captain Talbot. The latter took *Ariel* out to Shanghai in 110 days, and there loaded 1,221,500 lbs. of tea at £3 alongside the *Cutty Sark*. Both ships sailed on the same day at the beginning of September, but the little *Ariel* could not hold her powerful antagonist, and she arrived in the Thames on December 27th, 114 days out, and just a week behind Willis's crack ship.

In 1872 *Ariel* left London on January 31st, for Sydney, with a Captain Cachenaille in command. The beautiful tea ship never arrived, and no trace of her was ever found. She was always a ticklish ship to handle in the " roaring forties," and it was generally supposed that she broached to and foundered when running her easting down.

THE "MERMERUS."

THE *Mermerus* belonged to A. and J. H. Carmichael's Golden Fleece Line, and like all their ships was celebrated for her speed and good looks. She was specially built for the Melbourne wool trade; and though all the other ships of Carmichael's fleet traded to every part of the world, the *Mermerus* sailed regularly year after year between London and Melbourne, loading general out and the wool clip home, with the exception of one voyage to Sydney, when she went across to San Francisco from Australia and loaded grain home.

This splendid wool clipper was launched in May, 1872; she registered 1,671 tons; her measurements were : length 264 feet 2 inches, breadth 39 feet 8 inches, and depth 23 feet 7 inches. She had a poop 54 feet long, and a fo'c'sle head of 40 feet.

Carmichael's ships were celebrated the world over for their perfect sparring, a great feature being masts of unequal length, so that the dainty skysail yard at the main stood out by itself, and gave a lofty appearance which was very thorough-bred looking, and stamped a ship as a first-class clipper.

In the early 'seventies iron ships were being sent afloat with tremendous sail plans, very square, very lofty, and with as many as 7 yards on each mast. Many iron clippers were overhatted, with so much weight aloft that a hard squall brought everything down in one terrible crash; but though she was lofty enough (her mainmast was 161 feet from deck to truck) *Mermerus* was not oversparred. Her mainyard was 88 feet long, and her main skysail yard 32 feet. These are moderate measurements compared with many a clipper ship of her size and period.

Messrs. Barclay, Curle & Co., her builders, at first drew out plans for three skysail yards, which she carried for a voyage or two, but Carmichaels returned to the single skysail, which had been such an admired feature on their previous ships, *Golden Fleece* and *Jason*. The total area of the sail plan came to 34,997 yards, of which the headsails took 3,465, the staysails 4,965, and the spanker and spencer 2,719 yards; the rest being in the squaresails.

It is of interest to compare this sail area with that of a 4-mast ship of equal size. The *County of Peebles*, the first 4-mast ship, which was also built by Barclay, Curle & Co., had a sail area of 30,610 yards, 4,387 yards less than the *Mermerus ;* considering that the former had square yards on all four masts this is somewhat surprising. Her masts, however, were much shorter than those of the *Mermerus*, her main being only 134 feet from deck to truck.

The *Mermerus* could load 10,000 bales of wool; this cargo represented the fleeces of a million sheep, and was worth somewhere about £130,000. As she made over 20 passages with the season's wool clip and very rarely missed the sales, she must have been a very satisfactory ship for her owners. Indeed, Mr. Young, of the Australian Mortgage Land and Finance Company, once greeted one of the Carmichaels in Cornhill with the words : " That ship of yours is the most satisfactory ship in the wool trade."

In the palmy days of the Colonial trade, there was considerable rivalry between the shipping people of Melbourne and Sydney concerning the merits of their regular traders. The Melbourne supporters always put forward the *Mermerus* as a ship which their rivals could not beat, and certainly her records were very fine indeed.

She did nothing startling on her first two voyages, under a Captain McIntyre, but in 1874 Captain W. Fife took her over, and she loaded general for Sydney, her freight coming to £5,000. She also had two South Sea Island missionaries on board with their families. Captain Fife, who was a frugal Scot, did not hit it off too well with the missionaries, who complained that he starved them, whilst he declared that in a 72-day passage they ate 140 days of cabin stores besides six turtle, which the skipper, a great fisherman, had captured during a calm in the South Atlantic.

According to a letter which I received from one of the apprentices on this passage, Captain Fife had just cause for complaint, though he brought it on himself through being too sparing with the stores. Apparently the missionary families and ten Scottish apprentices conspired together, got at the stores in the lazarette, and spent their nights in secret feasting.

After making a splendid run out to Sydney, the *Mermerus* loaded coal at Newcastle, N.S.W., for San Francisco at 24s. a ton. The Pacific was crossed in the good time of 56 days; she then loaded 2,420 tons of wheat at £4 1s. 3d., and came home round the Horn, arriving Liverpool on May 25th, 1875, 104 days out.

On her next passage she went from Liverpool to Melbourne in 69 days. Her record outward passage was made in 1876, when she left London on June 25th, took in gunpowder at Gravesend, and arrived Melbourne on August 30th, the gunpowder being just 66 days on board.

In 1877 *Mermerus* went out to Melbourne from London in 79 days from anchorage to anchorage. She left Melbourne on November 24th with a wool cargo, was only 71 days to the Lizard, and anchored in the Thames, 80 days out.

Captain W. Fife handed the Carmichael wool clipper over to Captain J. B. Coles at the end of this voyage. Captain Coles, who had previously been in command of the little *Medea*, was one of the most trusted of the " Golden Fleece " skippers. His record in the *Mermerus* was hard to beat—20 years of freedom from mishap, and successful voyaging between London and Melbourne. And when at last the old ship was sold abroad, Captain Coles retired from the sea, knowing well that he could never find another ship to equal the peerless *Mermerus*.

In 1878–9 her passages were 85 days out and 83 home. The winter of 1878–9 was a terrible one. The Thames was frozen over, and a bitter north-east gale raged in the Channel for weeks. All the homeward bounders put into Falmouth or Queenstown, with the exception of *Mermerus* and the tea clipper *Normancourt*. These two ships beat up-Channel against snow-storms and head seas, the *Mermerus* arriving Gravesend on February 5th. Special tugs had to be chartered to tow the rest of the shipping from the Carrick Roads to London, so Captain Fife had reason to be proud of himself.

In 1879 the *Mermerus* left the Downs on March 26th, and reached Hobson's Bay on June 11th, 77 days out. This voyage she caught the March wool sales, with a passage of 90 days. And so her passages went on year by year, rarely much over 70 days outwards, and invariably catching the wool sales homewards.

Her best outward run in the 'eighties was 73 days in 1880 from Dungeness. Her best wool passage was 77 days in 1886–7. But it was her splendid average, made without a mishap of any sort, which endeared her to all who were connected with her; and she kept

"Mermerus"
Built 1872 Wool Clipper

this up until the end.   In 1896 she was only 76 days to Melbourne, and in 1897, her last voyage under the British flag, her time outwards was 77 days.

She was then sold to the Russians, but continued to make good passages.   In 1902 she arrived at Port Adelaide from Cardiff, on February 4th, only 73 days out.   In 1904 she made the best passage of the year from Australia, being 69 days from Adelaide to the Wight.

Her end came in December, 1909.   At 3 p.m. on December 12th she got ashore in a thick fog, about 10 miles from Christiansand, having left Frederikstadt timber laden for Melbourne on November 29th.   Though she lay in an exposed position with a rock through her bottom, the local tugs managed to get her off and bring her safely to an anchor.   Unfortunately, she was too badly damaged to be repaired, though her captain, Gustafson, contracted with a salvage steamer on the no cure no pay contract.   But her bottom was found to be split, her decks were sprung owing to the waterlogged cargo swelling, and her headgear had gone overboard.

Sailing ships were not worth spending money on in 1909, and so it came about that this beautiful and celebrated wool clipper was sold at Christiansand on April 28th, 1910, to the ship-breakers.

THE " PORT JACKSON."

THIS beautiful four-mast barque is best remembered as one of Devitt & Moore's celebrated cadet ships ; and there must be a great number of officers in the Mercantile Marine who look back to their time in the *Port Jackson* with that warm-hearted feeling which shore-goers keep for an old school.

The *Port Jackson* was built in 1882 by the famous firm of Hall, of Aberdeen, for the equally famous firm of Duthie Bros., who intended the vessel for the Australian trade, in which they had been amongst the earliest pioneers. She was designed by Mr. Alexander Duthie, and registered 2,132 tons, 286 feet 2 inches in length, 41 feet 1 inch beam, and 25 feet 2 inches depth of hold. She cost £29,000 to build, or at the rate of £13 a ton, and the Duthie Brothers, being expert shipbuilders themselves, overlooked every detail of her construction with the utmost care.

The fashion in four-mast barques had only come in a few years, and in the early 'eighties every builder of any repute was striving to produce a vessel which would prove superior to her rivals, not only in design and rig, but in strength and seaworthiness. Members of Lloyd's will, I know, bear me out in my testimony to the everlasting qualities of these iron ships, to the strength of their plates, the perfection of their riveting, and their perfect finish down to the most insignificant detail. One and all, these iron sailing ships have outlasted the later steel ships, which with competition ever growing keener and freights falling steadily, were jerry-built compared with their iron predecessors.

As a specimen of an iron ship of this era, the *Port Jackson* was certainly hard to beat. She was always celebrated for her good looks, and her performances equalled them. The *Port Jackson* spent most of her life trading to that wonderful harbour from which she took her name. Through the 'eighties she was commanded by Captain Crombie.

On her maiden passage she reached Sydney 77 days out from the Channel, being the first four-mast barque to make the trip in under 80 days. Her best run in the 24 hours was 345 miles. Her passages both out and home were very regular, averaging from 80 to 85 days outward, and 10 days or so more coming home.

There is very little incident to record in these steady passages to and from Australia until 1893. She arrived out on May 14th, and then nearly came to her end by fire. The damage sustained on this occasion is briefly described as follows :—" Ship scorched throughout, 13 hold beams very badly burnt amidships, about 100 feet of the lower deck burnt, main-deck plates bent and a good deal of the main-deck planking requiring replacement." Exclusive of sails, ropes and provisions, the repairs were estimated at £4,100. After being repaired, she loaded wool at Newcastle, and sailing on November 29th, reached London 107 days out.

During the 'nineties the *Port Jackson* was commanded by Captain Hodge. She continued to hold her own against the steam tramp until well into the 20th century. At last, with charters hard to get and freights at the very bottom, her owners reluctantly laid her up in the Thames. Here she lay idle for two years, before being purchased by Messrs. Devitt & Moore. In 1906 Messrs. Devitt & Moore contracted to take out 100 *Warspite* boys for the round trip to Australia and back in one of their sailing ships. This venture was arranged by the Marine Society for training fo'c'sle hands, and aroused a great deal of interest amongst those who had the manning of our Mercantile Marine at heart.

But Devitt & Moore were in somewhat of a quandary. They had only lately sold their *Macquarie*, and they had no other suitable ship available; thus they jumped at the opportunity presented by the *Port Jackson*, which lay in the Thames awaiting a buyer. As soon as the ship was taken over she was given a thorough refit, whilst a deck-house, 60 feet long, was erected between her main and mizen masts, where the 100 boys could sling their hammocks.

The start of her first passage as a Devitt & Moore training ship was not a very lucky one. To begin with, their most experienced and trusted Commander, Captain Cutler, to whom they had entrusted the ship, died about three weeks before she was ready to sail. A successor was found in Captain Ward.

Next, in hauling out of the S.W. India Dock on May 21st, 1906, the *Port Jackson* damaged some of her plates against the dock side, which necessitated the discharge of some 200 or 300 tons of cargo, sundry repairs, and a few days' delay in her start.

The third disaster was a much more serious affair. Whilst she lay at anchor in the Downs in a thick fog, the German steamer *Pyrgos* crashed into her and cut her down to the water-line. The *Port Jackson* heeled over under the shock, and at first it was thought that the ship was doomed. It was a trying situation for the *Warspite* boys on their first deep-sea passage, but they behaved admirably. Chief Instructor Glynn at once ordered the bugler to blow the "still," at which every boy stood to attention, silently awaiting whatever was to be. Then came the order: "Divisions fall in on the deck-house." The boys lined up, as steady as veterans, amidst the crash and rending of plates and timbers, whilst the towering bow of the steamer loomed up through the fog, apparently right on top of the sailing ship's topgallant fo'c'sle.

The sharp cutwater of the *Pyrgos* had in fact penetrated eight feet into the *Port Jackson*, making a hole just abaft the forward collision bulkhead which measured 10 feet by 12. Luckily the steamer had a clipper bow or it would have been all up with the sailing ship. As it was, the hole was above the water-line, the full force of the blow being taken by the starboard anchor and the heavy iron cathead. The cathead was bent double, whilst the anchor was stove right through the topgallant fo'c'sle, destroying all the bunks and seamen's chests. There happened to be only one hand in the fo'c'sle, and he had a marvellous escape.

Captain Ward's first order was, "Life-belts on and boats out." This was carried out swiftly but quietly and without any confusion; however, with no damage done below the water-line, it was soon realized that there was no danger of the ship sinking. Repairs, however, delayed the *Port Jackson* another month. She finally left the Downs at 6 p.m. on June 29th, and, after a very light weather passage, in which no attempt was made to carry on, reached Sydney 126 days out.

With regard to her regular crew, the *Port Jackson*, on this voyage, carried 3 mates, chaplain and doctor, 3 instructors, 3 stewards, 3 cooks, 4 quartermasters, bos'n, sailmaker, carpenter, and 14 A.Bs. This many an old sailing ship owner would have called "regular Blackwall fashion o' doing things." Though the result of this deep-sea-training voyage was eminently successful, it was undoubtedly too expensive an experiment to repeat, and on her return home the *Port Jackson* was put into Devitt & Moore's cadet-training service.

Of the *Warspite* boys, whose ages ranged from 14 to 18 years, 94 shipped straight away as ordinary seamen in the Mercantile Marine, the remaining six joining the Royal Navy.

"Port Jackson"
Built 1882 Wool Clipper.

Eight of the boys went away in sailing ships, 21 entered the Cunard employ, whilst the rest went into tramp steamers at a wage of £2 per month.

For the next seven years the *Port Jackson* sailed regularly to Australia with cadets under that well-known commander, Captain Maitland.

On the outbreak of the war she was laid up at Grimsby. But it was not long before every ship was wanted by the British Empire in this titanic struggle, and after only a few months of idleness the *Port Jackson* was towed round to the Thames with coal in her hold.

She next took in cement at Northfleet and sailed for Buenos Ayres ; from the River Plate she took linseed to New York, where she loaded case oil, which was safely delivered at Adelaide. From Adelaide she sailed to Nantes, where Captain Maitland retired from the sea and left her in charge of the mate. The mate took her safely out to Buenos Ayres in ballast. This time she loaded wheat for the United Kingdom.

The *Port Jackson* left Buenos Ayres on January 17th, 1917. So far she had escaped mine, submarine, and raider, but her luck was not to last. On April 28th, in 51° N. 16° 20′ W., she was sunk without warning by a German submarine. Her crew took to the boats, the mate and 14 men being eventually picked up and landed at Queenstown, but nothing was ever heard of her master and the remaining 12 men of her crew.

THE "TORRENS."

To this chapter the Editor, by courtesy of the late Joseph Conrad's literary executors, is permitted to append at page 87 the article from that famous seaman-writer's pen which appeared in "The Blue Peter" of October, 1923.

NO vessel had a better record in the Australian trade than the wonderful *Torrens*. For years she was the favourite passenger ship from London to Adelaide, and although several magnificent iron clippers were built, notably the *Harbinger*, specially to lower her colours, the *Torrens* remained the most popular ship in the South Australian trade until she was sold to the Italians.

She was built in 1875, by James Laing, of Sunderland, to the order of Captain H. R. Angel, who had previously commanded the *Glen Osmond* and *Collingrove*. Launched in October, her registered tonnage was 1,335 tons gross, 1,276 net. She had a length of 222 feet 1 inch; breadth, 38 feet 1 inch; and depth, 21 feet 5 inches. She was composite built, and Captain Angel had a great deal to do with her design. Her model, indeed, was worthy of being compared with those of such clippers as the *Thermopylæ* and *Cutty Sark*. She was beautifully built of teak planking over the iron frames and was very heavily sparred, with a skysail yard at the main. She was also one of the last ships to carry stunsail booms aloft. Indeed, she hung on to her fore topmast stunsails until long after every other ship in the Australian trade had done away with them.

Although she was so sharp forward, the *Torrens* was a splendid sea boat and an exceedingly dry one, even when running down the easting, when it was by no means unusual for her to make 300 miles a day, whilst her passengers were able to take their exercise on a dry deck.

But it was not in the "roaring forties" that she made her passages. In high latitudes her runs were no better than those of a score of the iron wool clippers. It was between the Tropics that she made up time, her powers of ghosting along when hardly an air could be detected being quite extraordinary. On such occasions, it was no unusual thing for her to pass other famous clipper ships as if they were at anchor. And her officers always said that the flap of her sails sent her along at two or three knots.

Here is the enthusiastic testimony of one of the many seamen who learnt their trade aboard her :

" We sighted the *Jenny Harkness*, obviously American, at daylight, right ahead in the S.E. Trades ; at noon we were alongside her, and our Foo-Foo band played ' Yankee Doodle ' as we passed her. She had ' Jimmy Greens ' and water-sails, flying jib topsails and what not aloft and we slid by her as if she was—well—sailing slowly, as she undoubtedly was, compared to our speed. We passed a large ship running the easting down. She was under upper topgallant sails, while we were under upper topsails, with weather upper and lower stunsails set.

" The old ship was never driven ; she did not need it, neither would she stand it. But she sailed rings round anything sighted. To sight a ship to windward and ahead on a wind, was to ensure the tautening of the weather braces, an order to sail a bit finer and to see her passing ahead and to windward of that ship by the early afternoon."

Her biggest run under Captain H. R. Angel, who commanded her for fifteen voyages, was 336 miles in the 24 hours, and her fastest speed through the water, according to his testimony, was 14 knots. The best day's run of her life was 370 miles, made under Captain Falkland Angel, the son of her old skipper, in 1897. She was running the easting down, and her positions were :

On December 29th, lat. 46° 15′ S., long. 77° 30′ E.
„ „ 30th „ 44° 30′ S. „ 85° 0′ E.

One of her apprentices, writing to me about this occasion, states as follows :

" I remember very well heaving the log twice on that day. The line was marked up to 14½ knots and the whole of it ran out before the glass was empty ; so we used a watch instead, and the mate with the line sung out ' Stop ' when the stray line was all out and again when the 14 knot passed his fingers. The Old Man with the watch took the time, and when worked out this gave us 16½ knots. Captain Angel could not believe in such speed. We hove it again and this time made the rate just under 16. Two hours later we hove the log again and made the speed 15½ knots at both times. We had a strong wind on the starboard quarter with a smooth sea, and all plain sail set except the mizen royal."

The evidence of the second mate, who was officer of the watch, amply confirms the above, though differing slightly in detail. This man was the present Captain Sydney Angel, late of the S.S. *Australind*. His description of the *Torrens* logging 16½ knots is as follows :

" I was second mate at the time, and had the middle watch. The captain had gone below at midnight with the warning not to break anything. It was described as a fine night, blowing hard, but with very little sea ; the wind slightly on the starboard quarter. I set the fore and main royals and had the fore topmast staysail in as it was not drawing ; the main topmast staysail and mizen staysail were set. I hove the log at one o'clock, and the line ran out before the glass ; I sent one of the apprentices for a watch, and they were so interested that the whole five of them came along to see what she was really doing. On heaving the log again I found that she was doing a good 16½, not 18. I could not believe this, and hove the log again and again. She kept up this speed until the end of the watch, when the wind was a trifle less, but I made her doing then just under 16. At 4 o'clock I reported this to the mate, but he could not believe it ; but the run at noon proved that she had averaged well over 15."

The *Torrens* followed up this big run by the following week's work :—245, 220, 298, 270, 280, 280 and 270. This was nothing out of the way, being just a fair sample of her usual running in the " roaring forties."

The *Torrens* was specially designed for carrying passengers and her poop, the break of which was only just short of the mainmast, was 80 feet long. With the exception of the famous " Lochs," she was the last sailing ship to carry passengers in the Australian trade.

Under Captain H. R. Angel the *Torrens* proved to be a wonderfully lucky ship. She set up the sailing-ship record for the shortest passage ever made between Plymouth and Adelaide, port to port—namely, 64 days—and her average for her first fifteen outward passages works out at 74 days from the Plymouth Breakwater to the Semaphore, Port Adelaide. Having a smart ship which he could handle like a yacht, Captain Angel always took her into St. Vincent's Gulf by the Backstairs Passage, east of Kangaroo Island, instead of through Investigator Strait.

Her wonderful record going out to Adelaide, whilst commanded by Captain H. R. Angel, has never been approached by any other ship in the Australian trade. It may, therefore, perhaps be of interest to give the actual dates :

"Torrens"

Built 1875. Passenger and Emigrant Ship.

Date left London.	Date left Plymouth.	Date arrived Adelaide.	Days Out.
Dec. 8, 1875	Dec. 12, 1875	Mar. 7, 1876	85
Oct. 26, 1876	Oct. 29, 1876	Jan. 18, 1877	81
„ 27, 1877	Nov. 4, 1877	„ 11, 1878	68
„ 26, 1878	„ 2, 1878	„ 18, 1879	77
„ 26, 1879	Oct. 30, 1879	„ 8, 1880	70
„ 28, 1880	Nov. 2, 1880	„ 6, 1881	65
„ 27, 1881	Oct. 29, 1881	„ 8, 1882	71
„ 26, 1882	„ 29, 1882	„ 16, 1883	79
„ 27, 1883	„ 29, 1883	„ 7, 1884	70
„ 26, 1884	Nov. 2, 1884	„ 25, 1885	84
„ 27, 1885	„ 1, 1885	„ 6, 1886	66
„ 28, 1886	„ 2, 1886	„ 15, 1887	74
„ 27, 1887	„ 8, 1887	„ 14, 1888	67
„ 27, 1888	„ 1, 1888	„ 14, 1889	74
„ 30, 1889	„ 7, 1889	„ 26, 1890	80

On his homeward passages, Captain Angel always took things easy, for the benefit of his passengers, calling in generally at Cape Town, St. Helena and Ascension.

The *Torrens* was managed by the Elder Line, who had an interest in her, though most of the shares were held by Captain Angel. The statement in my " Colonial Clippers " that the *Torrens* flew a special house-flag as Commodore of the Elder Line has been queried by several seamen. I had this information originally from the late Captain Sharpe, and it was confirmed by Captain H. R. Angel, who, in a letter to me, dated April 24th, 1912, wrote :

" Captain Sharpe is right, my house-flag as Commodore of the Elder Line was different from the other ships and was a white ground with red crescent and stars."

The Elder Line house-flag had a red ground and white crescent and stars. In each case the crescent was divided from the two stars by a vertical bar of blue.

As an example of her good luck whilst under Captain H. R. Angel's command, the old skipper used to tell the following yarn :

On one of her homeward passages the *Torrens* ran out of lamp oil just as she was approaching the mouth of the English Channel. This naturally gave Captain Angel a good deal of anxiety, as the prospect of navigating those crowded waters without lights was far from being pleasant. However, just before soundings were reached, a barrel was passed floating on the water. Captain Angel lowered a boat and picked it up. As soon as it was got aboard he had it tapped, when it was found to contain oil, and thus the *Torrens* was able to keep her side-lights bright until the end of the passage.

There are many people still alive who enjoyed a trip in the *Torrens* as passengers, and a few quotations may be of interest. Referring to the outward voyage of 1886–7, an old *Torrens* passenger writes :

" On the voyage under notice, the *Torrens* brought out 53 passengers in the saloon, including the captain's wife and daughter and young son, Clifford, who was then a boy of about 12. His eldest son had been killed, as I was told, by falling from aloft on the deck of the *Torrens* during a previous voyage.* The mate was Mr. Moore, a hard man with the crew, but a fine sailor. The second mate was Archie Flemyng, a delightful young Scotsman and a great favourite with everybody on board. We carried live-stock—cows and sheep—in pens on the main deck. Several Australians returning to Adelaide after a visit to the Old Country were among the passengers.

" No one who has not made a long voyage in such a ship as the *Torrens* can realize the ' lift ' and thrill of that form of sea travel. It was like riding a thoroughbred, whereas travelling by the steamship of to-day, with its deadening comfort and monotony, is as devoid of thrills as sitting on a tram."

* NOTE :—This is a mistake. The boy was killed on board the *Collingrove,* not the *Torrens.*

He then proceeds to give the log and a short account of the passage.   The *Torrens* was 20 days to the Equator from Plymouth, in spite of a bad gale in the Bay.   Madeira was passed 8 days out and at the same time the *Torrens* overhauled the *Wave Queen*, which was 15 days out from Plymouth.   On November 24th the coast of Brazil was sighted off Pernambuco, and about midday a catamaran, consisting of six large logs strapped together, came alongside, and its crew of two men and a boy undertook to post the ship's letters ashore for the modest fee of two bottles of Bass and 10s. in English silver.   All that afternoon the *Torrens* was passing Brazilian catamarans fishing.

The *Torrens* was not particularly favoured by wind on this passage and her biggest run was only 306 miles, made December 15th, the day on which she crossed the Greenwich Meridian.   Cape Willoughby light was made on January 13th and the *Torrens* arrived at the Semaphore at three o'clock that afternoon.

Here are a few extracts from a letter of a passenger referring to the next outward passage :

" I happened to be a passenger in the *Torrens* in 1887.   On that voyage, Captain Angel had his wife and his daughter, Mabel, with him, which, from the social point of view, greatly enhanced the enjoyment of the voyage.   The enclosed, which is a copy of the ship's runs, shows that with a little luck we looked like beating the record ; unfortunately the wind failed just as we neared Kangaroo Island and we went up the Backstairs Passage rather slowly at first ; the wind freshened shortly before we got up and we had a lovely time getting all her canvas off in time to drop anchor.

" She was a wonderful ship and I felt very distressed when I left her at Adelaide.

" About a couple of years after, I was coming up to London Bridge on one of the old penny steamers and looking over to the docks, I said to my friend ' Do you see that forest of masts ? Do you see that mast towering above the others ? It is just like the old *Torrens*.'   A sturdy slap on the back made me turn round, to face Captain Angel, who said, ' You are quite right, it is the old hooker. I know you used to like going aloft, but I did not think any passenger could pick out his own boat in such a crowd.' "

This passenger also gives the latitude, longitude, and runs, evidently from the *Torrens*' " *Gazette*," the usual passenger-ship newspaper, which was generally edited by one of the saloon passengers.   On this voyage the *Torrens* was only 19 days to the Equator, 36 days to the Greenwich Meridian, and 64 days to 37° 05′ S., 137° 52′ E.   During the passage, the ship made five runs of over 300 miles, the best being 321.

When Captain Angel retired from the sea, in the autumn of 1890, he handed over his ship to Captain W. H. Cope.   The good luck of the *Torrens*, at any rate for a time, seemed to have walked over the side with her old captain.   No doubt she owed this good luck as much to his fine management as to anything else.   Captain Angel, besides being a very fine seaman, full of courage and resource, was also a great disciplinarian.   He was not, however, a bully, and the *Torrens*, under him, was always a happy ship.   The Old Man could indeed relax on occasions ; he had all the seaman's love of a yarn and spent many a moonlight night in the Tropics relating the exciting adventures of his past life to a ring of admiring passengers.

The *Torrens*' first passage under Captain Cope was a very unlucky one.   Caught in a squall in 6° N. 27° W. on November 30th, 1890, she lost her foremast from the deck, everything above the cap of the main lower mast, also her mizen topgallant mast and all the yards on the mizen except the lower topsail and crossjack.   She was picked up by the *Ethiope*, of Liverpool, and towed into Pernambuco, the tow taking eight days and costing the owners of the *Torrens* £2,000.   New spars were sent out and the duty upon them at Pernambuco was no less than £700.

On this passage the *Torrens* had her usual full half-deck of high-spirited apprentices, and she had a fine crew, who also were full of life, so that Pernambuco was given good cause to remember the stay of the Adelaide clipper. Her crew earned the title of " the mad Englishmen on the doomed ship." The Spaniards looked upon the *Torrens* as doomed, because on top of her severe dismasting, she must needs catch fire. However, the steamer *Mariner* put her hose on to the sailing ship and the fire was got under.

Whilst the *Torrens* lay refitting at Pernambuco, Fernie's *Argomene* put in to the port with a hole in her bows you could have driven a 'bus through. The *Argomene* had been in collision with an American barque, which had been sunk with all hands.

When the *Torrens* at length resumed her voyage, her provisions were running pretty low and all hands had to be on short rations. One of her apprentices writing to me of the passage, remarked : " I remember Chips and myself eating a pound of butter, a loaf of bread and a good pound of chops each on our first day in Port Adelaide."

The *Torrens* did not reach Adelaide until April 26th, 1891, at which date she was 179 days out from London.

The next two voyages of the *Torrens* are of more interest to the *literati* than to the seafaring profession, for the late Joseph Conrad was doing the duties of chief officer, whilst, on the second voyage, W. H. Jacques made the round trip and John Galsworthy was a passenger from Adelaide to Cape Town.

It would be interesting to hear from those who served under him of Joseph Conrad's qualities as that responsible person, the chief officer of a first-class London ship. Was he a driver ? Did he hustle those unruly boys in the half-deck ? Was he a stern disciplinarian, or could he be hoodwinked by the malingerer ? Finally, was he the artist in seamanship that he was as a writer ?

These questions are answered in part by a correspondent of the " *Spectator*." After remarking that the kindly Captain Cope was inclined to be extra careful to take in sail at the first hint of a blow, after the unlucky dismasting during his first passage in command, the " *Spectator's* " correspondent goes on to say :

" Conrad used to pray for half a gale in the night, when the captain had his watch below, in order to make the old ship show her paces. I shall never forget his figure on deck, in his old reefer jacket, with a red silk handkerchief round his neck—swift, almost stealthy, and silent in his movements—with knees slightly bent, shoulders bowed—we knew that he had lately been captain of a Congo river steamer and was riddled with African fever !—his chin and alert face thrust forward, his keen eyes between half-closed lids noting everything, or constantly, in changeable weather, raised to sky and cloud and sails.

" His manner with his men was generally very quiet, though he did raise his voice excitedly when things went wrong or not so fast as they ought to. There was, of course, implicit and immediate obedience to his orders and I never heard a sound of grousing about them. The men could not fail to see in Conrad the keen and knowledgeable sailor. I do not know whether they loved him, but admire him they did, and trusted him completely."

W. H. Cope continued to command the *Torrens* until the autumn of 1896, his best passage being his last outward one, when he reached Adelaide on December 6th, 1895, 79 days out. He was succeeded by Captain Falkland Angel, a son of H. R. Angel.

Falkland Angel was a sail carrier. On his first outward passage he drove the *Torrens* out to Adelaide in 75 days, and on his second he was only two days longer.

On the ship's homeward passage in the autumn of 1898, she found herself, after a spell of easterly weather, becalmed, along with 13 other sailing ships, at the mouth of the Channel. Then one morning at daybreak, the wind came away from the south-west, gradually increasing, and every one of the other ships was speedily left out of sight astern. When off the Foreland, a tug came out and asked if a tow was wanted. Captain Angel sung out : " Yes, if you can catch us." But the tug was swept into the ship's wake and steadily dropped astern. Later, another tug came alongside, and it was now necessary for the ship to take one. The tug boatman wanted £65. " Fifty ! " offered the Old Man. " Fifty and a new hat ! " roared back the tug-master. Captain Angel nodded, and then the following words came clearly to those listening on the *Torrens :* " Give us your line. I'd tow you all round the —— world for a new hat."

It was on Captain Falkland Angel's third passage that the *Torrens* had a very curious experience. On February 5th, 1899, she arrived in Adelaide, 103 days out, with her bows smashed in, her bowsprit and jib-boom gone and nothing set forward above the lower topsail. In this condition she had run through the Backstairs Passage with a strong breeze on the quarter, and overhauled and passed a steamer named the *Federal.* On her arrival, it was stated that she had been foul of an iceberg on January 11th, 1899, but a rumour was spread through Adelaide that it was not an iceberg that she had struck, but the land, and people even declared that they had seen rocks sticking in the broken timbers of her bows and pieces of stone embedded in the yard-arms which struck the berg. As an explanation of these strange rumours, the following account, written by one of her apprentices, is of interest :

" At 9 p.m., when running with a strong breeze on the port quarter, in misty weather, we suddenly sighted the westernmost of the Crozet Isles right ahead. We just had time to clear it, and the Old Man ordered the topgallant sails to be taken off her and the mainsail hauled up. He then went below to look at the chart. After a few minutes, he came up again and gave the mate the course. This course was set to take us to the westward of the Penguin Rock, but the mate, thinking that the Old Man meant to go to the eastward and that he had not allowed enough, altered the course a point more to the east when the skipper had gone below again, with the consequence that we struck the rock. Luckily there was deep water right alongside, it rises straight up out of the water, and as the look-out reported ' Ice right ahead,' the man at the wheel at once put his helm down without waiting for orders, so that when we struck we were already coming up into the wind and only struck a glancing blow. It carried away our bowsprit and fore topmast and smashed a hole in the bows, but we were able to keep her afloat.

" At the inquiry, we all blandly swore that it was an iceberg that we hit. On the morning after the accident, whilst I was at the wheel, the Old Man pointed astern and told one of the passengers, ' That's what we hit,' and there was no ice in sight, only the Crozet Islands."

As against the above we have the evidence given in the inquiry at Adelaide in March, 1899. Besides all the officers and several of the apprentices, some of the crew and passengers were also cross-examined, and, as a result, the members of the Supreme Court of Admiralty came unanimously to the opinion that there was no evidence to justify the conclusion that the casualty was caused by striking Penguin Island.

As regards the rocks sticking into the bows of the *Torrens*, this rumour was said to have been spread in Adelaide by some shilling-a-month men who had fallen foul of Captain Angel.

The *Torrens* made four more voyages under Elder's house-flag before she was sold to the Italians. Her last passage under the Red Ensign was an unlucky one. Leaving Adelaide on April 23rd, 1903, she was caught in a bad storm before she was clear of Kangaroo Island, and if she had not been a weatherly ship she would not have managed to claw off the land. Again she caught it severely between Mauritius and the Cape.

Captain Angel put into Cape Town, as he had very little cargo on board from Adelaide. No cargo was offered at Cape Town, but there was a large dump of explosives of all sorts, relics of the Boer War, at St. Helena, and *Torrens* was chartered by the British Government to take those explosives aboard and bring them home.

Whilst the *Torrens* was towing up the Thames at the end of this passage a vessel attempted to pass between her and the tug, with the result that she was cut down by the *Torrens* and sank in three minutes. When it was seen that the collision was unavoidable, there was great apprehension aboard the *Torrens* for fear of her cargo of explosives. However, the old ship was uninjured, and no blame was attached to Captain Angel.

By this date the *Torrens* was beginning to eat up money for repairs, and Captain Angel, with great reluctance, decided to sell his beautiful ship to the Italians. The change of ownership was not a lucky one. The Italians soon ran the *Torrens* ashore, and after refloating her, decided that she was not worth the cost of repairs. The Genoese shipbreakers, however, were so struck by the beauty of her model and the perfection of her build that they repaired her and sent her afloat again.

In 1910 the Italians again bumped her on the rocks, and again she was refloated, but this time she was towed back to the shipbreakers for good and all.

THE "TORRENS."

A PERSONAL TRIBUTE BY JOSEPH CONRAD.

(Written for " The Blue Peter " of October, 1923.)

IT is one of the pleasant surprises of my accumulated years to be still here when the shade of that beautiful ship is being evoked for a moment by a sea-travel magazine before the eyes of a public which does its sea-travelling under very different conditions. Personally I cannot help thinking them not so much improved as needlessly sophisticated. However, that opinion of mine may be wildly wrong. I am not familiar with the demands of the spirit of the age. And, besides, I know next to nothing of sea-travel. Even of the people who do that thing I know but few. My two years in the *Torrens* is my only professional experience of passengers ; and though we—officers brought up in strenuous Indiamen and famous wool-clippers—did not think much of passengers, regarding them as derogatory nuisances with delicate feelings which prevented one driving one's ship till all was blue, I will confess that this experience was most fortunate from every point of view, marking the end of my sea life with pleasant memories, new impressions and precious friendships. The pleasant memories include the excellent ship's companies it was my luck to work with on each of my two voyages. But the *Torrens* had a fame which attracted the right kind of sailor, and when engaging her crew her chief officer had always a large and promising crowd to pick and choose from. There was in it always a certain proportion of men who had served in her before and were anxious to join again ; for apart from her more brilliant qualities, such as her speed and her celebrated good looks (which by themselves go a long way with a sailor), she was regarded as a " comfortable ship " in a strictly professional sense, which means that she was known to handle easily and to be a good sea-boat in heavy weather. I cannot say that during my time in her we ever experienced really heavy weather ; but we had the usual assortment of winds, up to " very strong gales " (logbook style), from various directions ; and I can testify that, on every point of sailing, the way that ship had of letting big seas slip under her did one's heart good to watch. It resembled so much an exhibition of intelligent grace and unerring skill that it could fascinate even the least seaman-like of our passengers. A passage under sail brings out in the course of days whatever there may be of sea love and sea sense in any individual whose soul is not indissolubly wedded to the pedestrian shore.

There are, of course, degrees of landsmanism—even to the incurable. A gentleman whom we had on board on my first voyage presented an extreme instance of it. It, however, trenched upon the morbid in its excessive sea fright, which had its pathetic as well as comic moments. We had not been more than ten days out from Plymouth when he took it into his head that his shattered constitution could not stand the voyage. Note that he had not had as much as an hour of seasickness. He maintained, however, that a few more days at sea would certainly kill him. He was absolutely certain of it, and he pleaded day after day with a persistent agonised earnestness to be put ashore on the first convenient bit of land, which in this case would have been Tenerife. But it is not so easy for a sailing ship to make an unexpected call without losing much time. Any deviation from a direct course of the voyage (unless in case of actual distress) would have invalidated the ship's insurance. It was not to be thought of, especially as the man looked fit enough and the doctor had reported that he could not find the slightest evidence of organic disease of any sort. I was sorry for my captain. He could not refuse to listen to the man. Neither could he accede to his request. It was absurd. And yet ! . . . who could tell ? It became worse when he began to offer progressive bribes up to three hundred pounds or more. I don't know why I was called to one of those awful conferences. The even, low flow of argument from those trembling lips impressed me. He exhibited to us his bank pass-book to prove that he had the means to buy his life from us. Our doctor stood by in grim silence. The captain looked dead-tired, but kept his temper wonderfully under the implication of callous heartlessness. It was I who could not stand the inconclusive anguish of the situation. It was not so long since I had been neurasthenic myself. At the very next pause I remarked in a loud and cheery tone, " I suppose I had better get the anchors ready first thing to-morrow." The captain glared at me speechlessly, as well he might. But the effect of the hopeful word " anchors " had an instantaneous soothing effect on our passenger. As if satisfied that there was at last somebody on his side he was willing to leave it at that. He went out.

I need not say that next day the anchors were not touched. But we sighted Tenerife at thirty miles off, to windward—a towering and majestic shadow against the sky. Our passenger spent the day leaning over the rail, watching it till it melted away in the dusk. It was the confirmation of a death-sentence for him, I suppose. He took it very well.

He gave me the opportunity to admire for many days an exhibition of consistent stoicism. He never repined. He withdrew within himself. Though civil enough when addressed directly, he had very few words to give to anybody—as though his fund of speech had been expended while pleading in vain for his life. But his heart was burning with indignant anger. He went ashore unreadable but unforgiving, without taking notice of anyone in the ship. I was the only exception. Poor futile creature as I was, he remembered that I at least had seemed to be " on his side." If I may take an Irishman's privilege, I will say that if he had really died he could not have abhorred the ship and everyone in her more. To have been exposed to live for seventy days under a sentence of death was a soul-searing outrage, and he very properly resented it to the last.

I must say that, in general, our passengers would begin very soon to look thoroughly at home in the ship. Its life was homely enough, and far removed from the ideals of the Ritz Hotel. The monotony of the sea is easier to bear than the boredom of the shore, if only because there is no visible remedy and no contrast at hand to keep discontent alive.   The world contains, or contained then, some people who could put up with a sense of peace for three months.   The feeling of close confinement in a sailing ship, with her propelling power working in the open air, and with her daily life going on in public sight, and presenting the varied interests of human character and individual exertion, is always less oppressive than in a steamer even many times her size.   Besides, in a sailing ship there are neither vibration nor mechanical noises to grow actively wearisome.   Another advantage was that the sailing passenger ships of that epoch were never crowded.   The cabins of the *Torrens* had two berths each, but they were roomy and not over-furnished with all sorts of inadequate contrivances for comfort, so-called.   I have seen the cabins of a modern passenger steamship with three or four berths (their very couches being numbered) which were not half as big as ours.   Not half as big—in fact, some of our passengers, who seized the opportunity of learning to dance the hornpipe from our boatswain (an agile professor), could pursue their studies in their own rooms.   And that art requires for its practice more space than the proverbial swinging of a cat, I can assure you.   Much more.

The *Torrens* was launched in 1875, only a few months after I had managed, after lots of trouble, to launch myself on the waters of the Mediterranean.   Thus we began our careers about the same time.   From the professional point of view hers was by far the greatest success. It began early, and went on growing for fifteen years under the command of Captain H. R. Angel, whose own long career as a ship-master was the greatest success of the three.   He left her in 1890, and people said that he took his ship's luck away with him.   The *Torrens* certainly lost some of her masts the very next voyage, by one of those sudden accidents for which no man can be made responsible.   I joined her a year afterwards, on the 2nd of November, 1891, in London, and I ceased to " belong to her," as the saying is (it was a wrench), on the 15th of October, 1893, when, in London Dock, I took a long look from the quay at that last of ships I ever had under my care, and, stepping round the corner of a tall warehouse, parted from her for ever, and at the same time stepped (in merciful ignorance) out of my sea life altogether.

I owed the opportunity of my close association with my famous contemporary to my acquaintance with Captain W. H. Cope, who succeeded Captain H. R. Angel.   I had known him some years before, but only slightly, in a social way.   I knew that he had been a Conway boy, that he had had much varied service in mail boats, and in the Hooghly pilot steamer before the command of the *Torrens* came in his way.   But I had no reason to believe that he remembered me particularly.   However, on hearing from his brother that I was ashore, he sent me word that the *Torrens* wanted a chief officer, as a matter that might interest me.   I was then recovering slowly from a bad breakdown, after a most unpleasant and persistent tropical disease which I had caught in Africa while commanding a steamer on the River Congo.   Yet the temptation was great.   I confessed to him my doubts of my fitness for the post, from the point of view of health.   But he said that moping ashore never did anyone any good, and was very encouraging.   It was clear that, as the saying goes, " my looks did not pity me," for he argued that, so far as appearance went, there did not seem to be anything the matter with me.   And I suppose I could never have been half as neurasthenic as our poor passenger who wanted to be put ashore, for I lasted out for two voyages, as my discharges prove, though Mr. Basil Lubbock, in his book, " The Colonial Clippers," credits me with only one.   But in the end I had to go (and even stay) ashore.   Thus my famous contemporary outlived me at sea by many years, and if she had perhaps a harder life of it than I, it was at least untinged with unavailing regrets ; and she escaped the ignominious fate of being laid up as a coal hulk, which so many of her sisters had to suffer.   Mr. Lubbock, who can put so much interesting knowledge and right feeling into his studies of our merchant ships, calls her

" The Wonderful *Torrens*."   She was ! Her fascinations and virtues have made their marks on the hearts of men.   Only last year I received a letter from a young able seaman, whom I remembered having in my watch, invoking confidently her unforgotten name.   " I feel sure you must be Mr. Conrad, the chief officer, in whose watch I was when serving in the *Torrens* in 1891, and so I venture to write to you. . . ."   A friendly, quiet, middle-aged seaman's letter which gave me the greatest pleasure.   And I know of a retired sailor (a Britisher, I suppose), in Massachusetts, who is making a model in loving memory of her who, all her life, was so worthy of men's loyal service.   I am sorry I had no time to go to see him, and to gaze at the pious work of his hands.

It is touching to read in Mr. Lubbock's book that, after her transfer to the Italian flag, when she was taken to Genoa to be broken up, the Genoese shipwrights were so moved by the beauty of her lines and the perfections of her build that they had no heart to break her up. They went to work instead to preserve her life for a few more years.   A true labour of love, if ever there was one !

But in the end her body of iron and wood, so fair to look upon, had to be broken up— I hope with fitting reverence ; and as I sit here, thirty years, almost to a day, since I last set eyes on her, I love to think that her perfect form found a merciful end on the shores of the sunlit sea of my boyhood's dreams, and that her fine spirit has returned to dwell in the regions of the great winds, the inspirers and the companions of her swift, renowned, sea-tossed life which I, too, have been permitted to share for a little while.

THE "THOMAS STEPHENS."

THE *Thomas Stephens* was one of the finest ships ever launched in the Mersey. She was built by Potter as an iron passenger ship, to run in the old Black Ball Line. Launched in the same year as the *Cutty Sark*, and owned by Thomas Stephens & Sons, of London, this beautiful passenger clipper never actually sailed under the Black Ball flag, owing to the collapse of the Line just before she was launched; but her building was superintended and she was taken from the stocks by one of the most experienced masters in the Black Ball Line. This was Captain R. Richards, who was almost the first man to receive his master's certificate from the newly-formed Board of Trade; he was then only nineteen. Amongst the ships that he commanded were the *Vanguard, British Empire*, the auxiliary *Great Victoria*, and the *Donald MacKay*. He left the *Donald MacKay* to take command of the *Thomas Stephens*.

Though considered a big ship in 1869, the new passenger clipper, which, after two passages from Liverpool, always sailed as one of Bethell & Co.'s London line of Australian packets, only registered 1,507 tons. Her dimensions were :—Length, 263 feet; breadth, 38 feet 2 inches; depth, 23 feet 1 inch. Her sail plan was a tall one. When she came out she crossed three skysail yards over single topgallants, and carried a full suit of stunsails. Later on, following the fashion, she was fitted with double topgallant yards, and the stunsail-booms were sent down, whilst she only retained the skysail yard at the main. The figure-head of this beautiful ship was a very good likeness of her owner, complete with top hat, as was the custom of the day. She had one or two unusual innovations amongst her deck fittings, such as an iron wheel, and stanchions and wire netting above her topgallant rail, which no doubt saved many a man from going overboard when she was filling her main deck running the easting down.

Her passenger accommodation consisted of first, second and third cabins, as they were called in those days. Under her poop was her first-class saloon, with the berths and bath-rooms opening into it. In this class, all cabin furniture, bedding and every convenience, according to the shipping advertisements, was provided. The ship was also advertised as carrying a surgeon.

On her maiden voyage the *Thomas Stephens* sailed from Liverpool on September 24th, full up with passengers and emigrants, and made the run out to Melbourne in 82 days. Like all iron ships, she found the homeward passage more difficult than the outward one, and, sailing from Melbourne on February 1st, 1870, did not reach London until May 15th, 103 days out.

On her second outward passage she again sailed from Liverpool. Leaving the Mersey on September 9th, 1870, she arrived in Hobson's Bay on November 21st, 73 days out from port to port. This passage was advertised in the shipping columns of "*The Times*" as 64 days, but it is sometimes difficult to agree with the transits announced in the shipping advertisements, in which the passages seem frequently to have been counted as from land to land.

On her third voyage the *Thomas Stephens* loaded in London, and, sailing on October 26th, 1871, made one of the best passages of her career. I have the log of this passage, and it may, therefore, be of interest to give a few details :

The Line was crossed on November 20th, in Longitude 29° 57′ W. The S.E. Trade had been picked up two days before, and the ship was making 12 knots. In the notes on the ship's work I find that the watch were employed refitting tacks and sheets, the sailmaker making a weather-cloth for mizen rigging, and the engineer cleaning out the boiler. (The *Thomas Stephens*, like all sailing passenger ships, carried a condenser and donkey-engine. There are constant entries throughout the log " the engineer condensing.")

The Greenwich Meridian was crossed on December 4th, in 39° S., the ship running to the S.E. by S. with all starboard stunsails set, and logging 8 knots with a pleasant west-nor'-west breeze. She made her best run in 44° 48′ S., 27° 57′ E., on December 10th, in a heavy westerly gale, which started at 11 a.m. on the 9th, when the topgallant sails, crossjack, spanker and outer jib were handed in heavy squalls with thick rain. At 4 p.m. Captain Richards reset his main topgallant sail, and at 9 p.m. his fore topgallant sail and the main topgallant staysail. During the night it blew a hard gale, with a high cross sea, and the ship plunged along with her decks completely flooded fore and aft. At 1 a.m. the main topgallant stay carried away. At 7 a.m. a big sea came over the starboard quarter, washed the starboard life-boat out of the davits, filled up the main deck, and took the main hatch house over the lee rail. By 9.30 a.m. the gale was moderating, and all plain sail was set, the run at noon working out at 315 miles. The log gave the *Thomas Stephens* 16 knots an hour for 12 hours, 13 for 2 hours, 10 for 2 hours, 9 for 3 hours, and 8 for 5 hours.

The worst gale on the passage was encountered on December 29th and 30th. At 4 p.m. on the 29th the strong N.W. breeze increased rapidly to a hard gale. All hands were called, and after the topgallant sails, upper topsails, courses, and jib had been taken in, Captain Richards hove his ship to under lower topsails. There was a very big sea running, and the *Thomas Stephens* took heavy water aboard. However, at 8.30 p.m. the wind veered into the sou'-west, and Captain Richards wore his ship off before the wind, and set his foresail and fore upper topsail. During the night the *Thomas Stephens* logged 13 to 14 knots, tearing along with her main deck under water, and her passengers having an exceedingly uncomfortable time battened down below. This breeze, however, carried the ship to Cape Otway, which was made at 11 p.m. on January 1st. At 7 a.m. on January 2nd the pilot came aboard, and at 1 p.m. the *Thomas Stephens* came to an anchor in Hobson's Bay, having made the passage from pilot to pilot in 66 days.

After discharging her passengers and cargo, the ship left Melbourne with walers in her 'tween-decks for Calcutta on February 1st, 1872. The Line was crossed on February 29th and the pilot brig at the Sandheads reached on March 17th, the *Thomas Stephens* anchoring in Garden Reach, Calcutta, on March 18th, 46 days out. On her homeward passage she loaded amongst the jute clippers, and, sailing on April 20th, had no chance to make a record run owing to encountering light southerly winds all the way until she got the S.E. Trades.

On her fourth voyage the *Thomas Stephens* raced out to Australia against the tea clippers *Cutty Sark*, *Blackadder* and *Duke of Abercorn*. All four ships sailed from London, the *Duke of Abercorn* on November 15th, *Blackadder* on November 21st, *Cutty Sark* on November 26th, and *Thomas Stephens* on December 4th. It will be noticed that the *Thomas Stephens* started some days after the other three, but they experienced a terrific sou'-west gale in the

"*Thomas Stephens*"

Built 1869 Passenger and Emigrant Ship.

Channel, whilst the passenger ship came away with a fair wind. The *Duke of Abercorn* was hove to in this gale from November 21st until December 2nd, when she was 80 miles S.S.W. of the Scillies. *Blackadder* was off the Start on December 3rd, while the *Cutty Sark* and *Thomas Stephens* took their departure from the Lizard on the following day. The *Duke of Abercorn* crossed the Line on December 22nd. She was closely followed by the *Cutty Sark*, on December 23rd; *Blackadder* came next, on the 24th, whilst the *Thomas Stephens* crossed in 27° W. on Christmas Day. The *Duke of Abercorn* and *Blackadder* crossed the Cape Meridian on January 20th, whilst the *Thomas Stephens* crossed the Greenwich Meridian on January 17th, a day ahead of *Cutty Sark*, which ship, however, was in 47° S., the *Thomas Stephens* being in 43° S. *Blackadder*, *Cutty Sark* and *Thomas Stephens* made a close race of it to the Australian land, but while running down her easting the *Duke of Abercorn* dropped a week behind. She and the *Blackadder* were bound for Sydney, and proceeded via the South of Tasmania. *Blackadder* rounded the South-West Cape, Tasmania, on February 10th, 1873, the same day that *Cutty Sark* and *Thomas Stephens* made the Otway. The *Duke of Abercorn* did not round Tasmania until February 17th, but she made a good run up the coast, and arrived at Sydney on February 23rd, the same day as the *Blackadder*. The *Thomas Stephens* actually beat the *Cutty Sark* into the Port Phillip anchorage, where she anchored at noon on February 11th, the *Cutty Sark* not getting in to Queen's Cliff until 11 p.m. Of the four ships, *Thomas Stephens* undoubtedly made the best passage, and she distinguished herself by bringing papers two days later in date than those by the last mail boat. She also landed a shorthorn bull in excellent condition.

In 1873 the Bethell Liner made an excellent run home with wool. Leaving Melbourne on April 5th she arrived in London on June 26th.

On her fifth voyage the *Thomas Stephens* made another 66 days' run from Soundings to Melbourne, arriving in Hobson's Bay on November 8th. This voyage she went up to Newcastle, N.S.W., and took 1,800 tons of coal to Petropavlovsk. Captain Richards then went to Moulmein for his homeward cargo, and leaving Moulmein on June 13th, 1874, arrived London, 117 days out, on October 8th.

Captain Richards handed over to Captain Harry L. Bloomfield, who commanded *Thomas Stephens* on her sixth and seventh voyages. On her outward passage in 1874–5 she again met *Cutty Sark*. She also had the crack City Liner, *City of Hankow*, against her. The *Cutty Sark* left Gravesend on November 14th, *City of Hankow* on the 17th, and *Thomas Stephens* on the 18th. All three ships had to beat down Channel against fierce sou'-west gales, and the *Cutty Sark* lost a man overboard, off St. Catherine's, on the 16th. *Cutty Sark* and the *City of Hankow* took their departure from the Lizard on November 21st, the *Thomas Stephens* being just a day behind. The three ships were constantly in company with each other on the way to the Equator. When the wind was light the *City of Hankow* seemed to have the advantage of the other two, being in beautiful trim, with a splendid London general cargo, consisting chiefly of liquids. *Thomas Stephens*, on the other hand, was loaded very deep, drawing 11 inches more than on her previous outward passage. All three ships crossed the Line on the same day, December 11th, the *Thomas Stephens* and *City of Hankow* being together in 29° W., and the *Cutty Sark* in 26° W. After this the *Cutty Sark* gradually went ahead of the other two. The order at the Cape Meridian was :—*Cutty Sark*, January 1st, in 43° 30′ S.; *City of Hankow*, January 3rd, in 44° 27′ S.; and *Thomas Stephens*, on January 5th, in 41° 15′ S. The *Cutty Sark*, being bound to Sydney, rounded the South-West Cape, Tasmania, on January 26th, only 66 days out. The *City of Hankow* anchored in Hobson's Bay at 3 p.m. on January 30th, 70 days out from the Lizard, and *Thomas Stephens* anchored on the afternoon of January 31st, also 70 days out.

Previous to 1875 the *Thomas Stephens* had been painted a rather ugly grey. This year she appeared in Port Phillip looking very handsome as a black ship with painted ports. Her wool passage this year was made in 96 days to Falmouth.

On Captain Bloomfield's second voyage, and the ship's seventh, the *Thomas Stephens* arrived in Sydney Harbour on December 30th, 1875, being 91 days out from London. She sailed for home as one of the last of the Sydney wool fleet, and did not reach London until June 8th, 1876, being 92 days out. That summer Captain Richards returned to his old ship, and took her out to Melbourne in 78 days. Her homeward cargo was loaded in Rangoon, and she made the run from Rangoon to Liverpool in 113 days, arriving June 14th, 1877.

On her ninth voyage she went out to Melbourne from Liverpool in 76 days, having one first-class passenger and thirty-eight second and steerage. On her homeward passage she left Melbourne on January 17th, and had a very close race with the *La Hogue*, which had sailed from Sydney on January 16th. In the end the *La Hogue* just beat her, arriving in London on April 16th, 90 days out, whilst the *Thomas Stephens* reached the Downs two days later, in 91 days.

In 1878 Captain Richards took 77 days between Plymouth and Sydney, the *Thomas Stephens* being only 19 days from the Greenwich Meridian to the South Cape, Tasmania. Her wool passage this year was made in 89 days. She arrived in London from Sydney on March 6th, 1879.

On her eleventh voyage the *Thomas Stephens* took emigrants out to Otago from London, leaving on April 26th, 1879. She then crossed to San Francisco, and loaded her first grain cargo. Leaving the Pacific port on November 8th, 1879, she made the fine run home of 99 days, arriving Queenstown February 18th, 1880.

In 1880 Captain Richards made his last voyage in the *Thomas Stephens*, and when he handed her over to his successor he was presented with a handsome service of silver plate by his owners. This last voyage was as good as any of the preceding ones. Leaving Liverpool on April 29th, he made the splendid run of 83 days to Rangoon. The passage home from the East of an iron ship, unless she had been in dry-dock at Calcutta, was generally spoilt by growth on the bottom, and this was probably the reason why the homeward passage was not equal to her outward one.

Captain Robertson succeeded Captain Richards, and had the ship for three voyages, his best passages being :

1881	London to Melbourne ..	86 days.
1882	Liverpool to San Francisco ..	124 ,,
	San Francisco to Falmouth ..	98 ,,
1882-3	London to Sydney	75 ,,
1883-4	San Francisco to Falmouth ..	120 ,,

In the spring of 1884 Captain Robertson was succeeded by young Captain W. Cross, who was another hard carrier of sail. His first voyage was not favoured by winds, and the *Thomas Stephens* took 115 days going out from London to Sydney, and 130 coming home from 'Frisco to Falmouth. The ship discharged at Dunkirk, and then took a hundred emigrants from Antwerp to Sydney. This time the passage was made in 87 days. Captain Cross held on to his canvas like grim death in his effort to make a good run, and on one occasion, when running her easting down, the *Thomas Stephens* was badly pooped, and her lee helmsman washed down on to the main deck. Loading wool in December, Captain Cross raced *The Tweed* home, and, arriving in London on March 21st, 1885, 100 days out, managed to beat her by a week.

Captain Cross's last outward passage was 79 days to Sydney in 1886. Captain Robert Johnstone, formerly of the *Abergeldie*, then took over and sailed from Sharpness for Melbourne. Off the Lizard the *Thomas Stephens* met her old rival, the *Cutty Sark*, on August 20th, the latter being bound out to Sydney. The two ships passed Madeira together ten days later, but after this the *Cutty Sark* gained rapidly on her antagonist, the *Thomas Stephens* being loaded very deep with salt. The Cape Meridian was crossed by the *Cutty Sark* on October 15th, but *Thomas Stephens* did not reach it for another week. On October 2nd *Cutty Sark* was dismasted, but with such a master as Woodget she soon had an effective jury-rig up, and passed the Otway on November 11th. The *Thomas Stephens* did not sight the Otway until November 24th, and anchored at Melbourne on the 25th, 97 days out ; the *Cutty Sark* had reached Sydney on the 17th, having given her a very bad dressing down.

In 1888–9 Captain Johnstone went out to Sydney and back, his passages being 93 days out and 111 home. Then Captain Cutler took the command for a voyage to Sydney, taking her out in 88 days, and returning in 108. He was followed in 1890 by Captain Davies. His Sydney voyage was a good one—88 days out and 96 home.

In the winter of 1891–2 the *Thomas Stephens* made the longish passage of 150 days from San Francisco to Fleetwood. On her homeward run in 1892 the old ship received her first bad damage from the weather. Leaving Melbourne with wheat on May 8th, she put into Callao on July 7th with the whole starboard side of her bulwarks carried away from the fore-rigging to aft of the main, her decks also being severely strained. After rounding the Horn, she again was in trouble, and put into Bahia, her destination being New York. From New York with a new captain, Captain Davey, in command, she went out to Melbourne again, making the voyage in 104 days.

Her last voyage under the British Flag was an unfortunate one. She sailed from Barry on December 27th, 1894, under Captain Belding, for Esquimalt, but Cape Stiff proved too much for her, for she was dismasted, and had to put back to the Falklands. Here Captain Belding refused the expensive estimate of the Port Stanley shipwrights, and boldly set sail under a jury-rig for Cape Town, where the ship arrived on May 14th, 1895. Here he refitted, and, leaving Table Bay on June 22nd, continued by the eastern route, and finally arrived at Esquimalt on September 24th, 271 days out.

At the end of this voyage the *Thomas Stephens* was sold to the Portuguese Government, and Captain Belding was ordered to take her out to Lisbon with a Portuguese crew. During the passage the ship caught fire, and it was chiefly due to Captain Belding's energy and skill that the fire was extinguished. The Portuguese were so pleased with him that they not only presented him with an Order and a service of plate, but they asked him to continue in command of the ship. For the next few years the *Thomas Stephens*, under the name of *Pero de Alemguer*, looking very smart, sailed the seas as a training ship, under the Portuguese flag, as did also the famous *Thermopylæ*. At last she was laid up in the Tagus, but in 1915 was once more fitted out and sent across to America. She arrived safely, but on her return passage to Lisbon in January, 1916, was either overwhelmed by a winter gale, a floating mine, or a Hun torpedo, being eventually posted at Lloyd's as missing.

THE "SAMUEL PLIMSOLL."

THE *Samuel Plimsoll* was the third iron ship built for the Aberdeen White Star Line by Hood, and she soon proved herself to be worthy of comparison with the dry-decked *Patriarch*, which held the record to Sydney, or Thompson's second iron ship, the wet but flying *Miltiades*, which was never much over 70 days on the Melbourne run. *Samuel Plimsoll's* registered measurements were :—Tonnage, 1,444 tons; length, 241 feet 3 inches; breadth, 39 feet; depth of hold, 23 feet 1 inch.

Captain R. Boaden relinquished the command of the famous *Star of Peace* in order to take the new clipper from the stocks, and at her launch in September, 1873, she was christened by Mrs. Boaden, in the presence of the great parliamentarian after whom she was named. Like George Thompson's previous iron ships, the *Samuel Plimsoll* was specially fitted for passengers and emigrants, and throughout the first ten years of her existence she usually took aboard from 350 to 400 emigrants at Plymouth. Her first fifteen voyages were made to Sydney; she was then put on the Melbourne run for the rest of her life under the Aberdeen White Star flag. Homewards she invariably loaded wool, but like all iron ships, she could never rival the earlier wood and composite built clippers on this passage.

Ever since *Thermopylæ's* famous record-breaking maiden voyage, Thompson's ships were always specially prepared and loaded for their first run out to the Colonies, and always signed on a crew of carefully picked men. As *Thermopylæ's* first voyage was easily her quickest, so also were those of *Patriarch* and *Samuel Plimsoll*. It will be recalled that *Patriarch* made Sydney in 67 days, pilot to pilot, and came home in 69 days. This was a record which no ship could be expected to rival without good luck with her winds both out and home, and though the *Samuel Plimsoll* was certainly the equal of the *Patriarch* under most conditions of weather, she failed to beat *Patriarch's* record Sydney voyage.

On November 19th, 1873, Captain Boaden left Plymouth with 180 emigrants in the 'tween-decks. In spite of very light N.E. trades, *Samuel Plimsoll* was only 22 days to the Equator, crossing the Line in 29° W. on December 11th. Another 22 days took her to the Greenwich Meridian, and the Longitude of the Cape was crossed on January 6th, 1874. The *Samuel Plimsoll's* best point was undoubtedly with strong winds on the quarter, and in running her easting down she always found her opportunity.

On the maiden passage her best 24-hour run was 340 miles, and she was only four days running from the Leeuwin to the S.W. Cape, Tasmania. On January 17th she passed the *Alexander Duthie*, an Aberdeen skysail-yard clipper with a good reputation for speed. *Samuel Plimsoll* arrived on February 1st, 1874, 74 days out from Plymouth. This was the best Sydney passage of that year, the only two ships to come anywhere near it being the *Cutty Sark*, 78 days, and *Patriarch*, 79 days. This maiden passage enabled the ship's agents to give the *Samuel Plimsoll* a good puff in the " *Sydney Morning Herald* " in the usual notice that she was ready for passengers and cargo. Special points were made of her lofty 'tween-decks and large side-ports, and the fact that she carried an experienced surgeon. The new ship was, of course, too late for the wool clip, but was quickly loaded, and sailing on April 14th, made the best run home of the whole fleet, arriving in the Thames July 5th, 82 days out.

Her second voyage could not compare with her first, as she took 88 days going out to Sydney, and 103 coming home.

In 1875 the *Samuel Plimsoll* left Plymouth on August 6th with 360 emigrants on board. At 11.15 p.m. that same night she came into collision with the Italian barque *Eurica* ; the barque sank, but Captain Boaden managed to rescue her crew and landed them at Falmouth. *Samuel Plimsoll*, whose thick iron plates came to no harm, left Falmouth again on August 8th, and the following are the dates of passing the usual points :

Aug.	21.	Passed Madeira.
Sept.	4.	Crossed Equator in 23° W.
„	25.	Crossed Meridian of Greenwich.
„	28.	Passed Longitude of Cape in 44° S.
„	30.	Fell in with a big field of ice and bergs extending for 100 miles.
Oct.	19.	Passed the Otway, only 21 days from the Cape Meridian.
„	20.	Passed Wilson's Promontory.
„	21.	Passed Gabo.
„	22.	Arrived Port Jackson, 75 days out from Falmouth.

Her run home this season was 83 days, leaving Sydney on January 2nd, 1876. The only two ships to beat this were the wonderful old stagers, *The Tweed*, which left Sydney on December 10th, and was only 69 days, and *Parramatta*, which was 79 days, leaving Sydney on February 1st.

On her fourth voyage *Samuel Plimsoll* left Plymouth on June 2nd, 1876, carrying 405 emigrants. She crossed the Line 26 days out in 22½° W. and the Cape Meridian 47 days out in 41° S. This year she put up a wonderful week's run between 41° E. and 97° E. in Latitude 41° S. The daily runs were as follows :—348, 330, 301, 342, 320, 246, 340, a total of 2,227 miles. The S.W. Cape, Tasmania, was rounded on August 9th, 68 days out, but Captain Boaden had his passage spoilt on the other side of Tasmania, and when he at length arrived within 30 miles of Sydney Heads on August 17th, was delayed another two days by a heavy S.S.W. gale, the passage totalling up to 78 days. This season the *Samuel Plimsoll*, for the first time, loaded amongst the November wool ships. Her passage home was not lucky, and she took 92 days ; the only vessel to make a good passage this year was the new green clipper, *Aristides*, which managed to get home in 81 days.

In 1877 *Samuel Plimsoll* left Plymouth on June 9th, with 78 single women, 105 single men, 72 married couples, and 133 children on board. The Equator was not crossed until July 7th, the emigrant clipper being held up by 8 days of calms. She got her chance, in the South Atlantic, and crossed the Cape Meridian on July 28th, after a week's run of 2,050 miles. The Longitude of the Leeuwin was passed on August 14th, the Otway on August 23rd, and Port Jackson reached on August 27th, 79 days out. Her wool passage was again only about the average. She arrived in London on February 12th, 1878, 96 days out. The *Mermerus* arrived on the same day, only 80 days out from Melbourne, also the *George Thompson*, 95 days out, and the *Romanoff*, 108 days out.

In 1878 Captain Boaden again embarked more than 450 emigrants, and left Plymouth on May 3rd, a month earlier than usual. The ship was not favoured by winds, being 13 days to the Latitude of Madeira, and finding very poor S.E. trades, with the result that she was 86 days on the passage. This was, however, made up for by the best wool passage of the year—80 days—during which she passed a number of crack ships, such as *Slieve More*, *Ben Cruachan*, *Miltiades*, *Cimba*, *Jerusalem* and *Ben Voirlich*.

"Samuel Plimsoll"

Built 1873 Passenger and Emigrant Ship.

On her next outward passage the *Samuel Plimsoll* was dismasted. Leaving Plymouth on March 21st, she made a smart run south. On the fifteenth day out she was within a couple of hundred miles of the Equator, when at 8 p.m. she was struck by a sharp squall from the southward. This carried away the bobstay, and before anything could be done, the bowsprit broke short off at the stem head, the foretopmast snapped at the lower cap, and came down with a crash, taking the main topgallant mast and yards with it. As usual with tropical squalls, the damage was done in a moment and left the ship lying like a wounded bird upon the water. And now we come to one of the classic tales of sailing-ship seamanship. It happened that there was a Yankee clipper in company, also bound to the Antipodes. Her skipper immediately altered his course for the dismasted *Samuel Plimsoll*, and sent a boat aboard her with an offer to tranship the passengers and take them on to their destination. This offer was refused, with thanks, so the American squared away, whilst the Aberdeen liner set to work refitting in mid-ocean. So thoroughly was the work done that the *Samuel Plimsoll* crossed the Equator on April 7th, only 17 days out, and was able to reel off over 2,000 miles in one week down in the " roaring forties." In the end the clipper was sailed into Sydney Harbour on June 12th, only 83 days out. The American arrived a few days later, and as soon as he could get ashore, reported leaving the *Samuel Plimsoll* dismasted in the North Atlantic; he also commented on Captain Boaden's foolhardiness in refusing to tranship his passengers. The story goes that the agent turned round, and rather unkindly imitating the slow drawl of the Yankee, replied with a chuckle : " If it's Captain Boaden you are talking about, I guess you had better see him yourself. He's in the next room." No doubt the American skipper was surprised ! Captain Boaden received a great deal of praise for refusing to put into one of the Brazil ports, as many a man would have done, and he was afterwards presented with an illuminated testimonial at a picnic given in his honour by the underwriters of Sydney.

The *Samuel Plimsoll's* passage home this year was a poor one—107 days ; the only consolation being that the beautiful *Salamis* (Thompson's iron *Thermopylæ*), which arrived in the Thames on March 8th, the day before *Samuel Plimsoll*, had taken two days longer from Melbourne.

In 1880 *Samuel Plimsoll* left Plymouth on April 29th, with 384 emigrants. On May 3rd, in 38° N. 18° W., a derelict was passed, a barque with her stern smashed in, her bulwarks and deck-houses gone by the board, and every sea making a clean breach across her main deck. Captain Boaden satisfied himself that this was the ill-fated *Queen of Hearts*, whose crew had been taken off by a steamer some three weeks before. Again the *Samuel Plimsoll* made a wonderful run to the Line, which was crossed in 25° 34' W. on May 15th, only 16 days out. The best work this passage consisted of the following runs in the " roaring forties " :— June 11th, 298 miles ; June 15th, 294 miles ; June 17th, 313 miles ; June 19th, 304 miles ; June 22nd, 291 miles ; June 23rd, 308 miles ; June 25th, 214 miles ; and June 26th, 300 miles. The ship was on the Meridian of the Cape on June 10th in 40°, off the Crozets on June 17th, Cape Leeuwin on June 27th, Otway July 5th, and arrived Port Jackson on July 9th, but had to be quarantined in Watson's Bay owing to having measles on board.

In 1881 Captain Boaden was not well enough to take the ship out, and Captain A. Simpson (late chief officer) took command for a voyage, being 79 days out and 91 home. Captain Boaden resumed command the next voyage, but did not come home in the ship owing to his poor health.

Captain Henderson, who had been mate of the *Samuel Plimsoll* on her first two voyages, and had then been in command of *Wave of Life, Moravian* and *Thermopylæ*, was appointed to succeed Captain Boaden, and under him the vessel continued to maintain her reputation for smart passages.

In 1883 *Samuel Plimsoll* made her best passage to Sydney, 72 days from Plymouth, whence she sailed at 4.35 p.m. on April 6th. The Equator was crossed on April 27th; Meridian of the Cape on May 19th in 40° S. Running her easting down the ship averaged 278 miles for 13 consecutive days, her best 24 hours being 337 miles. The Otway was sighted on June 10th, only 65 days out; Wilson's Promontory was passed on June 11th; but then, as so often happened in Sydney passages, no less than six days were wasted on the coast and the ship did not enter the Heads until 10 a.m. on June 17th.

In 1888 the *Samuel Plimsoll* made her first voyage to Melbourne. Leaving London on March 2nd the start of the passage was far from favourable, for a heavy westerly gale kept her hove to within 270 miles of the Start until March 15th. The Equator was crossed on April 5th, and a good run south was made, the ship averaging 218 miles a day from Trinidad Island to 130° East Longitude, the best distance in the 24 hours being 310 miles. The Otway was made at 9.30 p.m. on May 21st, and the ship reached the anchorage in Hobson's Bay the next day, 79 days out. Henceforward, until the end of the century, the *Samuel Plimsoll* was a regular trader to Melbourne under Captain Henderson, her passages being invariably above the average, as, for instance, Channel to Melbourne in 1889—81 days; 1890—84 days; 1891—78 days; 1893—79 days; 1894—79 days. In 1895 Captain Henderson made his best run to the Horn. In 15 days, from November 29th to December 12th, between 49° 50′ S. 179° 05′ W. and 55° 25′ S. 79° 59′ W., the old Aberdeen flyer covered 4,020 miles, her daily runs being 244, 286, 263, 259, 261, 273, 302, 290, 257, 253, 274, 264, 314, 235 and 245.

Samuel Plimsoll was sold at the beginning of the 20th century to a firm in Billiter Street, known as "Young Savill's," and in June, 1902, she sailed from Glasgow on what proved to be her first and last voyage to New Zealand. After an uneventful passage, and a fast run up the coast, the *Samuel Plimsoll* made Cape Saunders Light, a little over 90 days out. It was about 10 p.m. on a Friday night and the ship was now hove to as it was blowing very hard from the south-east. All the next day the *Samuel Plimsoll* was allowed to drift; then at seven bells on the Sunday morning the mainmast broke short off about four feet below the main deck. The result was perhaps the most extraordinary in all the annals of dismastings —the main cap carried away and the mast somehow leapt overboard, taking with it the fore and mizen topgallant masts, without doing any more damage than slightly bruising the teak topgallant rail. A good deal of water found its way below through the mast-hole, but this was soon plugged with old canvas, and the ship, under foresail and foretopsail, eventually made the land near Gable Head, North Island. Here a fair wind for Napier was picked up, and so rapidly did the lame duck slip along, that a small trawler which put out to her aid, could not catch her, and had to return. That evening, just as it was getting dark, a Union of New Zealand coasting steamer offered a tow, and took the green liner into Gisborne and afterwards to Port Chalmers. Here, after some deliberation, it was decided not to refit her, and she was sold for a coal hulk. She was then towed to Sydney at the end of a 120-fathom hawser, and later taken on to Fremantle, where she still lies.

THE "WINDSOR PARK."

WHEN the *Windsor Park* was launched in 1882, a tremendous boom in shipbuilding was going on, in which both sail and steam were receiving an equal share. This boom, which lasted until the middle of 1884, was practically the last really large output of iron-built ships, for steel plates were coming into fashion with a rush, such as threatened iron in its turn, just as iron had threatened and then conquered wood.

The *Windsor Park* was not amongst the first steel ships. She belonged to the type of iron full-rigged ship which was more a big carrier than a fast sailer. Thos. Royden and Sons, who built her, had reason to be proud of many a clipper of world-wide renown, such as the *Glengarry, Evesham Abbey, Knight of the Garter, Merioneth* and *Glenesslin*—each one of which could boast an outstanding performance in sailing-ship speed. I fear that the *Windsor Park* could not claim any kinship to these famous iron clippers. She was a sister ship, as a matter of fact, to the steady-going coolie ship *Orealla*, which belonged to Sandbach, Tuine & Co. She registered 1,761 tons, and measured 250 feet 5 inches in length, 40 feet 2 inches beam and 24 feet depth of hold. Royden built her on spec., and she was bought on the stocks by A. Howden & Co., her first commander, A. Bentley, also having a share in her.

The *Windsor Park* cost £40,000 to build, and Thomas Royden & Co. knew how to finish off a vessel, whether she was a clipper or a carrier; the ship's smart appearance was further improved by one of the mates of her early days, who did some beautiful carving on the teak panels at the break of the poop. When she first came out *Windsor Park*'s sail plan included a skysail at the main and stunsails at the fore.

Her first passage was quite a good one, 90 days to Saugar Light with a cargo of steel rails for the Indian railways.

After ten years in the Calcutta and Australian trades, *Windsor Park* was sold in 1893 to Geo. Gordon & Co., of Glasgow, and Captain Bentley was followed in the command by Captain G. Lambie, who had the *Windsor Park* to the end of the 19th century; finally A. Livingstone commanded her until 1911, when the old ship went to the Norwegians.

About the best passage of which I have any record was a cross-Pacific one of 37 days between Newcastle, N.S.W., and Valparaiso, where she arrived on August 9th, 1897. This passage was certainly a good one; the record being 29 days, made by the four-mast ship *Wendur* the year before, when she raced the famous *Loch Torridon* and beat her by six hours. But the *Windsor Park* was more notorious for her long passages in crossing the Pacific than for her short ones.

In 1900 she made the longest passage of the year between Newcastle, N.S.W., and San Francisco, taking 104 days. The best passage that year was made by the British ship, *Norfolk Islands*, whose time was 48 days. Nor was 104 days the worst that the old *Windsor*

Park could do on this favourite sailing-ship passage. In 1902 she arrived at San Francisco on April 5th, 113 days from Newcastle, N.S.W. This time, however, she was not the slowest ship of the fleet, for the *Clydesdale* actually took 125 days. It was evidently an unfavourable season, for the best passage was no better than 61 days, made by the four-mast barque, *Osborne*. It may be of interest to note that 80 ships made the Newcastle-'Frisco passage in 1900, and 71 in 1902. The usual sailing-ship round at the beginning of the 20th century was—out to Australia; across the Pacific with coal, either to the North-West Coast or the South-West Coast of America and then home with either grain, nitrate or guano.

The *Windsor Park* must have caused the underwriters a good deal of anxiety, for her homeward passages were usually longer than the average, and on three occasions she was listed amongst the vessels making unusually long trips homeward bound round the Horn from San Francisco. In 1901 she signalled the Lizard on January 11th—172 days from the Golden Gate. In 1902 she arrived at Queenstown on November 8th, 173 days out; and in 1905 she arrived in the Mersey on April 11th, also 173 days out from San Francisco. The best passage in 1901 was 101 days, made by the *Gertrude*; in 1902, the well-known four-mast barque *Muskoka* ran from San Francisco to the Bishops in 96 days; and in 1905, the best passage was made by the Frenchman, *Bossuet*, 129 days from 'Frisco to Runcorn.

On December 29th, 1906, the *Windsor Park* had a narrow escape from ending her days. When bound from Wallaroo to Port Elizabeth, she got ashore at Cape Recife. However, assistance was quickly on the spot, and she was refloated.

Bought by A. Meling, of Stavanger, in 1911, *Windsor Park* changed owners again in 1913, going to O. A. Fardig, of Nystad. When war broke out in 1914 the *Windsor Park* was on her way from New Caledonia to Hamburg, but she was diverted to the Clyde, whence she sailed to Picton, Nova Scotia, and back. But for the greater part of the war she kept out of the submarine area, trading between the United States and South American ports.

In 1920 the old ship was bought by G. W. Hellstad, of Nystad, and after being a stranger to British ports for some half-dozen years, she arrived in the Thames in May, 1921, 56 days out from Port Arthur, Texas. *Windsor Park* was laid up until September, then went round to Newport, Mon., but a profitable freight for a windjammer was practically impossible to come by and on October 20th, a Dutch tug towed her away to be converted into a coal hulk at Gibraltar. Soon after she was docked at Gibraltar a very strong gale blew up during the night, and the *Windsor Park*, which was moored alongside the Gun Wharf, broke loose and collided with the cable ship *Amber*, and also damaged part of the Mole. Later on the ship was dismantled and renamed *Saint James II*.

So much for the *Windsor Park*. She was one of those hard-working windjammers whose claim to history's recognition must always be that they trained thousands of superb seamen in a way which can never be approached by a mechanically driven oil or steam ship. The *Windsor Park* may have been a " workhouse," as some called her, and she may have been " a slow-going iron box," but she kept the seas with very few mishaps, and made a steady living for thirty-nine years.

"Windsor Park"

Built 1882 General Trader.

THE "FALLS OF HALLADALE."

D URING the middle 'eighties shipbuilders and designers were still experimenting with the recently devised four-masted rig for large sailing vessels. Owners were still undecided as to whether it was better to give a ship yards on all four masts or not, and whether skysails over double topgallants were worth the cost of additional hands. But on all sides it was agreed that interchangeable yards on fore, main and mizen were a very great economy and considerably eased both the rigger's and sailmaker's bills.

The Falls Line, of Glasgow, all of whose ships were built by Russell & Co., already owned six superb four-masters when they gave the order, in 1886, for the construction of the two fine sister ships, *Falls of Garry* and *Falls of Halladale*, but their previous vessels were square rigged on all four masts, with skysails over double topgallant sails on the main and mizen. In the design and rig of their new deep-watermen Messrs. Wright & Breakenridge, of the Falls Line, decided to sacrifice speed to carrying power, sail area to economy in man power; thus the *Falls of Garry* and *Falls of Halladale*, which were sent afloat in June and July respectively, came out with no yards on their jigger-masts, though they crossed the skysail yards on main and mizen, which yards, by the way, measured 34 feet in length. Though these were undoubtedly heavy yards to carry over 180 feet above the deck, in other respects the sail plan of the sister ships was extremely moderate for vessels of the 'eighties, when it was usual to send aloft yards of tremendous length and weight. The lower yards of the *Falls of Halladale* were only 82 feet long, which was some six or eight feet shorter than those usually crossed on a 2,000-ton four-mast barque of her type.

There was one great merit in the snug rig of the *Falls of Garry* and *Falls of Halladale* —their captains knew that they could carry on as long as the gear would stand, and this saved a great deal of sail handling on the part of the crew and anxiety on the part of the captain. The sister ships were large carriers, full-lined with square bilge and wall-sides —what used to be called the warehouse type—and they needed a favourable gale of wind to log 13 knots or make a 24-hour run of 300 miles.

It was not every captain who cared to carry on fearlessly in a gale of wind, especially when strict economy and careful preservation of gear were impressed upon him as the first consideration by his owner; and this probably explains why the *Falls of Halladale* was somewhat notorious for getting on the overdue list, whilst the *Falls of Garry* succeeded in making several outstanding passages.

The registered tonnage and measurements of the sister ships were as follows :—2,026 tons ; 275 feet 2 inches, length ; 41 feet 6 inches, breadth ; and 23 feet 9 inches, depth of hold. Their deck plans are worthy of remark, for they were two of the earliest ships to be fitted with fore and aft lifting bridges for bad weather. These bridges enabled the crew to get aft dry-shod in the worst of the Westerlies, when it would not have been safe to put a foot upon the main deck. It is hard for those who have never seen a sailing ship's main deck in a high following sea to understand the need for these bridges. Although they were cumbersome and unsightly when cocked up in harbour, latter-day windjammer owners were compelled by sheer force of wind and sea to admit their utility, for they saved the hands from death and injury again and again.

Iron and steel four-masters of over 250 feet in length could not keep clear of heavy water like their short wooden predecessors, with the result that quite an ordinary Southern Ocean sea would roar aboard and sweep irresistibly the whole length of the main deck. It was on such occasions that a watch who were hauling up gear or laying back on a brace had to leap for the boat-skids or poop ladders in order to save themselves from being hurled helplessly about in the flood. Men clutched madly at stanchion, loose rope's end or fife-rail as they felt themselves being bumped about from rail to rail ; sometimes, indeed, they were washed clean overboard, and on more than one occasion a whole watch was lost in this way. No landsman can visualize the scene. It was at such times that heroic deeds were done down there on the flooded main deck, when men risked life and limb in strenuous attempts to save their drowning watch mates. Deep-water seamen thought little of leaving the safety of the poop for the waist-deep flood of white water on a windjammer's main deck in an endeavour to drag sundry helpless bundles of humanity from the middle of a mass of tangled gear, wrecked doors, capstan bars and iron-shod buckets which were tossing about in the lee scuppers. Often and often the brave rescuers were caught in their turn by a hungry " greybeard " off Cape Stiff and, if they survived, only came through at the cost of a broken limb or cracked skull. But lucky ships with midship-bridges had no need to rig a maze of life-lines about their main decks. It was seldom that any heavy water reached the levels of the bridges, and even when it did these sturdy steel structures were built to withstand the worst of poopers.

Taking the bridges of the *Falls of Halladale* from forward aft, the first led from the forecastle head and, passing to starboard of the foremast, rested its after-end upon the fore boat-skids. The next bridge was a long one and landed up on top of the midship-house, from which an equally long bridge led to the top of the half-deck. These, like the fore-bridge, were on the starboard side, just clear of the hatches and fife-rails. The after-bridge, which led from the top of the half-deck to the poop, was placed amidships, and led right over the after-hatch.

The first commander of the *Falls of Halladale* was Captain George Bardo ; he was followed, in 1888, by Captain William Peters, who only handed over to Captain W. Fordyce a voyage or two before the ship was sold to T. Law & Co. in 1902 : whilst under the Shire house-flag the *Falls of Halladale* was commanded by Captain David Wood Thomson, who was unlucky enough to lose her on the coast of Victoria in 1908.

The *Halladale's* best passage, so far as I know, was 108 days between Calcutta and Falmouth in the spring of 1900, although she had been credited with a 100-day run from Swansea to San Francisco in 1895 ; but I have been unable to verify the latter figure.

The first occasion on which she gave the underwriters anxiety was in 1893. Captain Peters sailed from the Tyne on April 27th, with bricks, coke and pig-iron for San Francisco. Going north about round Scotland, the *Falls of Halladale* encountered nothing but head winds all the way down to the Line ; the usual weather was experienced off the Horn, where she spent the best part of a month head reaching under lower topsails ; finally, very light winds in the Pacific further delayed the passage, and the Golden Gate was not reached until October 31st, 187 days out. This was a specially hard passage for all hands, as owing to some mistake at Shields the captain's order for tobacco was not executed and the ship ran out of the precious weed before the Equator was crossed. At first the men were forced to dry their chews and smoke them, but in a very short time the chewing tobacco was all

"Falls of Halladale"

Built 1886 General Trader.

finished, and it was a case of sucking at an empty pipe or smoking some such concoction as tea or cut-up junk. In recounting his hardships in a letter, a member of the crew mentions one of those queer characters who were only to be found in the fo'c'sle of a sailing ship. This man, who was known as " Ropeyarn Jack," made a practice of gulping down a draught of paraffin before going on deck, in order, as he said, to keep out the cold. Needless to say that this method of warming his inside landed him in hospital on arrival at San Francisco. It was at the end of this long passage that the Falls liner shed her skysails, the main and mizen poles being cut off to match the height of the fore.

The *Falls of Halladale* spent most of her life in the Pacific grain trade to Europe, but I can find no homeward passages of under 130 days. In 1894, after lying up in Mission Bay for four months, she made the run to Grimsby in that time. In 1898 she again came on the overdue list, being 172 days out from San Francisco, when she reached Queenstown on April 2nd. Then in 1902 she was 169 days to Queenstown from Astoria.

Her worst passage, however, was the outward one in 1903–4. Captain Thomson sailed from Liverpool on July 25th, 1903. In attempting to round the corner the big four-master was so battered by a succession of Cape Horn " snorters " that she began to leak and it was found necessary to keep the pumps going. The battle to make westing continued for three terrible weeks, during which time 19 sails were blown to smithereens. Finally, on a bitter night in the midst of a raging snowstorm, a tremendous sea fell aboard the whole length of the main rail, and from such a height that it even smashed up the fore and aft bridges. This was the last straw. Captain Thomson put his helm up and resigned himself to the long run round the world via the Cape of Good Hope. This turning tail to the Westerlies no doubt eased the ship, but it did not lessen the hardships of her crew to any great extent. The grub was very short and bad, the pork green, the biscuit weevily, the peas mouldy, the sugar crawling, and the water rust red. As for the beef, witness the following doggerel, by a foremast hand :

> As the steam from the coppers poured
>   The cook he turned more pale,
> Till he lit his pipe and walked outside
>   And hung o'er the weather rail ;
> He hung all limp and loose,
>   And smoked like the very deuce,
> And said : " Great Scott ! it smells so strong
>   I'm chased from my own caboose."

By the time the longitude of New Zealand was reached all hands forward were in a state of open mutiny. No doubt they were desperate from sheer weariness of spirit, and refused duty in the hope of getting clear of the ship. At any rate Captain Thomson was induced to put into Invercargill on January 1st, 1904, and here a yacht seems to have intervened and made peace between skipper and crew. But on the passage being resumed the malcontents, under the usual fighting Irishman, by name Mooney, again refused work. This time Captain Thomson clapped seven of them, together with their ringleader, in irons. The stubborn Irishman stuck it out for 38 days, but the rest of the mutineers soon gave in and resumed work. At last, on March 19th, 1904, the *Falls of Halladale*, all rust-stained and battered, with her main royal mast gone and her mizen royal yard missing, struggled up to the anchorage in San Francisco Bay, being 238 days out from the Mersey.

On the voyage before her last, *Falls of Halladale* came to London with a cargo of 70-foot blue gum logs, and whilst these were being discharged at Purfleet Wharf the ship aroused a good deal of attention amongst London shipping people, for by this time big sailing ships had become somewhat of a rarity in the Thames. She afterwards took in a cargo of chalk at West Thurrock and then loaded explosives below Gravesend, sailing for the Antipodes on St. Patrick's Day, 1908.

The end came on November 14th, 1908, when the *Falls of Halladale* stranded about six miles west of Port Campbell, on the coast of Victoria, Australia. Captain Thomson had evidently no idea that he was so close in to the land, as he could easily have come round and headed off-shore on the port tack. As it was, the ship struck, bows on, in fine weather and became a total loss.

THE "ILLAWARRA."

THE *Illawarra* is chiefly remembered as one of Devitt & Moore's cadet ships. She and the *Macquarie* succeeded the *Harbinger* and the *Hesperus*, and were in their turn succeeded by the *Port Jackson* and *Medway*. But for twenty years before the *Illawarra* became a school ship she voyaged regularly to Sydney in Devitt & Moore's service. Built by Dobie & Co., of Glasgow, and launched in October, 1881, she registered 1,887 tons, and her principal measurements were :—Length, 269 feet 1 inch ; breadth, 40 feet 6 inches ; depth, 24 feet. Her poop was 54 feet long, and she was designed to carry passengers, though not on the scale of such ships as the *Rodney*, *Hesperus* and *Harbinger*, for in the early 'eighties the sailing ships were already losing most of their passengers and emigrants to the steamship companies, and a windjammer, in order to be able to earn dividends, had to be suited for any kind of cargo.

The *Illawarra* was, therefore, constructed as a first-class iron cargo carrier rather than a fine-lined wool clipper or a handsomely-fitted passenger ship. She was, indeed, of a very useful type, up to date in every way, with medium lines, easily capable of a 300-mile run in the " roaring forties," but slow, compared with the out-and-out clippers, in light and moderate winds. Her sail plan was moderate, and much less than those of many iron ships of her size, with double topgallant yards and nothing to worry her apprentices above the royals.

Devitt & Moore gave the command of their new ship to the veteran Captain David B. Corvasso, who had made his name in the old Blackwall frigates, *La Hogue* and *Dunbar Castle*. Captain Corvasso was a splendid seaman, with a very strong personality, and ruled his passengers as he did his crew, with more than a touch of the martinet. His pet expression, which he bellowed out in a reef-topsail voice when roused, was : " What the devil next ? "

On one occasion, when he had ninety single women and a few married couples as emigrants aboard the *Dunbar Castle*, he found himself up against a mutiny of his passengers. These girls chased their matron and the ship's doctor out of their quarters, with a shrill chorus of threats and a terrifying exhibition of muscular arms and legs ; and, when the captain came forward to see what was the matter, he was met at the foot of the women's companion by a sturdy North Country lass, who was stripped to the waist for battle and, shaking a huge fist in the martinet's face, dared him to advance. " What the devil next ? " roared Corvasso, and at once ordered the hose-pipe to be screwed on to the force-pump. This method of quelling a mutiny was too much for even the most courageous of the rebellious maidens ; they very quickly quieted down, and went to their bunks without any further trouble.

Captain Corvasso commanded the *Illawarra* throughout the 'eighties. On her first voyage the *Illawarra* left Liverpool on January 12th, 1882, had a rather lengthy passage to the Line, which she did not cross until February 17th, 36 days out, and reached Sydney on April 29th, 107 days out. It was not a sufficiently good passage to gain her a place amongst the wool clippers, but at this date the San Francisco grain trade with Europe was booming. So Corvasso loaded coal at Sydney for San Francisco, and proceeded to make the run across the Pacific in the splendid time of 51 days.

The *Illawarra* left San Francisco with a cargo of wheat and barley for Grimsby on October 31st, sighted Scilly on March 11th, 1883, 131 days out, and reached Grimsby on the 17th.

On her second voyage the *Illawarra* had a very much better passage out to Sydney. Leaving Plymouth with passengers, at 3.30 p.m. on May 3rd, she arrived in Port Jackson on July 28th, 86 days out. She again crossed to San Francisco—this time in 61 days—and, leaving the Californian port with a full cargo, signalled off the Lizard on June 4th, 1884, 129 days out. This was her last grain passage. Henceforth she loaded in the Colonies for home with either wool or wheat; on her first passage for the wool sales she made the very good time, for an iron ship, of 86 days to the Start. She loaded over 7,000 bales of wool. Between 1884 and 1899 15 voyages were made in the Sydney trade, out with general and home with a wool cargo. The best outward run was 85 days—good, but nothing out of the way, but it must be remembered that the *Illawarra* always left London in the height of the summer, and usually had a light weather passage to the Line. Homewards round the Horn her best run was 83 days from Sydney to the Wight, which was an exceedingly good piece of work for an iron ship. This run was made in 1893–4. Old Corvasso was succeeded by a Captain Smith in the 'nineties.

In 1890 Lord Brassey and Messrs. Devitt & Moore started a cadet-training premium scheme with the two magnificent ships, *Hesperus* and *Harbinger*. Besides carrying about 50 cadets apiece the ships were most liberally officered and kept up. In addition to five deck officers, they were given a surgeon, a chaplain, and a Naval Instructor, the last of whom was usually an ex-naval officer.

In 1899 the *Hesperus* was sold, and Devitt & Moore picked the *Illawarra* as the most suitable ship to succeed her. Captain Harwood Barrett, who had made his name as the commander of the *Rodney*, was chosen to command the new cadet ship, having previously had experience of cadets in the *Hesperus*. Unfortunately Captain Barrett was far from well, and he died at sea on his first voyage in the *Illawarra*, whilst she was outward bound to Melbourne.

Captain Maitland, Barrett's brother-in-law, who had just relinquished the command of the *Harbinger*, on her sale abroad, was ordered to proceed to Australia by mail-steamer, and take over the *Illawarra*. Maitland had only lately been married, and he took his wife out with him, and brought her home in the *Illawarra*. He commanded the *Illawarra* for seven years, and then took over the *Port Jackson*—thus he had a very long experience in training cadets.

The Brassey scheme, which came to an end during the war with Germany, when the last two training ships, *Port Jackson* and *Medway*, were taken out of the hands of Messrs. Devitt & Moore by the Government, was acknowledged to be the best system ever devised for training officers for our Merchant Navy. Though the parents of the boys were charged a stiffish premium, the cadets themselves lived in luxury, compared with the ordinary sailing-ship apprentice. At the same time they were taught their profession by picked instructors, with the added advantage of usually a start as junior officer in one of the first-class passenger lines as soon as they had passed their second mate's examination.

The boys of the *Illawarra* were divided into two watches, each of two divisions. During the day one division kept the deck, doing all the ordinary ship's work with the seamen, whilst the other division attended classes below for navigation, seamanship and nautical astronomy

"Illawarra"
Built 1881 Training Ship.

under the instructor.　Captain Maitland usually took the senior boys himself, and coached them in seamanship and that bugbear of all apprentices, " the Rule of the Road at Sea." With regard to sail-handling, the Brassey cadets, like the old-time Blackwall midshipmen, were made entirely responsible for the mizen mast, and considered themselves disgraced if it happened that they could not do without help.

During her years as a cadet ship the *Illawarra* was diverted from the Sydney run to that of Melbourne.　On her first passage to Hobson's Bay she went from Brixham to Melbourne in 83 days.　In 1900 she left London, under Captain Maitland, on October 1st, cleared the Channel on October 8th, had to tack off Pernambuco on November 9th, and crossed the Cape Meridian in 42½° S. on December 4th.　The longitude of Cape Leeuwin was crossed on Christmas Eve, and the *Illawarra* entered Port Phillip Heads on January 1st, 85 days out. On this occasion, besides her cadets, she had two consumptive passengers ;　both the latter died at sea.

A cadet ship was, of course, much better manned than an ordinary deep-water trader ; thus we nearly always find these ships making good passages, though they did not attempt to carry on ;　the *Illawarra's* best day's run in 1900 was only 301 miles.

In 1907 the *Illawarra's* career under Devitt & Moore's house-flag came to an end, and in July of that year she towed down the Thames with a Norwegian captain in place of Maitland, and the Norwegian flag instead of the Red Ensign.　The Norwegians loaded her with wood at Christiania, a deck cargo of deals taking the place of the old schoolrooms and cadet accommodation on the main deck.　Under Captain J. Jobson she made the run from Christiania to Melbourne in 104 days.

The end of the fine old ship came three years later.　On February 12th, 1912, she left Leith for Valparaiso, but met with disaster, being abandoned off the Old Head of Kinsale on March 7th, in a sinking condition, leaking after a storm.　Her crew were rescued by the British steamer, *Bangore Head*, and, though the shipping report does not say so, we may conclude that the ship sank off that rugged Irish coast.

THE "MEDWAY."

THE *Medway* was the last of Devitt & Moore's splendid fleet of ocean training ships. This magnificent, steel four-mast barque was built in 1902 by A. McMillan & Co., of Dumbarton, to the order of Sota & Aznar, of Monte Video, who gave her the name of *Ama Begonakoa*. From the first, she was designed to carry cadets, a large deck-house being built for their accommodation just aft of the mizen mast, this and the usual midshiphouse, aft of the foremast, being connected with the poop by flying bridges.

The new cadet ship registered 2,511 tons gross, 2,298 tons net and lifted a dead weight cargo of 4,000 tons. Her principal measurements were :—Length, 300 feet ; breadth, 43 feet 2 inches ; depth, 24 feet 8 inches. Her moulded depth was 26 feet 6 inches ; freeboard amidships, 5 feet 8 inches ; and length of poop, 42 feet. With the knowledge that she would be well manned with cadets aboard, Messrs. McMillan gave her a big sail plan, and though she had not the speed of the *Port Jackson* she was by no means an indifferent sailer. After eight years under the Uruguayan flag, the *Ama Begonakoa* was bought in 1910 by Devitt & Moore's Ocean Training Ships, Ltd., and renamed the *Medway*, Robert Jackson, the chief officer of the *Port Jackson*, being placed in command.

At the end of her first voyage under Devitt & Moore's house-flag, Lord Brassey gave a luncheon aboard the *Medway* to about forty prominent shipping people, at which the Marquis of Graham and Sir Thomas Devitt made speeches on the advantages of a training in sail for the future officers of the Mercantile Marine. Though their arguments were, of course, unanswerable by the advocates of steam training, the most interesting speech came from the captain of the ship. After testifying to the good qualities of his vessel, which had made the fine passage of 95 days to the Channel from Australia, Captain Jackson declared that a first-voyage cadet was fit to go through the second mate's examination, that a second-voyage cadet could pass the mate's examination, and that he would back a third-voyage cadet to beat any old shell-back at pure sailorizing. These were big claims, but the captain was scarcely exaggerating, for no better sailors were ever turned out than those trained in the Devitt & Moore cadet ships.

Until the outbreak of war the *Medway* voyaged regularly in the Australian trade, and her cadet accommodation was always fully taken up. Her cargoes were usually general out from London and wool and grain home from Sydney, N.S.W.

Though a full-built ship, the *Medway* often acquitted herself well against vessels which were noted for their speed ; for instance, on April 4th, 1912, the P.S.N. Co.'s liner, *Orissa*, spoke the *Medway* and the *Howard D. Troop*, in 2° N. 31° W. The *Howard D. Troop* was a very fast four-mast barque with a number of record passages to her credit, and a hard driving " Blue Nose " skipper in command. The two ships had left Sydney together on January 16th, and the *Medway* was making a splendid race of it against her formidable opponent. The year before she had raced the *Loch Etive* home, arriving in the Thames 101 days out from Sydney, whilst the Loch liner was about the same time to her port of call.

The *Medway's* outward passages were from London to the Colonies direct, except that of 1912, when we find her crossing the Atlantic from Lisbon to New York, and then making a longish passage out round the Cape.

In 1914 the cadet ship sailed from Sydney a bare fortnight before the declaration of war, and arrived at Falmouth, 116 days out, on November 13th. Very shortly after her arrival in Carrick Roads, Captain Jackson died. The ship was ordered to Cardiff to discharge, and she went round in charge of the veteran Captain McKay, who was well over 80 years old, and had once commanded the colonial clipper, *Ann Duthie*.

We now come to the *Medway's* war service. Captain David Williams was appointed to the command in December, 1914, and on April 22nd, 1915, the ship sailed from Liverpool for Hobart with a full cargo of rails (3,630 tons). She arrived at Hobart on July 27th, 96 days out. She next crossed in ballast to Portland, Oregon. With her water ballast tanks full, and an additional 500 tons of stiffening in the shape of road metal, the big four-master handled splendidly, and arrived at Portland on December 18th, 79 days out.

The *Medway* loaded a full cargo of grain and sailed from Portland under Admiralty instructions on January 5th, 1916, for Channel port of call. An average passage was made to Falmouth, the *Medway* being fortunate in escaping the German submarines, which were then thick off the mouth of the Channel. At Falmouth all her cadets were landed, and those who had put in 12 months' service were immediately drafted into the fleet as temporary midshipmen, R.N.R.

Meanwhile the *Medway* was ordered to discharge at Bordeaux, her grain having been bought by the French Government. This was a dangerous passage for a sailing ship to make, and Messrs. Devitt & Moore very properly asked for an escort. The Admiralty replied by placing a tug, which was armed with a 4·7 gun, and had lately returned from bottling up the *Konigsberg* in the Rufigi River, at the disposal of the *Medway*. But apparently such escort had to be paid for, and the owners of the tug wanted a fabulous sum to tow the *Medway* round to Bordeaux, so it was decided to do without an escort.

Captain Williams, like every other member of the British Mercantile Marine, was not to be stopped on " his " lawful occasions by any threat of mine or torpedo. He shipped a crew of runners, and sailed from Falmouth on July 2nd, 1916. The *Medway* fell in for a splendid slant from the N.W., and went flying through the danger zone, arriving at Bordeaux on July 5th.

On July 19th, still without escort or armament, the cadet ship left Bordeaux for Barry, with a cargo of pit props ; and again her luck held in extraordinary fashion, for this time she was actually becalmed for several days off the Lizard, during which time Captain Williams and his stout-hearted crew of runners enjoyed bathing over the side, notwithstanding the fact that they might expect a tin fish to send their ship sky-high at any moment. However, the *Medway* reached Barry all safe on July 31st. By this date the Admiralty had grown very much alive to the importance of cadet training, and they not only urged Messrs. Devitt & Moore to fill up their cadet quarters to the last bunk, but to keep their training-ships as much as possible out of the war zone. In such a case the *Medway* soon had her full complement of cadets on board.

Captain Williams loaded at Barry for St. Vincent and Santos, sailed on September 12th, 1916, and reached St. Vincent 22 days out. Sailing again on October 19th, he arrived at Santos on November 10th, 22 days from St. Vincent. This was the beginning of some remarkable sailing on the part of the *Medway ;* though she had never been reckoned a fast sailer, in the hands of Captain Williams her records were invariably much above the average, for he was one of those seamen who always managed to get the best out of a vessel.

"Medway"
Built 1902 Training Ship.

On her next passage she left Santos on December 9th, and arrived at Tocopilla on January 30th, 1917, having accomplished the difficult passage round the Horn from the Eastward in 52 days. At Tocopilla nitrate was loaded for Cape Town, on account of the Government.

Captain Williams sailed on February 19th, 1917, and arrived in Table Bay on April 3rd. This was a 43-day passage, which beat the previous record, held by a German sailing ship, by two days.

On May 1st, 1917, Captain Williams cleared for Tocopilla again, and running his easting down, he kept the *Medway* staggering along under a press of sail with the roaring westerlies behind her. It must have been an unpleasant passage for her crew and all her first-voyage apprentices, but the old ship made fine running and reached Tocopilla on July 2nd, 1917, 62 days out. Thus she had encircled the globe in 105 sailing days from Tocopilla, within the tropics, in Northern Chile, to the South'ard round the Horn, then Eastward Ho to the Cape, and on again round New Zealand and across the vast stretches of the South Pacific to her starting-point. This was truly a splendid sailing feat.

The *Medway's* next passage was to Durban : she set sail on July 21st, and reached port on September 20th, 61 days out. Once again it was a case of encircling the globe in the " roaring forties." This time Captain Williams cleared for Iquique, and made the run from Durban in 65 days, arriving on January 24th, 1918. The *Medway* had taken 126 days to encircle the globe, which was good enough.

Once again the ship was loaded for Cape Town. She sailed on February 14th, 1918, and arrived at the Cape on April 12th, a 57-day trip.

Though the *Medway* was never torpedoed, she fell a victim to the war as surely as if she had been torpedoed. It happened in this way. By 1918 the Ministry of Shipping was at its wits' end for oil carriers, and with unlimited cash at its demand began to buy sailing ships and convert them into Diesel-engined tramps. What this expensive method of obtaining tonnage cost the nation, I should not like to say ; however, several splendid sailing ships were changed as if by magic into the most hideous monstrosities in the way of cargo carriers that it would be possible to imagine, and amongst them was the poor old *Medway*. Messrs. Devitt & Moore fought their hardest to avoid losing their last ship— the *Port Jackson* had been torpedoed in April, 1917—and they had the support of the Admiralty, who were most anxious that the *Medway* should continue the useful work of training cadets. At first Devitt & Moore refused to sell ; then, after much pressure had been put upon them, they agreed to part with their vessel, provided the training of the cadets was continued. The Ministry of Shipping at first agreed to this proviso ; but when the sale was settled they backed down and refused to continue the training of cadets. On the *Medway's* arrival at Cape Town they took possession of the ship and landed the cadets. Of these boys who were thus turned adrift by a Government Department, which was evidently suffering from nerves, some had only been at sea a few months, whilst others were ready to sit for their second mate's examination.

The *Medway* was sent in ballast to Hong Kong, where her masts were cut down, Diesel engines were bedded in her hold, and she was converted into an oil carrier. By the time that the beautiful four-mast barque had been changed into an internal-engined nightmare of a ship, the emergency had passed, the Armistice had been signed, and there was no further need for her services.

Disguised as a twin screw motor schooner and under the flag of the Anglo-Saxon Petroleum Company the *Medway* still sails the seas as the *Myr Shell*.

THE "SALAMIS."

THOSE who knew the *Salamis* and her sailing capabilities, always declared that she was the fastest iron ship that was ever built, and I think her records in the Colonial trade show good cause for this statement. She was built by Hood, of Aberdeen, from the lines of the famous *Thermopylæ*, which were increased all round to produce the extra tonnage. The principal measurements of the *Salamis*, with a registered tonnage of 1,130 tons gross and 1,021 net, were :—Length, 212 feet 6 inches ; breadth, 36 feet ; depth, 21 feet 7 inches ; depth moulded, 23 feet 8 inches ; free-board, 4 feet 9½ inches ; rise of floor, 6 feet 6 inches. Forward, while tremendously sharp, she had a good spring ; aft her run tapered away to the same shaped symmetrical stern which was such a distinguishing characteristic of the *Thermopylæ*. As regards her rigging plan, her spars were said to be a foot longer all round than the *Thermopylæ's*. There is no sail or rigging plan of either ship in existence, but the masts and spars of the *Salamis* ; these were considered large enough in 1875 for a vessel of 1,500 tons. Following are the chief measurements :

Bowsprit and jib-boom	..	..	..	66	feet
Mainmast, deck to truck	..	..	..	150	,,
Main lower mast	..	..	..	..	66	,,
,, topmast	..	..	..	..	52	,,
,, topgallant mast	..	..	..	34	,,
,, royal mast	..	..	..	..	23	,,
,, masthead	..	..	..	..	2	,,
,, lower doublings	..	..	..	15	,,
,, topmast doublings	..	..	..	12	,,
,, yard	..	..	..	..	81	,,
,, lower topsail yard	..	..	..	72	,,
,, upper topsail yard	..	..	..	64	,,
,, lower topgallant yard	..	..	..	57	,,
,, upper topgallant yard	..	..	..	49	,,
,, royal yard	..	..	..	..	37	,,

This out-and-out clipper was intended for the same round as the *Thermopylæ*—outwards to Melbourne with general cargo, across the Pacific with coal to China, and home with the first teas of the season ; but when the *Salamis* arrived out in China on her second voyage in 1876 she found that all the first teas were being taken by the steamers, and that only one or two noted clippers, such as the *Cutty Sark* and *Thermopylæ*, were able to hold their own. Thus the *Salamis* never succeeded in loading a cargo of new teas for the English market and she made her name entirely as a Colonial wool clipper.

From 1875 to 1894 she had only two masters. These were Captains Phillips, Senior and Junior. Indeed, the little clipper was a regular home for the Phillips family ; at one time, when Captain Phillips, Senior, was commander, one son was chief mate and another third mate. Captain Phillips, Senior, gave up the command of the *Harlaw* to take *Salamis* from the stocks. In 1888, on his arrival in Port Phillip, he was asked to hand the *Salamis* over to his first mate, who happened to be his son, and to take command of the *Pericles*, Captain

Largie, of the latter ship, being obliged to give up owing to trouble with his eyes.   Captain Phillips, Junior, handed over the *Salamis* to Captain R. B. B. McKilliam in 1894.

With their white spars and green topsides the Aberdeen White Star clippers were all beautiful to look at, but the smallest iron ship of the lot, the little *Salamis*, was considered by many sailing-ship men to be the handsomest ship of the fleet.   Her outward passages to Melbourne have never been equalled by any other iron ship.   For 13 consecutive passages to Melbourne her average from pilot to pilot was 75 days, and as regards her wool passages, though the homeward run was never so suited to an iron ship as it was to a wooden one, 100 days being considered quite a good passage for anything built of metal, the *Salamis* managed to make an average of 87 days for 18 consecutive wool passages from Melbourne to London.   Between points her performances were very regular ;   her best time from London to the Line was 18½ days ;   she twice covered the distance from the Line to the Cape Meridian in 21 days ;   and no less than six times did she make the Otway from the Cape Meridian in 23 days or under.

On her maiden passage she made the run out in 68 days from Start Point.   She had very baffling winds to the Equator, which was crossed on August 2nd, 23 days out from the Start ; the S.E. Trades, too, were very shy, and she had to make a tack off the Abrolhos Rocks. The Westerlies also were very unsteady and changeable and she had no chance to make a big 24 hours' run, her best being 304 knots.   She loaded home as first ship of the Melbourne wool fleet, sailing on October 23rd, 1875, and reached London on January 25th, 1876, 94 days out.

Her second voyage started badly.   Whilst sheltering in the Downs from a severe gale of wind, the *Salamis* lost a man overboard, and three anchors and chains.   The third anchor had to be slipped and the vessel got hurriedly under weigh, or she would have gone ashore. After a hard time in the Channel she was compelled to put into Plymouth in order to replace the missing anchors and cables.   She finally left Plymouth on March 24th, and took her departure from the Lizard the next day.   The Line was crossed on April 18th, and the Cape Meridian on May 14th, in 43° S.   Whilst the ship was scudding with only a fore-topsail set, in 69° E., a heavy sea was shipped over the quarter, which broke up the wheel and smashed in the cabin skylight, and the *Salamis* had to be hove to for 14 hours whilst repairs were made.   She finally reached Melbourne on June 8th, 76 days from Plymouth.   After discharging, Captain Phillips went up to Sydney, loaded coal for Shanghai, and made the run across, Sydney to Shanghai, in the splendid time of 32 days.   Yet, in spite of her proved sailing powers, the *Salamis* failed to get a charter to load new teas, so she was compelled to run down to Hong Kong for a mixed Chinese cargo.   In the N.E. monsoon she made the passage through the Formosa Channel in 2 days and some odd hours, and her passage home from Hong Kong was made in 110 days.

On her third voyage, in 1877–8, *Salamis* went out to Melbourne in 76 days, and came home in 87 days.   On her outward passage in 1878 she was held up by violent S.E. gales, in 31° S., which compelled her to heave to ;   in fact, she had a very rough passage all the way to Sydney, and did not reach Port Jackson until she had been out 87 days.   This year Captain Phillips made a most determined effort to load a tea cargo, but it happened to be a year of depressed freights everywhere.   Twice the *Salamis* crossed from Sydney to Shanghai, but each time she had to return to Melbourne.   Her two runs from Australia to Shanghai were made in the good times of 43 and 37 days, but she was not so lucky on her return passages, which were more difficult.

On the first occasion *Salamis* left Shanghai on November 26th, 1878, in company with *Thermopylæ*.   After a ding-dong race down the China Sea, the two clippers arrived together

"Salamis"
Built 1875 Wool Clipper.

at the northern entrance to the Straits of Sunda on December 15th, only 19 days out. Here they found a fleet of 37 sail, either anchored under the coast of Sumatra or standing off and on, waiting for the strong N.E. current to ease up and allow them to get to the south-west of Thwart-the-Way Island. For the next 12 days ship after ship had a shot at the Straits, but was compelled, after two or three tacks, to run back to the anchorage under Sumatra. At last, on December 19th, *Thermopylæ* worked as far as Anjer, and eventually got through. *Salamis* was the second to clear the Straits, and taking her departure from Java Head on December 29th, she soon made up for lost time in the S.E. Trades, her best run being 336 miles ; she anchored off Queen's Cliff on February 17th, 1879, 61 days out.

On her second trip back from China she reached Melbourne on July 6th, 64 days out. After this, Captain Phillips was glad to load wool for London. On the wool passage *Salamis* once more had a tussle with *Thermopylæ*, but was once more beaten. *Thermopylæ* left Sydney on November 18th, whilst *Salamis* left Melbourne November 19th ; the former arrived in the Thames on February 7th, 81 days out, but *Salamis* did not reach London until March 8th, 109 days out. It is probable, however, that the *Salamis's* iron bottom was not as clean as *Thermopylæ's* copper one.

In the following list I give the times of *Salamis's* passages from 1880 until 1888, when Captain Phillips, Senior, handed over to his son :

		Out. Days.			Home. Days.		
1880–1	..	76	to Melbourne		88	from Melbourne	
1881–2	..	72	,,	,,	101	,,	,,
1882–3	..	71	,,	,,	92	,,	,,
1883–4	..	76	,,	Sydney	100	,,	,,
1884–5	..	82	,,	Melbourne	84	,,	,,
1885–6	..	74	,,	,,	77	,,	,,
1886–7	..	79	,,	,,	85	,,	,,
1887–8	..	85	,,	,,	75	,,	,,
1888–9	..	70	,,	,,	85	,,	,,

In 1882 the *Salamis* crossed the Cape Meridian, in 42° S., on the same day that the S.S. *Aberdeen* rounded the Cape. In the run from the Cape to Melbourne, the *Aberdeen* only beat the little clipper by 3 days. On her passage to Sydney in 1883 the *Salamis* was off the Otway 71 days out. It will be noticed how very steady her outward passages were, and that Captain Phillips's last two passages, homeward in 1887–8 and outward in 1888, were amongst his best. His son did not succeed in equalling his father's record on the outward run, but his homeward passages 1888-1894 were very good, his average being just under 86 days for the six.

On her outward passage in 1890, the *Salamis* had a queer time of it as regards weather. On June 17th, in 7° 32′ W., 38° 8′ S., she had the wind in furious gusts from every point of the compass in turn, whilst rain fell in torrents ; finally, at midnight, she was heeled by a squall of hurricane force from the N.N.E., which lasted, without any slackening, for 24 hours. Four days later, at 4.30 p.m., when scudding before the westerlies in a high cross sea, the *Salamis* was pooped by a heavy dollop, which washed the man at the wheel into the mizen rigging, where he managed to hold on, though badly injured ; broke the cabin skylight and flooded the cabin ; carried away the binnacle and took the compass with it, as it surged over on to the main-deck and so overboard.

Nine days later the *Salamis* was again in danger from the weather. This time she found herself in the path of seven water-spouts, which were working along the surface of the water, from east to west, at a tremendous speed. One of these passed close ahead of the ship, catching her aback with a fierce burst of wind and throwing the water over her in monster fountains. Whilst the ship was hove down by this furious mixture of wind and water, she was battered by torrential rain and hail as big as pigeons' eggs, falling at the same time. The gallant little *Salamis* came through this battle of the elements unscathed, but her passage was spoilt. It so happened that she was engaged in an interesting race with the *Cimba* and *Aristides*, whilst the *Cutty Sark*, starting over a week later, was coming up astern of the three iron clippers. Perhaps the times of this race will be of interest—I therefore give them in the form of a table :

Details.			*Cimba.*		*Salamis.*		*Aristides.*	
Left London	..	..	..	May	3	May	5	May	5
Off the Lizard	..	..	..	,,	8	,,	9	,,	9
Crossed the Equator	..	..	June	2	June	1	June	1
Crossed Cape Meridian	..	July	1	,,	29	,,	29
Crossed Leewuin Meridian	..	,,	21	July	20	July	18
Off Cape Otway	..	..	,,	30	,,	31	,,	24

The *Salamis* anchored in Hobson's Bay on August 1st, whilst the other two ships went on up the coast to Sydney, with the famous *Cutty Sark* on their heels. *Cutty Sark* sailed from London on May 14th ; crossed the Cape Meridian July 6th ; crossed the Leeuwin Meridian only one day behind *Salamis* and was up with her off the Otway. She caught and passed the *Cimba* off Wilson's Promontory on August 1st, and anchored in Port Jackson 80 days out at midnight on August 2nd, only four hours behind the *Aristides*.

Under Captain McKilliam *Salamis* continued to maintain her reputation, her passages, whether outward or homeward, being frequently the best of the season. Her wool cargo, by the way, was generally in the neighbourhood of 5,500 bales. She was not fitted for passengers, like the rest of the Aberdeen White Star iron vessels, being purely a racing ship.

The end of her long career in the Melbourne trade came in 1899, when she was sold to L. Gunderson, of Porsgrund, Norway. Though the Norwegians did not change her name, they removed the yards from her mizen-mast, and made no attempt to keep her in the aristocratic wool trade. Thus the poor little clipper found herself loading such second-class cargoes as guano, and it was in this trade that she was wrecked on Malden Island, in the South Pacific, on May 20th, 1905.

THE " SOPHOCLES."

THE *Sophocles* was launched in 1879, from Hood's yard, for George Thompson's famous Aberdeen White Star Line. With the exception of the beautiful little *Salamis*, the *Sophocles* was the smallest iron ship ever built for George Thompson, and she was practically a sister ship of the *Cimba*, which had been built in the same yard the year before for Alexander Nicol.

The registered tonnage and measurements of the two ships were as follows :

		Tons.	Length.	Breadth.	Depth.
			ft. in.	ft. in.	ft. in.
Cimba	..	1,174	223 0	34 6	21 7
Sophocles	..	1,138	223 4	34 7	21 7

They were also rigged alike, with double topgallant yards at fore and main, but single mizen topgallant sails. Yet, though the two ships were so much alike that it required a keen sailor's eye to distinguish the one from the other, their performances were very different. Both were regular Sydney traders and loaded the wool clip for London, but whereas *Cimba* was considered to be amongst the first flight, and rarely made a poor passage, it is hard to find a passage of the *Sophocles* that was not longer than it should have been. An instance or two will suffice :

In 1889–90 *Cimba* and *Sophocles* loaded wool in October for the January wool sales. The former sailed from Sydney on October 22nd, but the *Sophocles* was not ready to sail until the 26th. The *Salamis* left Melbourne on the day that *Cimba* left Port Jackson, whilst a small iron barque of 900 tons, named *Serica*, after the well-known tea clipper, sailed in company with *Sophocles*.

Other famous ships in that year's wool fleet were the following :

Derwent	..	left Sydney	..	October	14
Loch Vennachar	..	,, Melbourne	..	,,	17
Woollahra	..	,, Sydney	..	,,	22
Blackadder	..	,, Brisbane	..	,,	31
Rodney	..	,, Sydney	..	,,	31
Cutty Sark	..	,, Sydney	..	November	3

All these ships caught the wool sales except the unfortunate *Sophocles*. *Cimba* shared the honours with the *Cutty Sark*, both ships making the run in 75 days. Of the others, *Rodney* took 78 days, *Derwent* 80, *Blackadder* 83, *Serica* 84, *Salamis* and *Woollahra* 85, and *Loch Vennachar* 86 days.

The *Sophocles* did not reach London until March 14th, when she was no less than 139 days out. Yet it was a favourable year as regards winds, and even heavy box-shaped carriers were making the run home from the Colonies in under the hundred days.   One could account for a bad passage now and again, but the *Sophocles* seemed to be invariably whipper-in to the wool fleet.   Possibly she was unlucky in her captains ; it is hard to account for it otherwise, for Hood could not build a sluggard, and a ship cannot always be out of trim or badly stowed.

In 1888–9 the *Sophocles* had also been the last of the wool fleet to arrive.   This time she left Sydney on December 22nd, her nearest rival being the famous *Loch Garry*, which left Melbourne on December 21st.   The *Loch Garry* made a good average passage, reaching London on March 20th, 89 days out ; the *Sophocles* was actually 26 days behind her, and did not show up in the Thames until April 15th, when she was 114 days out.   Though she failed to uphold the Aberdeen standard as regards speed, the little *Sophocles* was a fine sea boat, an economical carrier, and a vessel that kept free of trouble.

Of the nine iron clippers built by Hood for George Thompson, only two ships, the *Salamis* and *Sophocles*, were not fitted for the passenger and emigrant trade.

Sophocles, which should have been a crack wool clipper in the Sydney trade, would never have filled her hold with bales of the season's clip if it had not been for her green sides and the White Star house-flag at her main truck, and when the sailing ships of the Aberdeen White Star Line were sold in the middle 'nineties she found her place amongst the general traders, and for thirty years sailed to and fro across the seven seas, barque-rigged, with the Italian flag flying from her spanker gaff, when she was broken up about 1925.

"Sophocles"
Built 1879 Wool Clipper.

THE "BENVENUE."

WATSON'S two *Benvenues* will be remembered for their tragic endings, the first becoming a total loss at Timaru, after being driven up on the beach from the inner anchorage during a fierce gale in 1882, and the second stranding with the loss of her master and an apprentice at Sandgate, near Folkestone, whilst towing down Channel on a passage to Sydney in 1891. The remainder of the crew were lashed in the mizen top for over fifteen hours and were eventually rescued by the Sandgate life-boat.

The first *Benvenue*, the subject of this article, was one of the smartest of the early iron clippers. She was launched by Barclay, Curle & Co., in May, 1867, and registered 999 tons, her dimensions being :—Length, 210 feet ; breadth, 35 feet 1 inch ; depth of hold, 20 feet 7 inches. She was an extremely handsome ship, crossing a main skysail. Her raised quarter-deck, which was 34 feet long, and her fo'c'sle-head were on a level with the main rail, thus showing the line of her sheer in its entirety.

During her early years the *Benvenue*, in company with Watson's other clippers, was employed almost entirely in the Melbourne trade, in which she had to compete with all the most famous clippers of the day. She was transferred to the New Zealand trade in 1876. Like all the early ships running out to New Zealand, she took her share of the passenger and emigrant traffic, and in the late 'seventies carried many a well-known New Zealander, both in her cabin and her 'tween decks.

Her best known commander was Captain William McGowan, who was nicknamed Mad McGowan by his crews on account of the daring way in which he carried sail. McGowan was one of those captains about whom many yarns were told. Like most sailormen of the old school, he was a man of very strong personality—one who had his likes and dislikes, and was not afraid to air his own opinions on any subject under the sun. Although his sardonic humour made him a most disconcerting and unpleasant antagonist in debate, yet all his ideas, especially those to do with his own profession, were right up-to-date. In looking after his men he was a long way ahead of most officers of his time, and his interest in their welfare made him very popular with foremast hands. After the wreck of the *Benvenue* he superintended the building of the *Gogoburn* by Birrell, in which ship he was able to carry out all his ideas with regard to improving the berthing and feeding of his men. Although the *Gogoburn* was only a little 1,000-ton barque, about the same size as the *Benvenue*, her deck-house was cut up into two and four-berth cabins for the accommodation of the bos'n, sailmaker, four quartermasters, ten A.B.'s and two O.S.'s. The cook of the *Gogoburn* had to provide three hot meals a day for all hands, and it was the duty of the officer of the watch to inspect each kid and make a report to the captain if there was any complaint. It is not surprising, therefore, to find foremast hands sailing with Captain McGowan for voyage after voyage. Yet, if he saw to it that his men were berthed and fed well, he also made them work. In the *Benvenue* he used to carry on until the last possible moment. He knew the breaking strain of each rope in his ship, and when he gave the order for sail to be reduced it was not until it was necessary; but it was at such a moment, when the order had been given to shorten sail, that he expected his well-fed hands to prove their worth and show their smartness in the matter of seamanship and sail-handling.

McGowan was a canny man, and on one voyage he tried a chequer-board crew, thus causing keen rivalry between the two watches in all matters to do with the working of the ship. This is how he got hold of his chequer-board crew:

Whilst the *Benvenue* was taking in cargo at Glasgow, McGowan put up a notice in the rigging with the challenging statement, " No Irish need apply." There was no Irishman living in those days—I speak of the 'seventies—who would put up with an affront of that sort, and the gauntlet thrown down by the captain was speedily picked up. The very next day the signboard became the target for all dead cats, rotten fruit and addled eggs in the neighbourhood, and when McGowan was ready to sail quite half his crew consisted of great husky Irishmen, fine sailors, who were determined to show the scornful master mariner the true worth of Irish sailormen. To a man they were big, powerful athletes, such men as are not seen in fo'c'sles nowadays, but Captain McGowan had also shipped a watch of big buck niggers, men from the Southern States of America, who had been trained and hardened under the bucko officers of Yankee Cape Horners. These were put in the port watch, whilst the Irish went into the starboard watch. Throughout the voyage it is said that the rivalry between the two watches was tremendous and even came to blows and, indeed, pitched battles, in which the Irish seamen, who had meant to teach Captain McGowan a lesson, and reform his opinion of their countrymen, invariably had the worst of it, in spite of the fact that they were all considered to be picked fighters.

Captain McGowan, who, previous to commanding the *Benvenue*, was the chief officer of the *Jessie Readman*, was one of the most experienced masters in the New Zealand trade. Nevertheless, although he knew the coast so well, he had more than one narrow escape from shipwreck. One of the ship's closest calls was on the passage out in 1880, when she was bound to Wellington. Tremendous weather was experienced whilst running the easting down, and with Captain McGowan carrying sail until the last possible moment, the *Benvenue* overran her distance. Thus it happened that during a hard westerly gale, and on a pitch-dark night, it was suddenly discovered that she was running full tilt on to the Snares. All hands were called, and Captain McGowan decided to wear the ship round in order to bring the wind on the other side. The *Benvenue* was running under a main topgallant sail. When the helm was put up the main topgallant sail and mizen lower topsail were blown away, along with the mainsail, which was torn out of the buntlines. There was a huge sea running, and as the wind came astern the vessel was pooped and the wheel damaged. As the *Benvenue* came to the wind the Snares showed on her lee bow, and it was evident to everyone aboard that it was touch and go whether she would clear the rocks. Captain McGowan was as calm as if there were no rocks in sight. Standing aft, he conned his ship in a quiet, steady voice. At last, when it seemed that she could only weather the Snares by a miracle, he took a pull at his pipe and called out to his crew, who were clustering along the rail of the poop with their eyes glued on the grey patches of surf which showed up through the darkness to leeward: " If she touches, boys, every man for himself." It is a curious fact, but on such an occasion a sailing ship will often accomplish prodigies of sailing which would be quite beyond her powers under less nerve-racking conditions. There are many instances of this, and old sailors firmly believed that the spirit of the ship fought her hardest to save her crew from drowning. Instances are recorded of ships coming about in half the time that they usually needed in order to scrape clear of rocks or icebergs, and in this case the little ship screwed out to windward in a way which amazed even her captain; and so she

"*Benvenue*"

Built 1867 Passenger and Emigrant Ship.

went clear; and a few days later, on June 8th to be exact, she arrived at Wellington, 94 days out.

In 1879 the *Benvenue* was the victim of one of the most curious ways of being dismasted that I have ever heard of. She had just made soundings in the English Channel after a splendid passage of 72 days from Lyttelton. The wind was easterly, and as she was heaving round in stays the main and crossjack yards interlocked, and the ship was dismasted. However, she was close to the land and right in the lane of the traffic up and down Channel, so she was soon picked up and towed into port.

Her best outward passage was made in 1881. The *Benvenue* sailed from Gravesend on February 11th, experienced heavy head gales in the Channel, and was not able to take her departure from the Lizard until February 18th. Strong north-west winds were picked up in the Bay of Biscay, and the Equator was crossed on March 7th, only 17 days from the Lizard. The Cape Meridian was crossed on March 31st, and Tasmania was passed on April 19th. On this occasion the Snares were sighted in light weather on April 26th, when the ship was only 67 days out. She was then becalmed for 24 hours on the coast, and did not reach Port Chalmers until the 29th, thus making a passage of 77 days from port to port, or 70 days from the Lizard.

On her last voyage the *Benvenue* went out to Newcastle, N.S.W. At Newcastle a cargo of coals was loaded, and the *Benvenue* sailed for Timaru, where she arrived on May 5th, 1882. A week later, whilst the *Benvenue* was discharging her coal cargo into lighters at the inner anchorage, it began to blow, and May 13th found the " Ben " clipper plunging bows under with both anchors down. Close to her lay another famous iron clipper, the *City of Perth*, of Smith's " City " Line, which was loaded and waiting for the storm to blow over before proceeding to sea. During the day the worst of the wind began to take off, but the seas which were rolling in grew steeper and steeper. These seas, as they hurtled shoreward in long ridges, put a severe strain on the cables of the two ships. About midnight, with the turn of the tide, which swung the vessels stern-on to the breakers, the sea became still heavier, and several breaking rollers swept over the poop of the *Benvenue*, bursting in the stern windows and doing other damage. The captain then ordered a stand-by call for all hands. No sooner were the men aft than an extra heavy comber struck the *Benvenue* under her counter and broke her rudder, at the same time taking one of the boats off the skids. The seas were now described as being " something fearful." The weight of the breakers, aided by the run of the tide, next caused the ship to fall off into the trough of the sea, where she rolled so badly that the shifting boards in the hold were insufficient to keep the coals in their place, with the result that the 500 tons of coal on board were thrown over to starboard, listing the ship down on her beam ends. At 9 a.m., whilst the crew were vainly attempting to trim the coal over to port, the starboard cable parted at the 135-fathom mark. With great difficulty a third anchor was got ready, on to which a steel hawser was bent. This had hardly been let go when the second cable parted. The ship was now practically adrift, and as she was settling further and further over, in spite of the efforts of the coal trimmers, Captain McGowan decided to get the boats over the side, ready to abandon ship. This ticklish job was managed successfully, and just before the *Benvenue* drifted into the broken water of the surf the boats left her side and managed to pull out to the *City of Perth*. At the same time the abandoned ship slewed round and headed directly for the shore, her last anchor having evidently parted. She headed through the outer breakers as steadily as if she had had a crack helmsman at her wheel, but immediately she struck the shore of Caroline Bay she was hurled broadside on by the terrific surf, and was soon a helpless wreck.

Meanwhile the two captains aboard the *City of Perth* were deliberating as to what should be done, for the " City " Line clipper, which had let go her third anchor about the same time as the *Benvenue*, had parted her two cables and was now entirely trusting to that third anchor. It was soon evident to everyone that the wire hawser to which the *City of Perth* was hanging would not last long under the tremendous strain which it had to take as each huge comber swept under her. It was now daylight, the sun was shining, and the wind had gone down, but the sea was worse than ever. It was so bad, indeed, that it was doubtful if any boat could live in it. Nevertheless, the two captains gave orders for their boats to be manned and the ship to be abandoned before it was too late.

And now begins a story of great heroism. Amongst those who were watching from the shore was a Timaru waterman named Philip Bradley. He got a volunteer crew together and put off to the rescue of the boats, which, as soon as they pulled clear of the *City of Perth*, seemed as if they must be swamped every minute. However, they survived and, guided by Bradley, were brought safely inside the breakwater. Shortly after this the sea began to show signs of going down, whereupon the harbour-master, Captain Mills, put off in a whale-boat for the *City of Perth*. He was followed by Captain McGowan, in the *Benvenue's* gig, and a third boat. All three boats managed to reach the vessel in safety, but the men were no sooner aboard the *City of Perth* than her wire hawser snapped, and swinging round she drifted stern on into the breakers. The boats were at once re-manned and hastily set off for the shore. The harbour-master's whale-boat and the other shore boat succeeded in making the breakwater, but Captain McGowan, in his gig, failed to stem the current and was swept into the surf, where he was soon hidden by the white crests of the rollers. Then a wail went up from those watching ashore as the gig was sighted upside down, whilst here and there the heads of her crew showed up against the frothing spume as they struggled in the breakers.

Without a moment's hesitation the two shore boats put out again, with the harbour-master's whale-boat leading. Captain Mills reached the drowning men, but before he had time to pull any of them into the boat, was himself capsized. Undaunted by the overturning of the whale-boat the gallant men in the other shore boat pulled steadily on, but she had no sooner entered the surf than she was capsized in her turn, and those ashore now had the terrible spectacle of between thirty and forty men drowning before their eyes. By this time it was quite calm, with hardly an air blowing, the sun was shining brightly, but the surf was, if anything, worse than ever. Nevertheless, a rush was made for the life-boat. She was launched safely, but was not half-way to the drowning men before she, too, was capsized. Her crew managed to right her and regain their places, but the next breaker turned her over again. Again she was righted, and for the third time was capsized.

Meanwhile a large surf-boat had been launched. This also proved quite helpless in the tremendous surf, and although her crew managed to avoid being turned over, they could not stem the seas, and were obliged to drop an anchor. The scene now baffled description. In the surf over forty men were battling for their lives, whilst four boats, including the life-boat, were tossing about keel up, and the only other boat available rode in imminent peril of sharing their fate. Ashore, the wives, mothers and sisters of the drowning men wildly implored the crowd to go to their assistance, but there was not another boat left in the place, so there was nothing to be done, although every single sailor on the beach was ready to volunteer had there been any way of reaching the men in the water. By this time it was nearly dark; a lull in the weight of the seas allowed the life-boat's crew to right their vessel again, and she succeeded in picking up a few of the drowning men, including Captain Mills, the harbour-master. With these on board she made for the shore, which was reached in safety amidst wild cheers. Some of her crew, however, were missing, and Captain Mills, who had been badly injured in the surf, died before he could be carried to his home.

It was now necessary to rescue the men in the surf-boat, and a new crew of volunteers was soon found to man the life-boat. This was once more successfully launched off the beach, and succeeded in reaching the surf-boat, but before all the latter's crew could scramble aboard the life-boat was swept away by a large comber and capsized. She could just be distinguished tossing keel up in the white water as night settled down, and a groan went up from the shore, which was quickly turned to a cheer when it was noticed that her crew had once more managed to right her. By this time the surf was certainly less, but it was pitch-dark. The life-boat made a safe landing and at once pushed off again to rescue the remainder of the surf-boat's crew. This she was successful in doing, and so ended the most tragic day in the history of the port of Timaru.

The *City of Perth* was afterwards salved, and sailed for many a long day under the name of *Turakina* and the flag of the New Zealand Shipping Co., but her partner in the tragedy, the poor little *Benvenue*, was too badly damaged to be worth the expense of floating, and the wreck, after everything movable had been taken off, was sold for the paltry sum of £150.

THE "CROMDALE."

THE *Cromdale*, sister ship of the *Mount Stewart*, was launched from Barclay, Curle & Co.'s yard on the Clyde in June, 1891. She registered exactly the same as the *Mount Stewart*—viz., tonnage, 1,903; length, 271 feet 6 inches; breadth, 40 feet 1 inch; and depth, 23 feet 4 inches.

Messrs. Donaldson, Rose & Co., her owners, put her into the Sydney trade under Captain E. H. Andrews, who had lately been mate, under his father, in the *Derwent*. *Cromdale* very nearly came to her end on her first homeward passage, owing to being embayed in a vast island of ice.

At long intervals the Antarctic regions experience an unusually hot summer, which, when combined with a succession of violent gales and rough seas, has a very destructive effect upon the great ice barrier bordering the continent of the South Pole. Great masses of this barrier break off and commence a drift of thousands of miles. The course of this drift is north-easterly, owing to the direction of the Antarctic current. But in the close neighbourhood of the Horn it is rare to find ice of any size. This is because the proximity of the land compels the current to set due east off the pitch of the Horn, and the ice is not able to make any northing until almost abreast of the Falkland Islands, from the longitude of which it soon drifts northward into the warm waters of the Atlantic, where it finally dissolves.

During the last hundred years or so there have been three great breakages of the barrier ice. This ice, in vast quantities, drifted into the South Atlantic in the years 1854–5, 1892–3 and 1908, where it proved a grave menace to all ships bound round the Horn. Between December, 1854, and April, 1855, a crescent-shaped ice island, which stretched no fewer than 60 miles in one direction and 40 miles in another, was reported by 21 ships during its drift between lat. 44° S., long. 28° W., and lat. 40° S., long. 20° W.

In December, 1854, the famous Australian auxiliary clipper, *Great Britain*, steamed for 50 miles along its outer edge. Another well-known Australian liner, the *Guiding Star*, was back-strapped under the huge ice cliffs and lost with all hands. Several other ships found themselves embayed and only extricated themselves by means of supreme seamanship. Never had such a mass of ice been met with in the experience of the oldest South-Spainer. But it was far surpassed by the 1892–3 ice. The 1854–5 ice was about 300 feet in height, but the stupendous sides of the 1892–3 bergs and islands were reported by numerous ships as rising to 1,000 and even 1,500 feet sheer out of the sea.

Let us now quote Captain Andrews's account of his narrow escape from the fate of the *Guiding Star* :

" We left Sydney on 1st March (1892), and having run our easting down on the parallel of 49° to 50° S., rounded the Horn on 30th March, without having seen ice, the average temperature of the water being 43° during the whole run across.

" At midnight on 1st April, in 56° S., 58° 32′ W., the temperature fell to 37½°, this being the lowest for the voyage, but no ice was seen, though there was a suspicious glare to the southward.

" At 4 a.m. on 6th April, in 46° S., 36° W., a large berg was reported right ahead, just giving us time to clear it.   At 4.30, with the first signs of daybreak, several could be distinctly seen to windward, the wind being N.W., and the ship steering N.E. about 9 knots.   At daylight, 5.20 a.m., the whole horizon to windward was a complete mass of bergs of enormous size, with an unbroken wall at the back ; there were also many to leeward.

" I now called all hands, and after reducing speed to 7 knots, sent the hands to their stations and stood on.   At 7 a.m. there was a wall extending from a point on the lee bow to about 4 points on the lee quarter, and at 7.30 both walls joined ahead.   I sent the chief mate aloft with a pair of glasses to find a passage out, but he reported from the topgallant yard that the ice was unbroken ahead.   Finding myself embayed and closely beset with innumerable bergs of all shapes, I decided to tack and try and get out the way I had come into the bay.

" The cliffs were now truly grand, rising up 300 feet on either side of us, and as square and true at the edge as if just out of a joiner's shop, with the sea breaking right over the southern cliff and whirling away in a cloud of spray.

" Tacked ship at 7.30, finding the utmost difficulty in keeping clear of the huge pieces strewn so thickly in the water and having on several occasions to scrape her along one to keep clear of the next.

" We stood on in this way until 11 a.m., when, to my horror, the wind started to veer with every squall till I drew quite close to the southern barrier, having the extreme point a little on my lee bow.

" I felt sure we must go ashore without a chance of saving ourselves.   Just about 11.30 the wind shifted to S.W., with a strong squall, so we squared away to the N.W., and came past the same bergs as we had seen at daybreak, the largest being about 1,000 feet high, anvil-shaped.   At 2 p.m. we got on the N.W. side of the northern arm of the horseshoe-shaped mass.   It then reached from 4 points on my lee bow to as far as could be seen astern in one unbroken line.

" A fact worthy of notice was that at least 50 of the bergs in the bay were perfectly black, which was to be accounted for by the temperature of the water being 51°, which had turned many over.   I also think that had there been even the smallest outlet at the eastern side of this mass, the water between the barriers would not have been so thickly strewn with bergs, as the prevailing westerly gales would have driven them through and separated them.

" I have frequently seen ice down south, but never anything like even the smaller bergs in this group."

This was the most exciting experience in *Cromdale's* career.   Her best passage was made in 1894, when she arrived off Prawle Point on April 10th, 80 days from Sydney.   In 1897 she was unable to get a homeward charter from Sydney, so she crossed the Pacific to San Francisco, making the run in 64 days, a fair average passage.   In 1898 we find Captain Sibley taking over the command, which he retained until just before her end.

A sailor, writing to " The Blue Peter," recalls " those pleasant days which I spent on board of her before the mast for more than three years, under the command of that gentleman, Captain Rice Sibley, and his two officers, Messrs. F. Catlow and Giles, both with most

"Cromdale"

Built 1891 Wool Clipper.

splendid seaman's qualities. She was one of those ships which could be called a home. Not because her crew was being coddled or caressed, none of that, but once a hand stepped on board of this fine clipper, he seemed to take all interest in her, especially in her smartness about her deck. A proudness used to exist amongst her crew, as she was being recognised as flagship at very near every port she would call on account of her tall mainmast with skysail yard, and the smart way her sails were furled and yards trimmed."

Her last voyage was made under Captain Arthur, of Dundee. From the start it was unlucky. The second mate was drowned whilst bathing at Monte Video ; the bos'n fell down the hold at Newcastle, N.S.W., and was killed ; whilst a seaman was killed by falling down the hold at Taltal, to which port she had crossed from Newcastle, N.S.W., in 44 days.

The *Cromdale* left Taltal for the United Kingdom on January 19th, 1913, and after a very long passage of 120 days reached soundings in a dense fog. The correct course for Falmouth was set from the dead reckoning, but unfortunately, during a temporary thinning of the fog, a blue-funnel steamer was encountered, which informed Captain Arthur that he was out of his course and needed to haul up two points to the northward. This advice was disastrous. Captain Arthur, relying on the steamer's knowledge of her position, altered his course, though he took the precaution of shortening sail.

It was very thick again on the night of Friday, May 23rd, but with a light wind and smooth sea the ship was jogging quietly along when a light was suddenly sighted through the haze ahead. It was so high above the ship that Captain Arthur knew at once that he was close inshore and suspected, as afterwards proved to be the case, that he was under the Lizard. He immediately ordered all hands to their stations for going about, but before the helm could be put down, and in less than five minutes from the first sighting of the light, which was at 10 p.m., the *Cromdale* struck right at the foot of the cliff.

From the way in which the water poured into her it was at once realized that she was badly holed, and the order was given to clear away the boats. These were safely launched, and Captain Arthur, his wife, and the crew of 23 hands pulled safely away from the ship's side, then rested on their oars, in the expectation that she would settle down at any moment.

Meanwhile those on duty at Lloyd's signal station noticed something looming in the fog below them and also heard the grating noise of the vessel grinding on the rocks, which they at first took to be the rattle of an anchor chain running out. Climbing down the rocks to a point where they could make out the ship with more distinctness, they shouted into the fog : " Are you in distress ? "

Immediately a faint cry of " Yes " came back, upon which Mr. John Perry, who was in charge of the signal station, fired the two-rocket signal for the Lizard and Cadjwith life-boats. These were speedily on the scene and took the shipwrecked men aboard. But, as the sea was smooth and the *Cromdale* still above water, the captain and a few volunteers from her crew asked to be put aboard the wreck again in order to salve what they could of their personal effects.

In this hazardous task an A.B., named Nightingale, specially distinguished himself. After salving all the fo'c'sle kits, he managed to break into the cabin and rescue the ship's papers, though in doing so he was constantly up to his neck in water. And scarcely had he succeeded in this before the ship suddenly settled down without any warning, until her deck was awash. For a moment those on board looked to be in grave danger, and they were compelled to take to the rigging until the life-boats could manœuvre within range. In the end the men, together with their bags and chests, were safely got aboard the Lizard life-boat, the only personal loss being a cash box containing £60, the savings of a Swedish A.B., which was dropped into the water between the ship and the life-boat. In such an exposed position there was very little hope of salving the *Cromdale*, and though the weather remained quiet, the Atlantic swell soon broke her up.

It may be of interest to collectors to know that several magnificent photographs were taken, by local professionals, of the ship as she lay half submerged at the foot of the cliff. These show her with her main lower topgallant sail, lower topsails, foresail and two headsails still set, whilst the upper topsails and topgallant sails and main course are roughly clewed and hauled up, which fact is very clear evidence as to the unexpected suddenness of the vessel's stranding.

THE " WAIMATE."

THE New Zealand Shipping Company, which has had so much to do with the populating and the prosperity of Maoriland, was really an amalgamation of two shipping concerns, both of which were financed by the Bank of New Zealand. These were the New Zealand Freight Company of Auckland, which was incorporated and registered on July 1st, 1872, and the New Zealand Shipping Company of Christchurch, which came into existence on January 6th, 1873. This company of enterprising colonists acted with energy from the very start. Until suitable ships could be built, four small vessels were bought and a number hired. Those bought were the Glasgow-built *Hindostan*, 833 tons, and *Dunfillan*, 853 tons, the *Scimitar*, of Hull, 1,188 tons, and the *Dorette*, of Hamburg, 848 tons. These were all given Maori names, and became, respectively, *Waitara*, *Mataura*, *Rangitiki* and *Waimea*.

The first two vessels to be specially built for the new company were the sister ships *Rakaia* and *Waikato*, launched from Blumer's Yard at Sunderland in the winter of 1873–4. Then in the summer of 1874 another pair of sister ships came from Blumer's slips. These were the *Waitangi* and *Waimate*, the first launched in June and the second in August. These two very handsome passenger-carrying iron clippers were not only the largest but the fastest of the sailing ships that were built for the N.Z.S. Co. Both had long, successful careers, with but few mishaps and no very serious accidents.

Waitangi made 25 voyages to the Colony before being sold to the Norwegians at the end of the 19th century ; the *Waimate's* record being 22 voyages before the Russians bought her in 1896.

The *Waimate* was considered the clipper of the New Zealand Shipping Company's fleet until the beautiful *City of Perth* came on the scene. Though it cannot be claimed that the *Waimate* was ever the equal of the *Turakina*, as the *City of Perth* was renamed, on any point of sailing, yet the former made the better outward passages of the two. The *Waimate's* passage from London to Lyttelton in 1880–1 was considered a record for many years ; her nearest rivals being *Scimitar* (later *Rangitiki*) and *Westland*. The following are the best times of the three ships :

Scimitar left Plymouth December 24, 1873, arrived Port Chalmers March 5, 1874	71 days.
From land to land	67 „
Waimate left London October 24, 1880, arrived Lyttelton, January 6, 1881	74 „
Took departure from Eddystone, October 30, to Lyttelton	68 „
From land to land	66 „
Westland left London April 13, 1888, arrived Dunedin June 25 ..	73 „
Took departure from Ushant, April 18, to Dunedin	68 „
From land to land	66 „

The N.Z.S. Co. have always justly prided themselves on the liberal way in which their ships were outfitted and kept up, and the *Waimate* was no exception to their rule. She was, in fact, a first-class ship in every respect, well built, splendidly fitted up for passengers, and smartly rigged with the old-time long jib-boom and the aristocratic main skysail. As regards measurements, she had a registered length of 219 feet 7 inches ; breadth, 35 feet 1 inch ; depth, 20 feet 7 inches ; and her tonnage came to 1,124 tons net and 1,156 gross.

All the N.Z.S. Co.'s ships were tiny vessels, according to modern standards, the largest in their fleet, the clipper *Turakina*, being only 1,189 tons net. Yet these ships took out from 300 to 400 emigrants, men, women and children, without being considered unduly crowded by the B.O.T. authorities. The British families that went out to stock the new Colonies and make great nations under the Southern Cross were a stout-hearted lot, for the voyage itself was quite a severe enough experience to daunt the weakling, or anyone at all deficient in backbone.

On her maiden passage Captain Rose took the *Waimate* out to Lyttelton in 89 days. On her second voyage Captain Peck took her over and the 74-day passage of 1880–1 was his seventh and last voyage.

After leaving Gravesend, on October 24th, 1880, the ship had a rough time in the Channel, until, when off Falmouth with the barometer down to 28.30, she was forced back by a furious southerly gale to the Eddystone, whence she took her departure on October 30th. The Equator was crossed on November 16th, only 16 days 8 hours from the Eddystone, a performance which could only have been accomplished by a really fast ship. Indeed, there is no doubt that, as long as the yards were off the backstays, the *Waimate* was a hard vessel to beat. She crossed the Meridian of the Cape in 44° S. on December 7th, which was also exceedingly good work. Captain Peck went as far as 48° S. when running his easting down, passed the Meridian of the Leeuwin on December 24th, and the South Cape, Tasmania, on December 30th, only a little over 60 days out. The Snares were abeam at 4 a.m. on January 4th, only 66 days from the Eddystone, and Lyttelton was reached on the evening of January 6th.

On her homeward passage this voyage the *Waimate* was very nearly wrecked in the neighbourhood of the Horn. Captain Peck was carrying a press of sail, running before heavy westerlies, and it was a dark and dirty night. Suddenly there came a wild cry from the look-out, and at the same moment that particular deep hollow roar of a big surf on a steep-to coast could be distinguished above the oratorio of the wind in the rigging. A minute or so later rugged cliffs, rising above a mist of spray, could be distinguished both ahead and on either bow, and all hands knew that the ship was rushing headlong on to an unknown shore. The *Waimate* must either have had a stronger current in her favour, or sailed better than the log allowed, for Captain Peck's dead reckoning was all adrift and he had had no sights for some days.

A more awful situation than being embayed or back-strapped on the Tierra del Fuegian coast on a black night, with the huge seas around one broken into spouts of foam by outlying razor-backed rocks, can hardly be imagined. Captain Peck took the only possible means of saving his ship. The cables were hurriedly ranged and shackled on to the anchors, which were unlashed and got outboard with all despatch. Then, as the helm was put down, and the ship rounded up into the wind with a fearful clatter of blocks and thunder of flogging canvas, both anchors were let go and 120 fathoms of chain veered, for the vessel was in deepish water, although close on the beam a ridge of rocks tore each sea into flying spume and froth. The anchors held, however, and the ship was saved. For which mercy all on board paid chief tribute to the gallant old bos'n, Ned Parker, who had the difficult task of getting the chains ranged clear and shackled on, and the anchors pinched off the bow, at the psychological moment. In the dark of that Cape Horn night, with its flying sprays and

"Waimate"

Built 1874 Passenger and Emigrant Ship.

screeching wind, it required a cool head and superb seamanship, on that slippery, reeling fo'c'sle-head, to get this heavy and dangerous work accomplished quickly and without a hitch—without something going wrong or someone getting hurt. The *Waimate* had to hang on in this desperate situation until an ease-up and a shift of wind gave her a chance of gaining an offing, then her chains were slipped, she managed to fetch clear, and resumed her passage.

At the end of this voyage Peck handed over to Captain Mosey, who had had the *Orari* from her launch in 1877. He was one of the most experienced masters in the New Zealand Shipping Company's employ, and had the *Waimate* for four voyages. On his first outward passage to Lyttelton, at the end of 1881, Captain Mosey managed to get a run of 354 miles out of the smart little ship, whilst running his easting down in 47° S. This, I believe, was her best 24 hours' work. In the fall of 1883 Captain Mosey brought the *Waimate* home from Port Chalmers to the Scillies in 71 days. This was the ship's best homeward passage. Her best run to the Horn was one of 18 days from Lyttelton in April, 1880.

In 1884–5, Captain Tribe had the *Waimate* for a voyage, during which she made her first passage to Auckland, which was also her longest passage, being 112 days.

After this Captain Canese took over, and ran her for six voyages, from 1886 to 1892, during which period the ship showed some splendid sailing, and made her best average. In the spring of 1886 she went out to Lyttelton from London in 82 days. Captain Canese beat this on his second voyage by going out to Port Chalmers in 78 days. Leaving London on October 20th, 1886, the *Waimate* crossed the Equator only 19 days out from the Thames and arrived on January 7th, 1887, 74 days from the Channel.

In 1889 she again made the run out in under 80 days from the Channel pilot, being 82 days to Port Chalmers from the Docks, and 78 from land to land.

On her last three voyages under the New Zealand Company's house-flag *Waimate* was commanded by Captain Worster, who had had the *Waikato* for six years. He took *Waimate* out to Port Chalmers in 92 days in the spring of 1893, to Auckland in 88 days during the summer of 1894, and his last trip was 104 days to Port Chalmers, between April 11th and July 25th, 1895.

In 1896 the clipper of the New Zealand fleet, as her officers used to call her, was sold to the Russians, and renamed *Valkyrian*, but she did not last long after her change of flag. In 1899 she sailed from Newcastle, N.S.W., with the usual coal cargo for Iquique, and was never heard of again. It is probable that her cargo became heated, that the fire got beyond control in rough westerly weather, and that thus the ship was lost, and all on board perished.

THE "BEN VOIRLICH."

THE two most noted passenger-carrying clippers of Watson's Ben Line, of Glasgow, were undoubtedly the beautiful 1,500-ton sisters, *Ben Cruachan* and *Ben Voirlich*, which were designed and built by Barclay, Curle & Co. in 1873. The second of the pair, the *Ben Voirlich*, was just an inch the larger all round, her registered measurements being :—Length, 255 feet 6 inches ; breadth, 37 feet 1 inch ; and depth, 21 feet 8 inches. Her tonnage, 1,474 tons, was larger, being six tons more than *Ben Cruachan's*. Both ships had the same sail plan, which was exceedingly square ; here are a few of the chief measurements :

Bowsprit and jib-boom, outboard	..	..	70 feet.		
Mainmast, deck to truck	..	..	143½ ,,		
Main and fore lower yards	..	..	84 ,,		
,, ,, ,, lower topsail yards	..	..	73 ,,		
,, ,, ,, upper topsail yards	..	..	70½ ,,		
,, ,, ,, lower topgallant yards	..	58½ ,,			
,, ,, ,, upper topgallant yards	..	56 ,,			
,, ,, ,, royal yards	..	..	44 ,,		

The *Ben Voirlich* was fitted with a very good labour-saving device consisting of a winch just aft of the midship-house, to which the fore-braces were taken by means of an endless chain, so that the winch took in on one side and gave out on the other. By this contrivance the fore-yards could be squared in quite easily by two men.

The *Ben Cruachan*, with her 'tween-decks full of emigrants, left the Clyde for Melbourne on October 5th, 1873, under that well-known commander, Bully Martin ; she was followed by *Ben Voirlich* on January 3rd, 1874, under Captain McPetrie. Captain Martin brought *Ben Cruachan* into Hobson's Bay, 67 days from the Tuskar, and McPetrie's passage in *Ben Voirlich* was also under 70 days. The latter was held up in the Clyde until January 26th, and after passing the Tuskar on the 27th was further delayed by a fortnight of head winds ; nevertheless, the Equator was crossed in 26° 30′ W. on February 19th, only 23 days from her pilot. She was on the Cape Meridian on March 15th, from which date until the 27th the new iron clipper averaged 12½ knots. The Otway was made on April 5th, and the anchor was dropped in Hobson's Bay on the 6th ; the ship being 69 days out from the Tuskar. Both ships loaded wool home, but their passages on this traverse were not so good, *Ben Cruachan* taking 100 and *Ben Voirlich* 108 days. These maiden passages proved that the new Ben Liners could be driven to the limit, and that they were at their best with yards off the backstays in strong winds and at their worst in light head winds.

It was on her second passage that the *Ben Voirlich* made her name, by breaking the iron ship record for the run out to Melbourne from the Channel. It was a specially favourable season for quick passages, and her record still holds good for iron or steel ships. Captain McPetrie left Gravesend on November 9th, 1874, was off Plymouth on the 11th, but did not clear the Channel until the 12th. The Equator was crossed in 31° 20′ W.

on December 1st, 20 days out from the Lizard. On December 24th the *Ben Voirlich* was in 45° S. on the Cape Meridian, and Captain McPetrie ran down his easting on the parallel of 46° 30′ S. *Ben Voirlich* possessed a very tough specimen of a mate, a bald-headed man with a great red beard, who drove the ship and her crew to the limit. Thus, whilst down in the " roaring forties," the *Ben's* main deck was under water most of the time, and the second cabin quarters, in a big house on deck, were continually being washed out. The emigrants below had an equally unpleasant time, but the ship herself delighted in the wild weather, and after making several 24-hour runs of over 300 miles, the best being 352 miles, she reached the Melbourne anchorage on January 14th, 65 days out from Plymouth. The *Loch Ness*, which passed the Tuskar on November 11th, and crossed the Equator on the same day as the *Ben Voirlich*, was beaten on the passage by 4 days. *Ben Voirlich's* jubilant crew even claimed the golden cock from the great *Thermopylæ*; but this claim was soon abandoned, for the *Thermopylæ* herself arrived on February 4th, only 64 days out from the Lizard, and her log-books showed two passages which were better than *Ben Voirlich's*. On her maiden passage *Thermopylæ* was 63 days from Gravesend and 62 from the Lizard to the Hobson's Bay anchorage; whilst in 1870–1 she was 65 days from the Downs, but only 60 from the Lizard.

The *Ben Voirlich* continued to distinguish herself on her outward passages, though she never had much luck homewards on her wool passages, which were steady and regular, without being spectacular.

During the years 1875 to 1879 *Ben Voirlich* was commanded by Captain Ovenstone, whose best passage was made in 1877—Achill Head to Hobson's Bay, 83 days. On this passage the *Ben Voirlich* made a run of 350 miles on July 26th in 35° 37′ S. 22° 10′ W.

In 1879 Captain Ovenstone handed over to Captain Douglas, late of the Blackwaller *Malabar*. On his first outward passage Captain Douglas took 87 days to Sydney, finding light head winds all the way up the east coast of Australia. On his second outward passage Charlie Douglas had a tremendous race with the Aberdeen clipper *Romanoff*, and beat her by one day, their times being :

			Ben Voirlich.	*Romanoff.*
Off the Lizard	..	.. ..	June 13	June 11
Crossed Equator	..	..	July 8	July 6
Crossed Cape Meridian	..	July 25	July 27
Passed Cape Otway	..	..	Aug. 17	Aug. 17
Arrived Hobson's Bay	..	Aug. 19	Aug. 18
Days from Lizard	..	..	67	68

Ben Voirlich's best 24-hour runs on this trip were 323 and 330 miles, made on July 21st and 22nd, in a hard W.S.W. gale to the southward of Gough Island. On August 17th, when in sight of Cape Schanck, Captain Douglas was obliged to heave to under reefed topsails, the wind blowing very hard, with terrific squalls from the N.N.W. and north; and he did not venture to make sail for Port Phillip Heads until the wind shifted to W.N.W., 48 hours later.

Captain Douglas's passages out in 1881 and 1882 were almost as good as his first. In 1881 he took his departure from the Lizard on May 2nd, and arrived Melbourne on July 15th, 74 days out. On this occasion the ship's best run was 349 miles and her best week's work 2,100 miles. In 1882, Captain Douglas took his departure from the Lizard on May 3rd, and anchored in Hobson's Bay on July 12th, only 70 days out from the Channel. This time the *Ben Voirlich's* best sailing performance was an average of 300 miles between Gough Island and Kerguelen.

"Ben Voirlich"

Built 1873 Passenger and Emigrant Ship.

In 1884 the captains of the two sisters, *Ben Cruachan* and *Ben Voirlich*, changed ships, Douglas going to the *Cruachan* and old Bully Martin taking over the *Ben Voirlich*. Though he did not succeed in equalling the records of her other captains when outward bound, Martin gave *Ben Voirlich* her best wool passage—this was 89 days in 1885-6. She left Melbourne in company with the *Rodney*, which beat her by two days to London. Their two passages were the best made for the March sales.

On her passage out in 1885 *Ben Voirlich* had a very unpleasant experience to the southward of the Cape of Good Hope. Captain Martin was driving his ship in a hard westerly gale. At 8 a.m. on August 6th a very vicious squall blew the fore-sail out of her. Two hours later the ship was scudding before a hurricane under fore and main lower topsails. At about 11 a.m. *Ben Voirlich* was pooped by a tremendous sea, which washed away the two helmsmen and Captain Martin, who was conning them. The lee helmsman caught in the mizen rigging, where he immediately lashed himself with the turned-up gear. A hen coop happened to be lashed to the bucket rail at the forward end of the poop, and Captain Martin and the quartermaster were hurled against this coop with such force that it was smashed to pieces. As soon as the water had run off, these two deep-sea warriors picked themselves up and clawed their way back to the wheel. This they found with half its spokes gone, smashed in two and only held together by the rim. It was also jammed in its own wreckage. This the two men managed to clear away in time to save the ship from broaching to. For the next twenty-four hours the *Ben Voirlich* was swept by mountainous seas, so that no one could put foot on her main-deck, and all the braces were led to the poop or on to the top of the deck-houses. That night the ship was stripped of her topgallant bulwarks, poop ladders, harness casks and hen coops. The port life-boat was smashed to matchwood, both standard and steering compasses swept overboard and not a handspike was left in the racks.

As soon as it was daylight Captain Martin, with great difficulty, had the second cabin passengers moved from their house to the poop, as he feared that the house would sooner or later be burst in and gutted by the seas. On this occasion *Ben Voirlich* weathered it out without loss of life. She had not been so lucky in 1878, when homeward bound. That time she was running before a very heavy sea, crossing the Banks to the westward of the Horn. The date was November 18th; a bigger sea than usual reared up like a mountain astern; the helmsman, a Dutchman, gave one look and let go the wheel with a strangled shout of fright. The ship immediately broached to, and as she lay over an avalanche of water broke over the poop and weather quarter, gutting the cabin and taking nine men overboard. Let me quote from my " Colonial Clippers " :

" For an hour the ship lay over on her beam ends, dragging her lower yards in the water, entirely out of control. Two men who happened to be at work on the lee-fore-yardarm were actually washed off it. One of them was lost overboard, but the other caught the rail and lay there head downwards, being held from going farther by the chain fore-sheet. An apprentice managed to get to him and grab hold, but the next moment a sea swept over them, and whilst the apprentice was washed inboard, the man was never seen again. This same apprentice happened to be washed up against the winch, to which he clung like a limpet; and then, as the old white-bearded sailmaker was hurled by him in the cross-wash of the sea, he caught the old man and held on to him, or the latter would have gone overboard.

" The brave ship struggled gamely : three times she brought her spars to windward and three times she was laid flat again. The whole of her topgallant rail and bulwarks were washed away, together with everything of a movable nature on the deck. At last, after a whole hour of desperate fighting, they managed to get the wheel up, and the clipper slowly righted herself as she fell off, and brought the wind astern."

This was *Ben Voirlich's* worst experience in the whole of her career. And it speaks well for her stability, her strength of build and rig, and general seaworthiness, for a less powerful ship would certainly have gone to Davy Jones's Locker.

In 1886 Captain Martin took the *Ben Voirlich* out to Sydney for the first time, but his passage was a poor one, 94 days.

In 1887 both *Ben Voirlich* and *Ben Cruachan* were removed from the Australian trade and sent out to San Francisco to take their part in the booming grain trade. *Ben Voirlich* arrived in 'Frisco Bay on September 23rd, 124 days out from the Channel. This passage was well above the average. *Ben Cruachan's* was not so good, being 164 days from the Tyne.

Ben Voirlich was sold to the Germans in 1891, whilst *Ben Cruachan* became the Mexican *Carmela*.

In 1903 Italian owners bought the *Ben Voirlich* and renamed her *Cognati*, and until the outbreak of war she was often to be seen in Australian ports, looking rather shabby, with the yards sent down from her mizen mast. In 1908 she was nearly sunk through collision with an iceberg in the neighbourhood of the Horn, but she managed to get into port.

Towards the end of the war *Ben Voirlich* turned up at Leith, where she was converted into an old-time prison hulk. But she was more comfortably fitted than any prison hulk of the Napoleonic Wars, with electric light and many other modern luxuries, while her mastless decks were covered with deck-houses, where the crews of the surrendered German ships were domiciled. The *Ben Cruachan*, which had been a hulk at Santa Cruz since 1904, was refitted during the war and did duty as a motor-ship through those stirring years. Thus both the famous *Bens* played their part in the titanic struggle.

THE "THESSALUS."

THE *Thessalus* was the largest, and perhaps the fastest of all the beautiful ships which were built by Barclay, Curle & Co. for the Golden Fleece Line, owned by A. and J. Carmichael, of Greenock. She was launched in July, 1874, at the height of the boom in iron clipper ships. By way of comparison, the following list of iron clippers built in that year may be of interest:

Ship.	Tons Gross.	Builder.
Belfast	1,957	Harland & Wolff.
Star of Bengal	1,870	Harland & Wolff.
Thessalus	1,865	Barclay, Curle.
Old Kensington	1,817	Potter.
Lochee	1,812	Stephen, of Dundee.
British General	1,810	Royden.
Cape Verde	1,786	Wingate.
Blair Athole	1,777	Elder.
Eastern Monarch	1,769	Mounsey.
Senator	1,768	Mounsey.
Duchess of Edinburgh	1,766	Mounsey.
Udston	1,764	Barclay, Curle.
Castle Roy	1,754	Elder.
Peterborough	1,740	Richardson, Duck.
Charlotte Croom	1,716	Connell.
Lammermoor	1,710	Reid.
Baron Aberdare	1,708	Watson.

The *Belfast* and the *Star of Bengal*, the only sailing ships built in 1874 which had greater tonnage than *Thessalus*, were jute clippers, but the *Thessalus* was intended for no special trade. She went everywhere, and her passages, whether as a jute clipper, a wool clipper, or a San Francisco grain carrier, were equally good. Though not fitted to carry a great many passengers, her poop being only 31 feet long, she had a number of spare cabins, and very often had half a dozen first-class passengers when going out to Melbourne or Sydney. Her registered measurements were :—Length, 269 feet; breadth, 41 feet 1 inch; depth, 23 feet 6 inches. Although she was certainly as speedy as any of the ships launched in 1874, the *Thessalus* was not overmasted, and she kept extraordinarily free from accidents. For instance, on her third voyage she encountered a very severe cyclone on August 31st, 1876, when close to the Sandheads. Captain Bennett, on recognizing the well-known signs of the coming storm, stood away to the extreme east side of the Bay of Bengal, and considered himself lucky to escape with the loss of his topgallant masts, repairs only costing the ship £380. In this cyclone the total damage done to shipping was reckoned to have cost the underwriters £100,000. The *Thessalus* was taking out a pack of foxhounds for the Calcutta Jackal Club, and these were housed in a large kennel on top of the main hatch. Knowing that the hounds would undoubtedly be drowned if left in the kennel, Captain Bennett let them out. Not long afterwards the kennel was washed clean over the lee rail without touching it. Nobody had time to notice what had happened to the foxhounds, and it was thought that they had all been swept overboard; but when the cyclone had passed they reappeared unhurt from beneath the lower fo'c'sle bunks, where they had taken refuge during the storm.

The *Thessalus* only had two captains during the whole of her life under the Red Ensign. Captain E. C. Bennett took her from the stocks, and had her until he retired from the sea at the beginning of the 'nineties. He was succeeded by Captain J. Henderson, who remained in the ship until she was sold.

On her maiden voyage the *Thessalus* went out to Calcutta. Thence she sailed for London on January 21st, 1875, arriving April 28th, 97 days out. This was not her best jute passage, which was made on her third voyage, when she left Calcutta on December 6th, 1876, and reached London on March 6th, 1877, 90 days out.

On her second voyage the *Thessalus* left London for Melbourne on July 6th, 1875, with six cabin-passengers. On this occasion she was by no means favoured by the winds. She was off the Lizard on July 8th, crossed the Equator on August 7th, was on the Cape Meridian on September 3rd, and reached Melbourne on September 29th, 83 days out. On September 5th, in 42° S. 30° E., the main upper topsail yard, which was of iron, was broken in halves during a furious squall, and the weather was so bad that it could not be sent down for two days, and afterwards took a whole week to repair.

On her first wool passage Carmichael's big ship left Melbourne on October 30th, 1875, and arrived London on January 31st, 1876, 93 days out.

The best Melbourne passage made by the *Thessalus* was on her fifth voyage, the spring of 1878. Sailing from Gravesend on March 2nd, Captain Bennett had a hard beat down Channel, and did not take his departure from the Lizard until March 8th. The Equator was crossed in 29° W., 20 days out from the Lizard, and the Cape Meridian in 43° S. on April 20th, only 23 days from the Line. The *Thessalus*, in spite of being very deeply loaded, arrived at Melbourne on May 14th, 73 days from port to port, and 67 days from the Start. From Melbourne Captain Bennett took walers to Calcutta, and made a very smart run, being only 48 days from anchorage to anchorage (July 8th to August 25th). She loaded jute home and, leaving Calcutta on November 7th, was off Deal on February 8th and reached Dundee on February 18th, 103 days out.

On her sixth voyage, in 1879, the *Thessalus* sailed from Penarth Roads to Calcutta, anchor to anchor, in 98 days (April 3rd to July 10th), and leaving Calcutta on September 22nd, passed Dover, bound for London, at 8.30 a.m. on December 28th, 97 days out.

In 1880 Captain Bennett made a long passage from London to Melbourne, being 86 days from the Start; but the *Thessalus* had no chance except between the Cape and the Leeuwin (May 3rd to May 23rd). Otherwise she encountered either very light winds or heavy head gales. Then she took 69 days (July 7th to September 14th) with horses to Calcutta, but although the passage was longer than her previous one, Captain Bennett was congratulated because he landed all his horses alive and in prime condition. The *Udston*, which reached the Hooghli shortly after the *Thessalus*, had only four horses alive. During bad weather in the Bay of Bengal the horses had broken loose in the 'tween-decks, and in a frenzy of terror kicked each other to death. This voyage, the *Thessalus*, instead of loading jute for home, loaded wheat bags, wool packs and camels for Melbourne. The camels, which could not have been a very pleasant cargo, were also landed in good condition, after the quick run of 47 days. At Melbourne Captain Bennett loaded wool at 1d. per lb. for London, and sailing on January 14th, 1881, arrived home on April 28th, 104 days out.

"Thessalus"
Built 1874 General Trader.

Thessalus made her first grain passage in the spring of 1883. After running out to Australia in 80 days, and crossing the Pacific from Sydney to San Francisco in the good time of 55 days (September 27th to November 21st), she sailed from San Francisco with the usual grain cargo on January 10th, 1883. She was followed by the big Harland & Wolff clipper, *British Merchant*, which was then on her third voyage, on January 21st. No doubt there was some keen betting as to which ship would reach home first. E. J. Molony, the master of the *British Merchant*, had as great a reputation as Bennett for making passages, and on this occasion the *British Merchant* had the best of it. This was due to the quick run to the Horn made by Molony's ship, for the two vessels were in company to the southward of Cape Stiff in terrific weather. The Horn was rounded by both of them on March 6th in a heavy gale and tremendous sea. In the log of the *British Merchant* the loss of boats and a man is recorded. Neither captain thought of heaving to, and the *British Merchant's* run on March 6th was 242 miles. Captain Molony, in his synopsis of the passage, writes :

" On March 4th, in 77° W., a gale commenced blowing from W.N.W. to W.S.W. for three days, with steadily falling barometer. This raised a tremendous sea, especially on the Burdwood Bank, where we lost bulwarks, boats, etc. Several other vessels met with disaster in the same gale and more than one foundered."

The two ships made a close race of it from the Horn to the Channel, where they fell in with a hard S.E. gale. The *British Merchant* passed Saltees Light at 1 p.m. on April 25th, on her way to Liverpool. *Thessalus* was off the Lizard on the same day, being 105 days out, as against the *British Merchant's* 95 days. Captain Bennett had a hard beat up Channel, and finally arrived off Gravesend on April 29th.

The Carmichael clipper's next voyage was to Calcutta and back, her jute passage taking 101 days to London. In 1884–5 *Thessalus* made the following passages :

	Left.		Arrived.	Days out.
The Downs	April 11, 1884	Sydney	June 27, 1884	77
Sydney	Aug. 1	San Pedro	Oct. 6	66
San Pedro	Oct. 28	San Francisco	Nov. 6	9
San Francisco	Nov. 25	Newcastle, N.S.W.	Jan. 9, 1885	45
Newcastle, N.S.W.	Feb. 4, 1885	San Francisco	May 8	93
San Francisco	July 27	Hull	Nov. 29	125

In 1886 after running out to Sydney from the Downs in 85 days, *Thessalus* crossed the Pacific from Newcastle to San Francisco (June 10th to July 30th) in 50 days, and sailing from San Francisco on October 5th, reached Havre in the good time of 104 days.

In 1887, on his thirteenth voyage, Captain Bennett made the run out to Sydney in 78 days, the dates being :

> Took departure from the Start, March 29th.
> He had left Docks, March 25th.
> Crossed Equator, April 20th.
> Crossed Cape Meridian, May 15th.
> Off the Otway, June 11th.
> Signalled Wilson's Promontory, June 13th.
> Off Cape Howe, June 14th.
> Entered Sydney Heads, 9 a.m., June 15th.

Whilst running her easting down on this passage *Thessalus* covered 3,007 miles in 11 days, her best 24-hour run being 322 miles. Her homeward passage in 1888 was made from Portland, Oregon, and was the quickest of her career from a North Pacific grain port. Leaving Portland on January 8th, she arrived at Queenstown on April 16th, 98 days out. It should, however, be stated that the season was a very favourable one, no less than five other ships, *Micronesia*, *Eurasia*, *Brownrigg*, *Merioneth* and *Eleanor Margaret*, making the run in under 100 days. The *Thessalus* very nearly equalled this run in 1889, on her next voyage, when she left San Francisco on January 5th, and arrived at Queenstown at 5.30 a.m. on April 20th, just under 105 days out.

With the 'nineties commenced a keen rivalry between the two Carmichael cracks, *Thessalus*, under Captain Henderson, and *Argonaut*, at first under Captain Thomas and then under Captain Hunter. On June 14th, 1890, *Thessalus* left Swansea, and the *Argonaut* left London, both being bound for San Francisco. The Golden Fleece clippers made splendid times for the difficult passage outwards round the Horn. *Thessalus* arrived at San Francisco on October 6th, 114 days out, and the *Argonaut* on October 10th, 118 days out. Of the two, the *Argonaut* was the first to complete her grain cargo. She sailed on November 17th, but the *Thessalus* did not get away until December 5th. The latter again had the best of it, and passing the *Argonaut*, was off the Lizard on March 24th, 109 days out, on her way to Dunkirk. The *Argonaut* arrived at Falmouth on April 3rd, having taken 137 days for the passage.

Three other well-known fast sailing ships were beaten by the *Thessalus* this grain season. These were: *Evesham Abbey*, which sailed from San Francisco on December 2nd for Dunkirk; *Romsdal*, which left on the 3rd for Havre; and the *Glenalvon*, which left on the 6th for Antwerp. All three took over 120 days, arriving at their port of discharge at the beginning of April.

The contest between the *Thessalus* and the *Argonaut* was continued in 1891–2. Between May and September, 1891, no less than 155 big sailing ships left the United Kingdom or Continent for San Francisco. The *Argonaut* loaded at Swansea and sailed on May 20th, the *Thessalus* following on May 26th from Barry. This time their passages were not quite so good, the *Thessalus* arriving at San Francisco 119 days out, and the *Argonaut* 128 days out. Nor was it such a favourable season for the homeward run. The rivalry between the two ships must have been very keen, for we find them sailing from San Francisco within a day of each other, but once again Captain Thomas, of the *Argonaut*, was unable to get the better of Henderson in the *Thessalus*. The latter sailed on November 11th, and arrived at Hull on March 19th, 128 days out, whilst the *Argonaut*, sailing on November 12th, passed Dover, bound for Dunkirk, on March 31st, 139 days out.

On her eighteenth voyage, in 1892–3, the *Thessalus* again loaded Welsh coal for San Francisco, sailing on May 17th. Although her outward passage was not good enough to figure amongst the best of the year, her homeward one was only beaten by that of the big four-masted barque *Andelana*. *Thessalus* left San Francisco on November 19th, 1892, and arrived at Queenstown on February 28th, 1893, 101 days out. *Andelana's* passage was one of the best ever made, as she was off Brow Head on May 21st, only 89 days out from San Francisco. She afterwards put into Holyhead to await sufficient tide to get her into Fleetwood. This 101-day run of the *Thessalus* was her last grain passage. Her next five voyages were out to Sydney by way of the Cape, and home with the wool clip.

On April 20th, 1893, Captain Henderson sailed from Cardiff, and arrived at Cape Town on June 7th, 47 days out. After discharging at the Cape the run of the *Thessalus* from Table Bay to Sydney was one of the finest performances of her career. She left Cape Town on Saturday, July 15th, the wind being moderate at S.S.E., which kept her plying to windward till July 19th, by which time she was off the Cape of Good Hope. The wind then came north-easterly, and from a light air increased to a strong breeze, finally causing Captain Henderson to shorten sail. For the next six days the *Thessalus* maintained the wonderful average of 317 miles per day. Then on July 26th the wind petered out and left the Golden Fleece clipper knocking about in the usual swell for 24 hours. After this the wind set in north-west, and gave the *Thessalus* another fine week's run. In his statement to the Press

Captain Henderson credits the *Thessalus* with covering 1,900 miles in the six days beginning July 27th, on which day her 24-hour run was 208 miles. I think, however, that the reporter got his account wrong, and that the best six days, totalling 1,900 miles, were selected from the 17 days between July 27th and Saturday, August 12th, when at 11 p.m. the Otway Light was sighted. The ship's fastest run was made on August 6th, and came to 369 miles. This, so far as I can find out, was the best 24-hour run of her career. To the Otway Light she took 23 days 20 hours from the Cape, and 27 days 11 hours from the anchorage in Table Bay. Captain Henderson reported off Wilson's Promontory at 3 p.m. on August 13th, and was then held up by baffling winds, calms, and squalls until 6.30 p.m. on August 15th, when the wind came out of the S.W. *Thessalus* took a tug at 3 p.m. on August 16th, and anchored in Port Jackson at 5.30 p.m. on the same day.

In 1895 Captain Henderson very nearly beat this passage. Leaving London on April 11th he took his departure from the Lizard on April 13th, and arrived within 100 miles of Cape Town on the fortieth day out, but was then held up for 3 days by light easterly airs, and did not reach the anchorage until May 27th, 44 days out from the Channel. The *Thessalus* was 22 days discharging cargo and taking in ballast at the Cape. This time she was only a day to the Cape of Good Hope from Table Bay, and running down her easting in about 38° S., had fine weather and good winds to the Leeuwin, after which it was unsettled and dirty. The ship again made many runs of over 300 miles a day, and averaged 10.1 knots between the Cape and the Otway. Wilson's Promontory was signalled on July 18th, and *Thessalus* came to anchor in Watson's Bay on July 23rd, her days under sail from the Channel to Sydney totalling again 78 days.

Leaving Sydney in October, 1896, with 8,633 bales screwed into her hold *Thessalus* made the best wool passage of her career, and won a very hard race with the *Cimba* by only a few hours. Her old antagonist, the *Argonaut*, which was now commanded by Captain Hunter, also sailed the same day as the *Cimba* and the *Thessalus*, October 17th, but Hunter, who was a great sail-carrier, and whose previous wool passage had been one of the best of the year, was very unlucky with his winds, and dropped a long way behind the *Thessalus* and the *Cimba*, which two vessels were twice in company during the passage. I will take the occasions from the abstract log of *Cimba* :

Date. Nov.	Lat.	Long.	Course.	Dist. Miles.	Winds.
3	54° 36′ S.	152° W.	N. 73° E.	143	Light to calm, with heavy, confused sea. *Thessalus*, *Anna*, and *Itata* in company.
4	54° 23′ S.	149° 41′ W.	N. 81° E.	83	Light north - westerly airs. *Thessalus*, *Anna*, and *Itata* still in company.
24	38° 28′ S.	36° 31′ W.	N. 31° E.	190	S.W. to S.E. moderate and fine to noon, then light and cloudy. *Thessalus* in company.
25	35° 53′ S.	34° 6′ W.	N. 37° E.	195	S.S.E. to N.N.W. moderate to fresh, increasing fast. Midnight very strong gale. *Thessalus* in company.

With regard to these encounters Captain Holmes (*Cimba*) wrote to me as follows :

" I left Sydney in company with the *Thessalus* and the *Argonaut*, and was twice in company with the former, having come up to him in light winds, but when he got the breeze he just romped away from me as if I was at anchor. *Thessalus* was a wonderfully fast ship, and I think that the five-masted German, *Potosi*, was the only one I have seen that could touch her."

Although the little *Cimba* was not nearly so fast as the *Thessalus* in strong winds she was quite her equal in light weather, and kept very close on her heels all the way up the Atlantic, and when the *Thessalus* was signalling the Start at noon on December 31st, 75 days out, the *Cimba* was making her number off the Lizard.   By taking steam, however, at 9 a.m. on January 2nd, when off Beachy Head, the *Cimba* was able to dock on January 3rd, the same day as the *Thessalus*, both ships being 78 days from Sydney.   These were easily the best wool passages of that year.   On the previous passage in 1894–5 *Thessalus* had managed to beat the *Cimba* by over a week, their times being as follows :

	Left.	Arrived.	Days.
Cimba ..	Sydney, Oct. 16	London, Jan. 19	95
Thessalus ..	Sydney, Oct. 20	London, Jan. 13	85

The well-known Devitt & Moore ship, *Derwent*, sailed on the same day as the *Thessalus*, and did not arrive until January 27th, 99 days out.

On her arrival home from Sydney in the spring of 1898 the *Thessalus* was sold to the Swedes, and left London on May 17th for Sundsvaal to load for Adelaide.   For the next 10 years she sailed in the Baltic and Australian timber trade, but apparently her new captain made no attempt to drive her, for I cannot find any outstanding passages to her account whilst under the Swedish flag.   The grand old ship was finally broken up about five years before the war.

THE " DUNTRUNE."

IN these days it is interesting to look back and see how our fathers and grandfathers set about the great adventure of emigration and a voyage of five or six months' duration in a sailing ship to the Colonies. It required a stout heart on the part of both men and women to face that long sea journey round the Cape in square-riggers which rarely exceeded 1,800 tons burthen. Even in the best appointed of these emigrant ships it was a journey of such hardships as I fear few present-day emigrants would be willing to face.

Amongst the finest and fastest of the iron clippers which took emigrants to Australia and New Zealand in the 'seventies and 'eighties, were the 1,500-ton sister ships of David Bruce's Dundee Clipper Line. These vessels carried out passengers of the sturdy Scottish and North Country stock at extraordinarily low rates—witness the following shipping advertisement from the " Dundee Advertiser " of 1883 :

The magnificent clipper *Duntrune*, Captain Rollo, will sail from Dundee for Brisbane (with liberty to call at Plymouth) on Tuesday, 28th August, taking approved passengers for £5 steerage, £15 second cabin.

The *Duntrune* and sister ships, *Southesk* and *Maulesden*, belonging to this line, have made some of the fastest passages on record to Australia. The appointments of the ship are specially designed to ensure the comfort and safety of the passengers.

Special railway arrangements have been made from Aberdeen, Keith, Elgin, Forres, Nairn, Inverness and the North, also from stations south as far as the midland counties of England, for passengers travelling at reduced rates to Dundee.

For particulars as to freight apply to MESSRS. F. S. C. GREEN & CO., 13 Fenchurch Avenue, London. Or MESSRS. DAVID BRUCE & CO., 3 Royal Exchange Place, Dundee. And for passages, to Queensland Government Emigration Agent, P. FLEMING, 44 High Street, Dundee.

No less than 448 assisted emigrants, including infants and children, were embarked aboard this 1,500-tonner. The emigrants were all berthed in the 'tween-decks, the single men forward, married couples and children amidships and single women aft, each class being kept strictly apart. The crew, under Captain J. Rollo, numbered 49 all told.

The *Duntrune* towed away to sea on Saturday, September 1st, 1883. Large crowds assembled to witness her departure and she went down the Tay dressed rainbow fashion with flags, and firing her signal guns. After being towed as far as Aberdeen, *Duntrune* had light winds and did not gain the Atlantic Ocean, *via* Fair Isle, until Thursday. From the start the fresh water condensing plant gave trouble and the clipper was spoken 73 miles south-west of Tory Island with her condenser broken down. The water in the tanks also proved none too good, so that Captain Rollo decided to put in to Madeira, which was reached on September 28th, after a rough and trying passage. Here the condenser was patched up by the engineers of the Cape Liner *Norham Castle* and of Sir Thomas Brassey's famous yacht, the *Sunbeam*. Lady Brassey, in her yachting log, " In the Trades, the Tropics, and the Roaring Forties," records the incident as follows :

" From the yacht we could see an emigrant ship, bound for Australia, which had put in here to renew her water-supply. She had had a very rough and prolonged passage from Scotland, and the poor emigrants had suffered great discomfort. The captain had appealed to the Consul, who, in his turn, had appealed to Tom and Mr Humphreys, as holding masters' certificates, to hold a formal inquiry into the state of the water-tanks, the contents of which were condemned as unfit for consumption.

" Tom thought I should be interested to see the vessel and we therefore boarded her on our way to the shore from the *Sunbeam*. Our approach evidently created great excitement and directly we drew near we were received with ringing cheers and waving of handkerchiefs. The emigrants appeared to be greatly interested in the children, and would all have shaken hands with us if they could. One man clapped Tom hard on the shoulder, and said, ' Well, sir, you have got the Missus out safe, and the wee bairns ; God bless them and you too ! ' I went into every hole and corner of the ship with the doctor, including the hospital, where one dear little child was lying, looking dreadfully ill, but where two new-born babies and their mothers seemed very bonny."

This delay naturally spoilt the *Duntrune's* passage. There was also a good deal of sickness amongst the children, which obliged Captain Rollo to take his ship along carefully in the " roaring forties."

The *Duntrune* arrived in Moreton Bay on Christmas Day, and anchored off Brisbane three days later. After discharging her emigrants she went down the coast to Newcastle, and there loaded coal for San Francisco, making the run across the Pacific in 68 days. At San Francisco she loaded a grain cargo and sailing on July 2nd, 1884, arrived off Roches Point on November 3rd, 124 days out, and at Havre, her port of discharge, on November 9th. Amongst the *Duntrune's* apprentices on this voyage were Captain Sir Franke B. S. Notley, K.B.E., R.D., R.N.R., the lately retired Marine Superintendent of the P. & O. S.N. Co., and Captain W. Jarvis, who has recently coiled down after commanding Charles Barrie's sailing ships *Decca* and *Dundee* and several of the Den steamers, having served that firm as master for over a quarter of a century.

The *Duntrune* was launched in May, 1875, from the Dundee slips of Alexander Stephen & Sons. This firm had long been known as the builders of Dundee whalers, but in the sister ships, *Airlie*, *Camperdown*, *Duntrune*, *Panmuir* and *Maulesden*, all launched in 1875, they showed that they were able to build iron clipper ships that would bear comparison with those of Aberdeen, the Clyde or the Mersey. The *Duntrune* and her sisters were as sharp as a knife below the water-line forward and then flared out, like the present-day destroyer ; in fact, many shipping people declared that in their clipper ships Messrs. Stephen & Sons anticipated the present-day destroyer designs. The stern of the *Duntrune* was almost square, but here again the lines were very fine. As regards her sea qualities, the *Duntrune* possessed that most unusual quality in an iron ship, of being able to keep her decks dry when running in the " roaring forties." She would always run and never had to be hove-to owing to the following sea. Also she steered so easily that a lee wheel was never needed. It was rare that anything heavier than the tops of seas ever came aboard, and sailors who had been a lifetime at sea pronounced her to be the best sea boat that they had ever been in. For a sharp ship, the *Duntrune* was fast in light winds and would steer so long as her sails would flap. Although she was undoubtedly as fast as her record-breaking sister, the *Maulesden*, I cannot find any unusually good passages until the year 1887, when she made the run from Port Augusta to Valparaiso in 31 days.

During her early years she was kept in the Australian trade, usually sailing from London or the Clyde in November, the best time in the year for making a good passage out to the Antipodes. In 1879 we find her taking 94 days from Gravesend to Sydney. On her next

"Duntrune"

Built 1875 Passenger and Emigrant Ship.

voyage she took 83 days from Portland to Sydney, and came home from Port Jackson to Dover in 85 days.   These passages are by no means worthy of the ship and we must, therefore, conclude that her early captains were very unfortunate in their winds and thus unable to get the best out of her.   But in 1891 the *Duntrune* was handed over to a very well-known Dundee skipper, Captain J. C. B. Jarvis, who had made a great reputation whilst in command of the fast four-mast barque, the *Earl of Dalhousie*.   Under Captain Jarvis the *Duntrune* not only became noted for her smart passages, but she was known, wherever deep-water shellbacks collected, as a happy ship.   In confirmation of this statement I need only add the testimony of one of the apprentices under Captain Jarvis.   He writes :

" Some of the men forward had sailed two or three voyages with him.   They used to say to us apprentices, ' You do not know what going to sea is ; this is only a —— floating home.' "

It must not be supposed that this happy state of affairs was brought about by slack discipline.   Captain Jarvis was a disciplinarian if ever there was one and he stood no nonsense of any sort from anyone aboard.   Standing well over six feet in height, this consummate seaman seemed stern and unbending to a degree at first sight, yet both officers and men soon discovered that he was absolutely just and infinitely kind, and what was even rarer in the old-time shipmaster, he never, under any provocation, showed the least sign of temper. Captain Jarvis commanded his ship on quite different lines from the general run of sailing-ship masters.   He picked his officers carefully ; he would not have a bully, nor would he put up with a poor seaman, with the result that he was well served, and foremast hands used to admit that his mate, James Shearer, was a worthy second to Old Man Jarvis.   Captain Jarvis was noted for his common sense, he concentrated on essentials and he had no use for some of the stupid old sailing-ship methods.   For instance, he would not allow his men to be worn out or washed about by such silly work as holystoning off the Horn, where many a good man has been caught and broken up by a sea whilst fooling with a holystone.

The *Duntrune* always had a good bogey-stove in her fo'c'sle, so that the men could dry their gear.   Also in severe weather Captain Jarvis invariably had coffee served out to the crowd at midnight.   As regards the feeding of his men, Captain Jarvis was away ahead of his times, for he saw to it that all the provisions put on board were of good quality.   He even bought flour in the Colonies so that the men could have fresh bread every day as well as the usual hard tack.

Captain Jarvis invented many of what would nowadays be called gadgets, to ease the working of his ship, both aloft and on deck.   He will chiefly be remembered for his brace winches, which were made from his design by Bullivants of London.   One of these was placed within the main fife-rail and had six cone-shaped drums ; when the handles were put in, the fore yard and two topsail yards could be hauled round together and automatically trimmed with the greatest of ease.   A winch controlling the main yard and topsail yards was just abaft the mizen mast.   By means of these winches the watch could readily square in with any sort of wind.

Captain Jarvis carried no reefs and all his sails, except the royals and mizen topgallant sail, clewed up to the yard-arm.   The *Duntrune* only had gaskets on her royals and mizen topgallant sails.   On the other yards on the after-part a jackstay with points attached was fitted.   If the points could not be reached someone hung on to the jackstay, bent down and threw the ends up.   The sail was then made fast in no time.   In loosing a sail made fast in this fashion a hand just slid along the foot-rope and slipped the points almost as quickly as he could move out along the yard.   With these points it was claimed that the *Duntrune's* sails could be made fast in half the time that it would take with the ordinary gear.

For ease in hauling up the main and fore courses, Captain Jarvis fitted a strong wire midship buntline. When this buntline was hauled up two blocks there was not much kick left in a course, even in blowing weather. Another of Jarvis's tricks, when running hard, was to ease his foresail by heaving in on the midship buntline. Being a hard driver, Captain Jarvis insisted on having the very best of gear and all his improvements were designed to speed up the work aloft, and also to make it safer.

His apprentices were devoted to the old skipper, for they knew that he would not put up with any hazing or silly ragging or unfair treatment. Yet a boy flew when he was spoken to, for the slacker knew that his punishment would be unpleasant, although never vindictive or brutal. When, as sometimes happened, an apprentice proved really unsatisfactory, Captain Jarvis used to report the lad to his owners and frankly advise his parents to start him in some other walk of life. In cases of sickness or accident the stern, unbending skipper was kindness itself and it is small wonder, therefore, that his apprentices and foremast hands were devoted to him.

Captain Jarvis took charge of the *Duntrune* at Dundee in the summer of 1891 and loaded coals at the Northumberland Dock on the Tyne for Valparaiso. Off the River Plate the cargo was found to be much heated, and in order to save his ship Captain Jarvis was obliged to jettison about 500 tons of coal. When between Staten Island and the Horn, the *Duntrune* fell in with the *British Empire*, also bound for Valparaiso. The *British Empire* was one of the smartest sailers in George Duncan's fleet. The *Duntrune* was lying within a point of her course, going close hauled on the starboard tack into a big head sea. It was a very even match between the two vessels as they raced along under royals, bows under at every plunge. That night it blew hard and the clippers got separated but, within three days' sail of the port, they were again in company. It was a ding-dong match, and after passing and repassing each other several times, the *Duntrune* had the luck to anchor twenty minutes ahead of her rival.

The *Duntrune* loaded at Iquique and cleared for Plymouth to call for orders. One pitch-dark, rainy night, when the ship had rounded the Horn and was some distance east of the Falklands and going about 11 knots under courses and upper main topsail, with the wind strong on the port beam, an iceberg was sighted right ahead. It was so dark that the berg·was close aboard before being seen by the mate, and though he just had time to order the helm hard over, it was too late to clear the berg. There was a sickening crash, and everything forward went, up to the knight-heads, whilst the fo'c'sle-head was piled with blocks of ice. It appeared that the sturdy *Duntrune* had cut a corner clean off the iceberg and then gone clear. In the darkness it was difficult to see what damage had been done aloft, but shortly after the iceberg had been left behind, the fore topmast carried away at the lower cap. For the next four days the *Duntrune* was jogged along through a succession of icebergs, large and small, covering about 100 miles a day, with her forepeak full of water and only the foresail set forward. After the usual strenuous time, Captain Jarvis managed to get a jury fore topmast and topgallant mast on end and rigged, and a condemned topsail yard was shipped as a bowsprit.

It is not surprising that the *Duntrune*, in this condition, made a longish run from the ice to the Equator, but from the Equator to Plymouth she took only 27 days. After discharging at Dunkirk, the ship was towed round to Cardiff, where she was repaired, and coal was loaded at 9/– per ton for Colombo. From Colombo, Captain Jarvis went across to Newcastle, N.S.W., in ballast. From here he took a cargo of coal to Valparaiso, where he loaded a cargo of manganese, barley and hay, at a freight of 23/–, for Liverpool.

The times were hard for sailing ships and the *Duntrune* made a small loss on the voyage. Nevertheless, her owners decided to send her out again.

Captain Jarvis then loaded general cargo at Liverpool for Sydney, and from there brought wool home to London. The *Duntrune* sailed from Sydney the same day as the *Earl of Zetland*. The two ships did not see each other once during the passage, but when the *Earl of Zetland* was towing up to Gravesend she was passed by the *Duntrune*, which had the luck to have the better tug.

The next voyage was to Melbourne and back. On the outward passage the *Duntrune's* owners were highly delighted when she was reported in 26 degrees south latitude, being only 26 days out from London. The *Duntrune's* time from Gravesend to the Line on this occasion was 19 days, which has not often been beaten. Her managing owner, of course, expected her to make a record passage, but Captain Jarvis had no luck in the "roaring forties" and the *Duntrune* took 76 days to Melbourne. With a little luck she would have had a chance of equalling the *Maulesden's* famous passage, when she crossed the Line 18 days out from Greenock and passed the South Cape, Tasmania, 61 days out.

On her homeward passage this voyage, the *Duntrune* towed out between Port Phillip Heads along with the *Timaru*, which was loaded with frozen meat, and she gave the latter vessel, which was considered a very smart ship in the New Zealand trade, a bad beating, for the *Duntrune* had discharged at London and loaded a cargo of cement at Northfleet when the *Timaru* was reported as having put in to one of the Western Isles. *Duntrune's* passage on this occasion was just over 90 days.

On his last outward passage in the *Duntrune*, Captain Jarvis made one of the finest passages ever known between the Thames and the Columbia River, the vessel being only 106 days out when she arrived off the Bar, having come up the Pacific from the Horn in the extraordinary time of 41 days.

Wheat was loaded at Portland, Oregon, and discharged at Cork after a homeward passage of 121 days. This was in 1896. Messrs. David Bruce & Co. now decided to sell all their sailing ships, and the *Duntrune* went to Messrs. Woodside, of Belfast, for the sum of £4,000, whereupon Captain Jarvis left her and until September, 1899, when he took charge of the *Lawhill* for the Anglo-American Oil Co., was a partner with Captain Alexander Wood in the Dundee Navigation School. He was succeeded in the *Duntrune* by Captain G. Winterton.

The end of the *Duntrune* can only be conjectured. In the autumn of 1899 the famous Dundee clipper was dismasted to the westward of the Horn, and the same night that she was dismasted Captain Winterton died, his wife and two children being on board. The carpenter, who had been in the *Duntrune* with Captain Jarvis, and was recommended by the latter to Captain Winterton, seems to have assumed charge of the vessel at this point, and after rigging up a jury-mast, ran her in to make the land on the west coast of Tierra del Fuego, where the ship anchored in 45 fathoms of water on a lee shore. The boats had apparently been broken up by the furious Cape Horn seas, but the carpenter managed to repair one of them, and in this he and seven men went off in the hope of reaching Sandy Point and obtaining assistance. They lost their way and drifted about for 17 days in the usual Cape Horn weather, during which time three of them died from exposure. The survivors were eventually picked up by a sealing schooner commanded by the notorious Captain Wilson, the man who went poaching in Russian waters in company with the *Black Diamond*. Wilson landed the carpenter and the other three men at Sandy Point. A Chilean gunboat was then sent to look for the *Duntrune*, but could find no sign of her and she was eventually posted at Lloyd's as missing.

The carpenter afterwards joined Captain Jarvis in the *Lawhill* and the above is his account of the *Duntrune* tragedy. Punta Arenas is a great place for the wildest rumours concerning wrecks off Cape Horn, and the gossips of the port added some lurid details to the carpenter's story, some of which undoubtedly were set abroad by Wilson, the sealer. There seems to have been no doubt, however, that a steamer was not far from the *Duntrune* soon after she had anchored, for the former's smoke was seen, and Mrs. Winterton and her children hurriedly got their clothes ready in order to go off to her, but, alas, the steamer failed to see the disabled sailing ship and the smudge of smoke grew less and less as she steamed away over the horizon, leaving those aboard the *Duntrune* to their tragic fate. It was generally concluded, after the Chilean gunboat had failed to find any signs of her, that she must have foundered soon after the carpenter's boat had left her side.

THE " MARLBOROUGH."

AWAY back in the 'forties we find the Whigs and Tories sharply divided on the matter of Naval administration. The old hands, led by the extremely able Admiral, Sir George Cockburn, who was First Sea Lord from 1841 to 1846, were all against new ideas and inventions, such as steam and heavy ordnance, and considered the small and handy frigate the most important vessel on the Navy List. The Reform Party, it is almost needless to add, were equally in favour of big ships, heavy broadsides and paddle-wheels. It is probable that Admiral Cockburn's loudly expressed opinions influenced Messrs. Green and T. and W. Smith, and caused them to lay down the *Prince of Wales* and *Queen* in 1842, the *Monarch* in 1844, the *Marlborough* in 1846, and the *Blenheim* in 1848.

These Blackwallers were some five hundred tons larger than the average London passenger ship of that date. The sister ships, *Prince of Wales* and *Queen*, were considered a very great advance in merchant ship designing. They were built with the scantlings of naval frigates, were pierced for fifty guns, and were flush-decked, this being considered a great attraction for passengers, as providing a delightful promenade. They were specially fitted for troops, and were ready at a moment's notice to be taken on the strength of the Navy as fifty-gun frigates. The *Monarch* was slightly larger all round, but in design was modelled closely on the other two. It may be of interest to describe the arrangement of her cabins, as showing the most up-to-date accommodation in a first-class passenger ship of 1844. On the main deck she had twelve cabins, each 11 feet by 10, opening into a saloon which was 36 feet long by 18 feet wide. On the lower deck she had sixteen cabins of the same size, and two after-cabins, with stern windows, which were each 18 feet by 16 feet.

These three ships from the Blackwall yard were by far the finest merchant ships built since the Honourable East India Company ceased to operate in 1834. Messrs. T. and W. Smith, of Newcastle, built and ran the only passenger-carrying sailing ships in the Eastern trade which could in any way compare with these of Green and Wigram. The rivalry between Blackwall and the Tyne was very keen. All three firms aped the lordly ways of the East India Company, and their method of carrying on came to be called Blackwall Fashion. The Smiths were not slow in taking up the challenge of Dicky Green, and their first reply to his big ships was the *Marlborough*. The only way in which the *Monarch*, the finest of Green's three ships, differed from a fifty-gun frigate was in lack of beam, the famous Symondite frigates of that day being noted for their tremendous measurements in this respect. The *Marlborough*, therefore, was given an extra foot of beam. She was also much deeper than Green's ships.

The following table of measurements will show the difference between the so-called Blackwall frigates and the Symondite frigates. The Navy ships in this list were all fifty-gun frigates, *Vernon*, *Constance* and *Arethusa* being designed by Sir William Symonds, and their great rival, the *Phaeton*, by White, of Cowes :—

		Tons.	Length.		Breadth.		Depth of hold.	
			ft.	in.	ft.	in.	ft.	in.
1832	H.M.S. *Vernon* ..	2,082	183	0	52	8½	17	1
1842	Green's *Prince of Wales*							
	and *Queen*	1,223	179	4	39	7	22	9
1844	Green's *Monarch* ..	1,444	175	0	40	5	23	5
1846	H.M.S. *Constance* ..	2,132	180	0	52	9	16	4
1846	Smith's *Marlborough*	1,402	175	5	41	5	29	1
1848	H.M.S. *Phaeton* ..	1,942	184	11	49	6	15	10½
1848	Smith's *Blenheim* ..	1,314	175	0	42	0	29	4
1849	H.M.S. *Arethusa* ..	2,127	180	0	52	8½	16	3½

The difference in tonnage between the Navy ships and the merchantmen is noticeable, but tonnage, especially in those days, was a very tricky subject. For instance, the displacement of the *Vernon*, according to Edye, was 1,386 tons at her launch, but when down to her constructed load-water line, was 2,564 tons. The most noticeable item in the measurements of the Tyne-built ships is their great depth of hold. The *Marlborough* and *Blenheim* were considered by the Naval authorities of their day to be a decided improvement on Green's three vessels. In the great Exhibition of 1851 they were pronounced to be the finest ships in the British merchant marine, and were awarded silk ensigns and house-flags on that account by the authorities of the Exhibition. Like the other three, they were specially surveyed by the Admiralty and certified as fit to carry armaments as hired frigates in the event of war. Like all the Blackwallers, the *Marlborough* was built of the finest English oak and Malabar teak and, along with her slightly larger sister ship, cost as much as £40 a ton. One of the most important measurements in a passenger ship of sailing-ship days used to be the height between decks. In the 'forties 5½ feet was by no means unusual. The height between decks of the *Marlborough* and *Blenheim* was 7 feet 2 inches.

The *Marlborough* was commanded during her early years by Sir Allen Young and, like all Smith's ships, carried passengers and troops between London, Madras and Calcutta. In 1853 both she and the *Blenheim* were diverted for one voyage to Australia, owing to the great need for passenger ships to take gold-seekers out to the Antipodes. On this occasion she was manned by a crew of Lascars. This innovation in a first-class passenger ship may have been due to the *Marlborough's* captain, for it was certainly not usual for Smith's frigates to be manned as if they were country ships.

Captain Young sailed from London with 325 passengers, and made the run out to Port Phillip in 78 days from the Lizard. This was splendid work for a ship which, as Captain Whall used to declare, was shaped like a serving mallet. Her return passage was equally good : she sailed from Hobson's Bay on July 4th with 72,000 ounces of gold-dust, valued at about £288,000, and 60 passengers. The *Marlborough* ran through Bass Strait before a strong north-west gale, which steadily increased until, at 4 p.m. on July 6th, the ship was being hurled along by a wind of hurricane strength. The barometer dropped to 28.90 in the worst of the blow, when the wind was so strong that it was impossible to remain upright on the deck, and a dense mist of spray was blown over the ship as the fury of the gale cut the tops off the seas. She was then running like a scared hare off the south-west coast of Tasmania, with the wind on her quarter. In the midst of a screeching squall she was struck by a heavy sea under the counter and broached-to. As the ship went over on her beam ends the main topsail blew to ribbons, and no doubt this saved her from destruction. Captain Young got his ship under command again before any serious damage was done.

A month later, a couple of days before the *Marlborough* rounded the Horn, she had a narrow escape from a large iceberg. She was travelling fast at the time, with a fresh

"Marlborough"
Built 1846 Passenger and Emigrant Ship.

nor'-nor'-west wind and a rough sea. The berg, which was 525 feet high and about half a mile in length, was surrounded by loose ice, through which the *Marlborough* had some difficulty in picking her way. There was probably no real danger, except in the minds of timid passengers, but this encounter with an iceberg was made much of in the newspaper descriptions of the vessel's passage after she had arrived home. The *Marlborough* rounded Cape Horn on August 8th, and made her number off the Start on September 26th when 83½ days out. Her officers declared that, had she had a European crew, the passage would have been made in at least a week less time.

Captain Young was succeeded in the command of the *Marlborough* by Joseph Toynbee, brother of Henry Toynbee, the famous commander of the Smith's *Hotspur*, and the successor, in 1866, of Admiral Fitzroy as Marine Superintendent of the Meteorological Office. Towards the middle of the 'sixties Captain Toynbee handed the *Marlborough* over to T. L. Porteous, another very well-known commander in the Blue Cross Line.

About 1869 the *Marlborough* was withdrawn from active service and converted to a coal hulk at Gibraltar. Here, in company with other celebrated hulks, of which the *Java*, *Orient*, *Light Brigade* and *True Briton* are still to be seen swinging to their moorings, she carried out her grimy duties until the year 1888, when she was broken up.

THE "CUTTY SARK" AND "THERMOPYLÆ"
IN THE TEA RACE OF 1872.

THOUGH the famous tea clippers *Cutty Sark* and *Thermopylæ* were rivals throughout their racing careers, and often loaded together, and left port within a few hours of each other for the same destination, the only instance that I know of where they were in company and actually racing within sight of each other was in the 1872 tea race.

When it became known that the two rivals were loading alongside each other at Shanghai, everyone in the tea trade realized that here, indeed, was going to be a battle of the giants, where seamanship and sail craft would reach their very highest level.

In these days cargo is thrown into a vessel's hold, and a stevedore's business no longer demands the skill that it did in the days of the tea clippers, when there were no water ballast tanks. The stiffening or ballast necessary with a light tea cargo had to be just the right amount and no more, no less, if a vessel was to be in her best trim.

The captain himself settled this knotty point, and if he had enough strength of character he dictated how much cargo his ship could take in. Thus we find Kemball, of *Thermopylæ*, so influencing his agents that the green clipper only loaded 1,196,400 pounds of tea instead of her usual 1,390,000. *Cutty Sark* also took in a lighter load than was her custom, her cargo weighing 1,303,000 pounds—in 1876 she stowed 1,375,364 pounds.

There was the usual race as to which should be first away.

The two clippers lay moored in the tiers off Hongkew, along with *Sir Lancelot*, *Undine*, *Argonaut*, *Doune Castle*, *Taitsing* and *Thyatira*.

As soon as the cargo came down each ship became surrounded by tea lighters, for they were loaded in the stream.

Sweating coolies, standing on stages, rigged along the *Cutty Sark's* black and the *Thermopylæ's* green sides, hove the chests aboard to their mates in the holds amidst a continual sing-song of guttural Chinese chantying.

It was hot, steamy, S.W. monsoon weather, with sharp bursts of rain alternating with a damp fog, so that sail bending was left to the very last moment.

Cutty Sark was the first to finish loading, the last chest being hurled aboard on the afternoon of June 17th. She got under way at 7 p.m., and dropped down as far as Halfway Point, where she had to bring up for the night.

Thermopylæ put the tarpaulins on her hatches some time after dark that same night. The Woosung bar was crossed by both vessels the following morning, *Cutty Sark* being in the lead, and the beautiful *Sir Lancelot*, on her way to load at Foochow, was also in company.

Here was a splendid start for the race home, with the chance of a trial of speed down the coast with *Sir Lancelot*.

But the weather spoilt it all. The wind was blowing at gale strength from the S.E., with heavy rain and thick weather, and by nightfall on the 18th the fog was so thick that the pilots of all three vessels insisted on anchoring close to the lightship.

On the 19th it cleared sufficiently at noon for the racing ships to up anchor, and they were able to drop down the Yangtze estuary for some six or seven miles with the ebb before the fog blotted out every landmark, and they were obliged to anchor again. The same exasperating weather held on the 20th. It cleared for about five hours after noon, when the ships made sail, but they were obliged to anchor again before night.

However, the 21st broke with a clear horizon, and the wind moderate from East to E.N.E. The pilots were dropped, and the clippers made sail. They speedily lost sight of each other in the fog, which came on about noon, and *Cutty Sark* and *Thermopylæ* did not see each other again until 1 p.m. on June 26th, when abreast of Hong Kong.

The wind was then very light from the S.W.; *Thermopylæ* came up on *Cutty Sark's* port quarter.

Both ships hoisted their ensigns, and the excitement aboard each rapidly grew to fever heat.

Captain Moodie, of the *Cutty Sark*, with young Willis, one of his owners, at his elbow, became like a bear with a sore head as he watched the green clipper slowly creeping up abeam.

The *Thermopylæ* was undoubtedly the faster ship in light winds. And this is what one would expect from a comparison of their lines. Of course, the crew of the *Cutty Sark* swore that *Thermopylæ* was holding a better wind—there was no other way of accounting for the fact that the clipper with the golden cock at her main truck was slipping through the lee of their own peerless vessel.

By sundown the *Thermopylæ* was hull down on the *Cutty Sark's* port bow.

It must have been a hectic night in that squally, uncertain monsoon weather. His officers declared that Captain Kemball was so nervy and pernickety that life was hardly worth living aboard the green clipper. And we may be sure that it was no better aboard the *Cutty Sark*.

There is nothing more trying or irritating to the nerves than racing under sail, whether it be in a dinghy, a metre boat, a J-class yacht or a tea clipper. On such occasions of concentrated excitement even the most self-controlled give way to heated words.

The *Cutty Sark* seems to have sailed better at night than she did during the day, or else her officers were more wide-awake than those of the *Thermopylæ*, for when daylight broke on the 27th *Thermopylæ* was once more hull down on the *Cutty's* port quarter.

But once again the *Cutty Sark's* crew had the irritating experience of seeing their rival creeping closer and closer, and what was still harder to bear, eating out to windward.

Both vessels were as close as they would lie on a wind, heading about S. by E., with all plain sail set. It was typical S.W. monsoon weather. Masses of heavy, rain-filled clouds were piled up in the sky like so many mountain ranges.

"Thermopylae" and "Cutty Sark"
in the Tea Race of 1872

Out of these at times came tearing squalls, through which the racing craft had to be carefully luffed, with a tremendous flogging of canvas and clatter of blocks.

Then, after a few minutes, down would come the rain in sheets, and the wind would be snuffed out to a faint air.

It was certainly *Thermopylæ's* weather; and before the end of the afternoon watch she was out on the *Cutty's* starboard bow, six miles to the S.S.W. of her, having come right through her weather.

Thermopylæ was noted for being unusually close-winded, but no one who has ever sailed in the *Cutty Sark* will admit that she could be beaten to windward unless by a fluke.

All through the night of the 28th the wind was light. The following morning the racing ships, with *Thermopylæ* leading, passed to leeward of the Macclesfield shoals; and as soon as the Egeria Bank, the easternmost limit of these reefs, was astern, each ship came round in turn on to the port tack and headed in for the Cochin China coast.

The night of the 29th was almost calm, but on the 30th the wind came away again strong and squally from the S.S.W., " a dead muzzler," and, to the delight of the *Cutty Sark*, when last seen at about noon the *Thermopylæ* bore north.

The two clippers did not meet again until July 15th. *Cutty Sark* was abreast of Direction Island, off the coast of Borneo, when *Thermopylæ* was sighted about eight miles to the N.N.W.

The wind was very light indeed from the eastward, and to the satisfaction of Captain Moodie, and his eager crew, the green clipper not only failed to gain, but slowly dropped astern. However, at daybreak on the 16th she was still in sight astern; and as soon as the racers hauled their wind for the Stolze's Channel, Gaspar Strait, she began to gain steadily, the wind, such as it was, being S.E. and right in their teeth.

The narrow channel was entered early on the 17th, and all day *Cutty Sark* and *Thermopylæ* were beating through with the wind slowly freshening from E.S.E.

Though *Thermopylæ* gained appreciably in the short tacking, she was still well astern when *Cutty Sark* passed Shoalwater Island at 11 p.m.

On the 18th, the wind, though still ahead, was very unsteady, with violent squalls followed by short spells of calm, when the flapping of sails was all that gave the vessels headway.

Cutty Sark was still leading when a slice of bad luck robbed her of the satisfaction of being the first to make her number off Anjer.

A crop of waterspouts, with their attendant whirlwinds, appeared right in her course, and she was compelled to take in sail and run away to leeward. And when she hauled to the wind again, there was her rival nicely placed upon her weather bow.

At 6 a.m. on the 19th *Thermopylæ* ran past Anjer with her number flying, having a lead of one and a half miles from *Cutty Sark*, which hove-to for a couple of hours whilst Captain Moodie went on shore for letters. But the weather in the Sunda Strait was so fluky and baffling, calms alternating with airs all round the compass, that noon on the 20th found the two racers still within three miles of each other.

Thermopylæ was still ahead ; and three miles was a valuable lead when the S.E. trades were expected at any moment.

Thermopylæ dropped *Cutty Sark* below the horizon that night, and the latter did not get the trade until the 26th, when she was abreast of Keeling Cocos Island.

The two clippers saw each other no more, though *Cutty Sark* passed *Thermopylæ* somewhere in the Indian Ocean, the latter again taking the lead when *Cutty Sark* lost her rudder.

The race, owing to this misfortune, ended in the green clipper's favour ; but the honours went to the loser, which, after carrying away her rudder on August 15th in 34.26 S., 28.1 E., and lying hove-to for a whole week whilst a jury-rudder was being fitted, towed up the Thames on October 18th, only just a week astern of her rival.

When Spurling's picture of " Thermopylæ " and " Cutty Sark " (now reproduced) first appeared in " The Blue Peter " some critics objected to one or two details. Taken independently the drawings of the ships are correct. Spurling's picture is so excellent in general treatment that it is well worthy of reproduction.

THE "CALIFORNIA."

THE last sailing ships built by Messrs. Harland & Wolff were the four majestic sisters, *Sindia* and *Holkar*, for Messrs. T. & J. Brocklebank ; *California*, for Messrs. Ismay, Imrie & Co., the owners of the Oceanic Steam Navigation Company, better known as the White Star Line ; and *Lord Templemore*, for the Lord Line of the Irish Shipowners Company, which was managed by Messrs. Thos. Dixon & Sons, of Belfast.

The *California* was launched in April, 1890, in the midst of what came to be called " the four-poster boom," and she was Harland & Wolff's 225th ship.

She was a steel four-mast barque of 3,099 tons gross and 2,991 tons net. Her measurements were : length, 392 feet 3 inches ; breadth, 45 feet 2 inches ; depth, 26 feet 7 inches. Her poop was 38 feet long, and she had a topgallant fo'c'sle 35 feet long.

From the lines plan, which I have reproduced in " The Last of the Windjammers," it will be seen that these four sister ships were typical full-built carriers of the 'nineties, with box-shaped midship sections, but in their handsome appearance all the characteristic hallmarks of Harland & Wolff's designing were preserved, such as a graceful sheer giving a strong hint of power, beautifully modelled ends, raking masts and very effective sail plans.

Though invariably on the moderate side, the spar plans of Harland & Wolff's ships were always most efficient, besides being very taking to the eye.

In the case of these last four ships, lower and topmasts were in one steel tube, divided by the tops at fore, main and mizen into the following two lengths : deck beams to top, 55 feet 6 inches ; top to cross-trees, 41 feet ; making a total of 96 feet 6 inches from deck beams to cross-trees, above which the topgallant mast extended 51 feet, with a pole of 11 feet.

The spike bowsprit stretched 40 feet outside the knightheads, and the yard lengths for fore, main and mizen were : lower yards, 88 feet ; lower topsail yards, 76 feet 6 inches ; upper topsail yards, 68 feet ; lower topgallant yards, 60 feet ; upper topgallant yards, 51 feet 6 inches ; royal yards, 41 feet.

When the *California* came out, Ismay, Imrie & Co.'s sailing fleet consisted of the lordly *Garfield*, considered by many to have been the finest full-rigger ever launched ; the Whitehaven-built four-poster *Gilcruix ; Dawpool*, sister ship of Beazley's *British Merchant ;* the two lovely steel barques, *Callao* and *Santiago ;* the full-rigger *Copley ;* and three old Mersey-built ships, *Hoghton Tower, Castlehead* and *Esmeralda*.

The smaller vessels of the fleet were engaged in the West Coast trade, whilst the larger sought homeward cargoes of Indian jute or Californian grain. During her short existence under the White Star flag, the *California* was one of the great fleet which assembled at San Francisco in the 'nineties in order to load wheat and barley for the United Kingdom or the Continent.

She has been dubbed by John Masefield : " The *California* huge, as slow as Time," but, as a matter of fact, like all Harland & Wolff's designs, she could do excellent work under conditions that suited her, and her records in the grain trade showed a very steady average, as, for instance :

> 1890   Liverpool to San Francisco—130 days.
> 1891   San Francisco to Liverpool—121 days.
> 1892   Newcastle, N.S.W., to San Francisco—53 days.
> 1894/5 San Francisco to Liverpool—130 days.

On this last passage she had the honour of showing her paces against the *Cutty Sark.* I find the incident recorded in the personal log of the late Captain Woodget, as follows :

" Feb. 28, 1895.   Gentle Easterly breeze and fine.   Noon, Lat. 0.55 S., Long. 31.18 W.   Course N. 11 E.   Distance 98 miles.   Passed and spoke the 4-mast barque *California,* 2,991 tons, from San Francisco, photographed the ship."

On her run up the Atlantic, besides the *California,* the *Cutty Sark* passed the following vessels : *Lady Wolseley, Pass of Killiecrankie, Flintshire, Knight of St. Michael's, Dawpool* and *Earl of Dalhousie.*   In spite of very ragged, worn copper, the *Cutty Sark* easily outdistanced every one of these ships ; and out of them all, the *California* made by far the best showing against her, being only beaten to the mouth of the Channel by a day or two—*Cutty Sark* making the Start on March 24th and docking in London on the 26th, only two days before the *California* reached the Mersey.

The first commander of the *California* was T. Dickinson, and he was succeeded, in 1892, by Captain J. Blair.

The boom in sail tonnage which raged between 1888 and 1892 soon resulted in a depression in sail freights, caused by over-building, and amongst the many owners who decided to sell their sailing ships through this cause, were Messrs. Ismay, Imrie & Co.

The *California* was sold to Messrs. Ritson & Livesey, of Liverpool, in 1896, but a year later their manager, Harold A. Sanderson, sold her to Sloman, of Hamburg.

The Germans were quick enough to buy British tonnage directly the price cheapened, and the *California,* under the name of *Alster,* became the name ship of a fleet which consisted almost entirely of ex-Britishers, including *California's* sister ship, *Lord Templemore.*

Amongst these were :

Alsterkamp	*ex Flotow*
Alsterschwan	*ex Alcedo*
Alsterufer	*ex North Star*
Alsterfee	*ex Oranasia*
Alsterdamm	*ex Somali*

The *Lord Templemore* was renamed *Alsternixe.*   In November, 1906, she left Callao for Melbourne in ballast, and was posted as missing.

In 1912 the whole of the Alster fleet was bought by E. C. Schramm & Co., and formed the nucleus of the Vinnen fleet, which at the outbreak of the war consisted of the following :

Christel Vinnen	*ex Alster*	*ex California*
Adolf Vinnen	*ex Alsterdamm*	*ex Somali*
Albertus Vinnen	*ex Alsterthal*	*ex Othmarschen*
Arnoldus Vinnen	*ex Alsterkamp*	*ex Flotow*
Berthold Vinnen	*ex Alsterschwan*	*ex Alcedo*
Carl Rudgert Vinnen	*ex Dunfermline*	
Helwig Vinnen	*ex Persimmon*	*ex Drumrock*
J. C. Vinnen	*ex Osborne*	
Lucy Vinnen	*ex Alsterfee*	*ex Oranasia*
Magdalene Vinnen	*ex Dunstaffnage*	
Susanne Vinnen	*ex Alsterufer*	*ex North Star*
Werner Vinnen	*ex Forteviot*	

"California"
Built 1890 General Trader.

The onset of the war found the *Christel Vinnen, ex California*, in Valparaiso, where she was interned. The crews of most of the German ships caught in this way did their best to wreck their vessels alow and aloft, and those aboard the *Christel Vinnen* were very thorough in this work of destruction.

At the Peace she was allocated to the Italians, but they made no attempt to refit her for service.

At last, in 1926, she changed hands and, under Captain T. H. Kirkwood, was given a complete overhaul, afterwards loading 5,000 tons of nitrate at Caleta Coloso for Norfolk, Virginia. After she had sailed from the nitrate port on January 10th, 1927, nothing further was heard of her for 77 days, 10 guineas per cent being paid. However, she reached Panama on March 28th all safe and sound, and was towed through the Canal at a total cost of 4,302 dollars, her actual Canal dues being 3,476.40 dollars.

She sailed from Colon on April 11th, and on April 15th stranded on the Island of Old Providence, where she was abandoned to the underwriters, and became a total loss.

The *California* was the last survivor of the four Harland & Wolff sisters. *Sindia*, when homeward bound from Kobe, Japan, to New York, was piled up on the beach at Ocean City, New Jersey, during a blizzard at the end of December, 1901.

Lord Templemore, as already recorded, was lost in 1906, and the *Holkar*, after being renamed *Souverain*, *Odessa* and, finally, *Hippalos*, was broken up in the summer of 1924, her last passage being from Melbourne to Havre.

THE "TAMAR."

AT the beginning of the last great sailing-ship boom in 1889, when so many sailing-ship owners were being induced to go in for the cheaply-built Clyde four-poster, the aristocratic Blackwall firm of Devitt & Moore asked Messrs. Napier, Shanks & Bell to build them a steel, full-rigged ship which should be worthy of all the great traditions of the London River.

The result was that handsome ship, the *Tamar*, of 2,112 tons gross register. British shipowners of the last fifty years have rather prided themselves on not being influenced by sentiment or conservatism, hence some very ugly seagoing craft, which are a constant offence to the eyes of old seamen, but in the building of *Tamar* that experienced shipowner, Sir Thomas Devitt, does seem to have bowed his head, if not to sentiment, at least to old conventions.

Men who had seen the zenith of wood and iron shipbuilding and cared for the sailing ship as a work of art and beauty, were very slow in sacrificing appearance to expediency, perfection of build to economy and " Blackwall fashion " to the merciless " pound and pint."

Though Sir Thomas could not but admit the economy of big tonnage, he was by no means enamoured of the new box-like, jerry-built, steel four-poster, as the four-mast barque of the Clyde was contemptuously called, nor was it recognized in the boom year of 1889 that the three-masted full-rigger of over 2,000 tons was not going to be a good dividend earner.

Owners, indeed, were very slow to realize some of the drawbacks in the big three-master of over 2,000 tons.

For one thing their masts were too far apart, necessitating tremendous yards if the drift between was to be filled up by canvas. Then with such huge yards their circumference was so great that ordinary-sized seamen, even with very short-stirruped foot-ropes, could not reach over them to pick up the sail. For this reason big full-riggers were decidedly unpopular with foremast hands.

And as a rule they were heavy working ships, requiring more hands than four-masters of the same tonnage.

Nevertheless, they always possessed one great attraction—they were a delight to everyone with a sailor's eye.

*   *   *

The *Tamar* was launched at Yoker, Dumbarton, in June, 1889. Her classification was, of course, 100 A1, and she retained this until her end at the ship-breakers.

Her registered dimensions were: length, 286 feet 6 inches; breadth, 42 feet 5 inches; depth, 24 feet. When fully loaded her freeboard amidships was 5 feet 7½ inches. She had the short poop—33 feet—of the general carrier and her forecastle head was 42 feet in length.

In her sail plan *Tamar* crossed six yards on each mast, royals over double topgallants.

At the date of her launch Messrs. Devitt & Moore's fleet consisted of the three famous cadet ships, *Macquarie, Hesperus* and *Illawarra,* and the *Derwent,* all of which are to be found in previous volumes of " Sail."

Tamar was not the first ship of her name to be loaded by Devitt & Moore in the Australian trade. Between 1846 and 1862 there was a smart little 500-ton wood barque of that name, for which they acted as brokers.

Nor must this big steel full-rigger be confused with the troop-ship of the same name, which was barque-rigged with a big sail plan and, after many years of carrying troops (1863 to 1894), became a depot ship at Hong Kong.

Tamar's first commander was Captain J. R. Brown, who had her until 1896. Though intended for the London General and Australian wool trade, *Tamar* was too full-built to be able to equal the passages of the famous iron wool clippers, and she needed strong fair winds in order to make a good passage.

Her best under Captain Brown, both outward and homeward, were made in 1895.

On March 15th, 1895, she made the Scillies 84 days out from Sydney, and on her next outward trip she reached Adelaide on August 16th, 77 days from Barry.

In 1896 Captain H. N. Forbes succeeded to the command. His best wool passage was made in the following year, when he passed St. Catherine's Lighthouse, Isle of Wight, 87 days out from Sydney with 7,428 bales of wool. The best passage that year was *Samuel Plimsoll's* 78 days from Sydney to the Lizard.

Captain Forbes, who had trained many a young officer in the old *Harbinger,* continued his good work in the *Tamar,* and many a fine present-day commander has to thank Captain Forbes and the *Tamar* for his success in life ; nor must we forget that the late Mr. Spurling served his time aboard her.

In the last years of the 19th century the Australian trade was one of cut freights and severe competition ; with steamers breaking into even such favoured sailing-ship lines as wool, wheat and coal ; we thus find Captain Forbes actually loading coal at Newcastle, N.S.W., in 1898, for San Francisco. However, he had the satisfaction of making the best trans-Pacific passage of the year out of a fleet which numbered, perhaps, over fifty ships. The *Tamar* arrived San Francisco on February 8th, only 51 days out.

In 1900 Mr. T. A. Shute, of Liverpool, bought the *Tamar* and sent her out to the West Coast of South America, under Captain J. C. Amberman. In 1903/4 the big full-rigger had a great race from the Tyne out round the Horn to the West coast against the four-mast barque *Endora,* considered the fastest vessel in Shute's fleet.

The *Tamar* was the first away. She passed Dover on November 24th, whilst *Endora* was off the Eddystone at 10.30 p.m. on November 30th. The latter ship made a very exceptional passage. On her 42nd day out she was off the Horn, and she reached Coquimbo on January 27th, only 57 days 16 hours out.

Tamar, with further to go, arrived at Callao, 68 days out from Dover, which was a very fine passage, though unfortunately put in the shade by *Endora's* record one.

It was on her very next voyage that the *Tamar* had one of those adventures which were more common in the days of sail than in the more hustling, less lonesome days of steam.

She sailed from Hamburg bound on the long, hard passage round the Horn and up the Pacific to Seattle. In the Channel she was making good time, when her new captain appeared on deck, mad with drink, and, suddenly drawing a revolver, fired without any warning at the helmsman, an able seaman named Albert Whitley. It was the mate's watch

"Tamar"
Built 1889 Australian Trader.

below, and about two in the afternoon, but the noise of shooting and furious language brought Mr. Madsen, the mate, on deck in double-quick time. It was at once perceived that the captain was so drunk that he could scarcely keep erect.

The two mates, in this difficult situation, did their best to humour their commander, but nothing could prevent him from altering the course of the ship more to the southward, with the result that as soon as it was dark the mate was scarcely surprised to see what he took to be the Vierge Light, near Ushant, over the port bow.

To be sure that he had made no mistake, the mate went into the chart-house and asked the captain if he might see the light book.

It was about 5.30 p.m. and, seeing the state of his skipper, Mr. Madsen, having verified his suspicion, reported that the flashing light seen was the Vierge and that the ship was heading straight for the rocks. At this the drunken man first of all tore up the light book and other navigation books and then, again drawing his revolver, swore he would shoot if the mate attempted to alter the course.

The ship swept on, heading straight for the shore, with all hands standing irresolute and the helmsman with one eye on the skipper, ready to dodge a bullet.

When the ship was within two miles of the rocks the mate plucked up courage and begged the captain to alter the course before it was too late. " I will shoot you if you interfere with the management of the ship. The whole ship can go to the bottom. I am responsible here," roared the drunken man ; then, raising his pistol, fired directly at the mate. The bullet whistled past the latter's ear ; but it put the mate's blood up and saved the ship.

After a little trouble the captain was overpowered and clapped in irons, whilst the course was altered just in time to take the *Tamar* out of danger. She was then headed back to Plymouth, where the Magistrates had to deal with the case.

Captain J. H. Hughes then had the *Tamar* for a voyage, and following him came Captain G. N. Rogers, who was eight years in the ship, during which time a very steady average was made, the *Tamar's* usual voyage being out to Chile with Welsh coal and home with nitrate.

The War took great toll of British sailing ships, both deep-water and coasting, but *Tamar* was one of the lucky ones which escaped ; indeed, she was the last of Shute's fleet, her old rival, the *Endora*, being sunk by the German submarine U 83 on February 14th, 1917, when 30 miles S.S.W of the Fastnets.

Captains Mahoney and Auld had her through the War. Right at the end of the War the old ship arrived out in Sydney, N.S.W.

Whilst running her easting down she had been badly pooped, and Captain Auld was washed off the poop. He was picked up under the forecastle-head when the water ran off and, though alive, it was found that both his legs were broken.

With his master condemned to hospital for some months, Mr. Thomas Shute had to find someone in Australia who would sail his ship home. One of his old employees, Captain James P. Barker, an ex-captain of the famous *British Isles*, who had " swallowed the anchor " in order to go into the Newcastle pilotage service, was found willing to take over the command, being anxious to get back to the Old Country with his family.

After her rough experience in the Westerlies it was found necessary to give the *Tamar* a thorough refit, including a new main lower mast. She next loaded a cargo of wheat. In the year after the War the wheat fleet was not confined to the ships of that enterprising Finn, Captain Gustav Erikson, and there were still a few British sailing ships taking advantage of the short boom, which was so soon to give way to black depression.

The previous ship on the loading berth had been the Shire liner, *Elginshire*, commanded by the well-known Captain C. C. Dixon. She sailed a fortnight ahead of the *Tamar*, both ships being bound to Queenstown for orders.

The latter towed through the Heads on June 18th, 1919, and rounded the Horn on July 30th, with a run of 250 miles. At 2 p.m. that afternoon the wind came ahead, and the *Tamar* was 60 miles South of the Diego Ramirez Rocks at 4 p.m. The usual Cape Horn weather was encountered—strong winds with snow and sleet showers ; short, dark, gloomy days ; the deck-houses waterlogged ; all clothing sodden ; the men worn out ; sea-cuts and salt-water boils, bruises and sprains, the lot of all hands ; and the ship most of the time under short canvas. The worst day seems to have been August 7th. Daybreak found the ship rolling along at 12 knots before a gigantic sea—the chasing greybeards being estimated by Captain Barker to raise their foaming crests from 50 to 60 feet about the trough, which lay like a valley on either side of each long ridge of water. At 7 a.m. the ship was hove-to, and as her head came round she lay down with the huge seas breaking all over her. There were the usual casualties from the raging flood which poured aboard—the cook and an A.B. were nearly drowned, one apprentice sprained his ankle, another was severely bruised and cut about (there were five boys serving their time in the half-deck), and hardly a man escaped scot-free from the ordeal. But the *Tamar* put up a good fight, and at 10 a.m. Captain Barker went below after having been over fifty hours on deck.

The old ship had a companion during this strenuous time—a sperm-whale, which, while she hurtled along before the wind at an easy 12 knots, kept up with her without any apparent difficulty ; and, when she was hove-to, remained under her lee, not more than 100 yards away. It is probable that the whale took the ship for one of her own kind.

The south-east trades were taken on August 20th and the Line crossed a week later. The old sail trade routes in these days are empty of ships, and it was not until September 7th that the *Tamar* encountered her first vessel—this was the American five-mast auxiliary schooner *Cora F. Cressy*.

The very next day, with the wind very light, great excitement was caused by a white shaft on the horizon astern, which soon resolved itself into a square-rigged ship bringing up the wind. By 1 p.m. she was near enough to be recognized—she was the *Elginshire*, lying over on the starboard tack, going a good 11 knots with everything drawing. By six bells in the afternoon watch she was less than a mile away on the *Tamar*'s port quarter, and the usual flag conversation took place.

Captain Dixon was evidently not too pleased at being overhauled by the *Tamar*, which had sailed a fortnight after the *Elginshire*, and he was carrying sail, though the weather was very squally ; in fact, just as the four-master drew abeam of the full-rigger, her main royal sheet carried away, and the chuckling crew of the *Tamar* watched *Elginshire*'s royal blow to ribbons. During the night a shift of wind in *Tamar*'s favour robbed the *Elginshire* of her position in the lead and the two wheat ships slowly drew apart until the horizon separated them.

September 27th found the *Tamar* becalmed in a fog surrounded by thousands of jelly-fish. That night the south-west wind came away strong and sent the ship rolling and pitching towards Queenstown at the rate of 14 knots. The wind held, and during the night of October 3rd the light on the Old Head of Kinsale was made right ahead, and by daybreak the *Tamar* was lying at anchor off Queenstown.

As the light spread, every eye looked eagerly round the anchorage to see if the *Elginshire* had arrived ; and, sure enough, there she was inside the *Tamar*, being towed into the harbour.

She had apparently been inshore of the *Tamar* and anchored just two hours ahead of her.

When the orders came off it was learnt that *Elginshire* was to proceed to Liverpool and *Tamar* to Sharpness. The passage was not to end without one last excitement. Early on the morning of October 9th, when in tow of a tug, the *Tamar* collided with a steamer. Luckily it was only a glancing blow, which buckled the bowsprit and spoilt some of the new paint, but at one moment things looked very serious aboard the helpless sailing ship.

The captain roared out an order to let go the tow-line. His family was swung out in the port life-boat, as the towering hull of the steamship *Mercedes de Larinaga* seemed about to sink the *Tamar,* and for a few moments it was feared that the sailing ship had been holed below water.

However, when the excitement died down, the tow-rope was picked up again, and at 9.45 p.m. on October 10th the *Tamar* was tied up at Sharpness alongside a grain elevator.

The old ship was soon overwhelmed by the post-war shipping slump, and in October, 1921, she was laid up amongst a large fleet of idle sailing ships at Bordeaux.

On May 22nd, 1923, the well-known Dutch tug, *Roode Zee,* appeared at Bordeaux and took the *Tamar* off to Holland, where she was broken up at Hendrik Ido Ambacht in the same year.

THE " STAR OF INDIA."

LLOYD'S Register shows three well-known ships under the name of *Star of India*. The last of these, however, was the old New Zealand trader, *Euterpe*, renamed by the Alaska Packers' Association. She was an iron vessel of 1,197 tons, built at Ramsey Bay, Isle of Man, in 1863, and notorious as being the slowest sailer in Shaw Savill's fleet. In the 'nineties she was bought by the Chilians, and from them she went to San Francisco to form one of the salmon canners' fleet. At the present date I hear she is moored in an artificial lake at San Diego as a show ship, an historic relic of the past glories of the sea, something to rouse wonder in the breasts of small boys and a heartache in old seamen.

The other two *Stars of India* were both launched in the same year, 1861. The larger of the two was a big New Brunswick-built full-rigger of 1,697 tons, which found her way to Liverpool and the ownership of W. Herron. This *Star of India* possessed a very unenviable reputation amongst seamen, for she was commanded for a time by the notorious Captain Bailey, about the hardest bucko and most unpopular skipper under the red ensign during the 'seventies and 'eighties.

He was murdered in the end by his own much-abused steward—a coloured man, who got off with a life sentence, chiefly owing to the testimony of the murdered man's own wife and daughter—which added to his terrible reputation.

We now come to the third *Star of India*, the subject of Mr. Spurling's picture. There is no doubt that this *Star of India* was by far the finest of the three ships, the best built and the fastest sailer.

Launched in July, 1861, from the well-known yard of Stephen at Dundee, she was frigate-built, a superb wooden passenger ship intended for the first-class Indian trade, where she at once took her place amongst the famous Blackwallers.

Her owner, Joseph Somes, was one of the biggest and most successful shipowners of the first half of the 19th century. He began his career as an India husband, that is to say, he owned East Indiamen, which were taken up and employed by the Honourable East India Company.

He must have been a most remarkable man in an era of remarkable shipping men, such as Sir Robert Wigram and George Green, partners in the ownership of the ancient Blackwall yard.

Sir Robert Wigram was a veritable city patriarch, the father of twenty-four children, who rode from his shipyard to his brewery and from his brewery to his rope-walk, surrounded by an escort of never less than seven sons. George Green, whose proudest boast was that he once buckled on King George III's spurs, is said to have been the origin of Hogarth's model apprentice.

These two men were the shipping rivals of Somes's youth. Then came Dicky Green, the East End philanthropist, and Money Wigram, their sons and successors, and the great

Duncan Dunbar, one of the builders of the Australian Commonwealth ; Smith of Newcastle, owner of the famous *Hotspur ;* John Willis, father of the owner of the *Cutty Sark ;* George Thompson, of the Aberdeen White Star Line of clippers ; Anderson of the Orient Line ; and George Marshall, of Marshall & Sons.

All these men were rivals of Joseph Somes in the London trade, which boasted the pick of the world's Mercantile Marine.   But Somes did not confine his energies to the first-class passenger trade.   He launched out in every direction, and his services to the Government were so valuable that he was granted the privilege of flying a special house-flag, which only differed from the white ensign in having an anchor in the canton instead of a Union Jack.

In the early years of the century, back in the war-time, he owned South Sea whalers, such as the *Perseverance*, built in Quebec in 1801, and a number of apple-cheeked West India sugar droghers.   Later, in the 'thirties and 'forties, he practically had the transporting of convicts to the Antipodes in his own hands.   His convict ships, which were lumbering, slow coaches, registering no more than 700 tons, but specially built for the purpose, were chartered by the Government at from five to seven pounds per ton per voyage.

When the H.E.I.C. charters expired, Joseph Somes bought the pick of their ships—such superb Indiamen as the *Earl of Balcarres, Thomas Coutts, Lowther Castle, George the Fourth, Abercrombie, Robinson* and *Java*.   This last, by the way, is still to be seen swinging to her moorings among the coal hulks at Gibraltar.

These big East Indiamen were replaced in course of time by a succession of smaller ships, such as the *Europa*, launched in the Thames in 1851 ; *Merchantman*, a Sunderland-built ship ; *Canning*, built at Moulmein ; *Eastern Monarch*, the pride of his fleet, which was built at Dundee in 1856 and burnt at Spithead, when just arrived home with troops in 1859 ; *Tyburnia*, Glasgow-built, a very well-known ship in her day ; *Dartmouth*, built by Stephen in 1859, and the *Peeress*, built the same year at Sunderland.

Then, in 1861, the *Star of India* was added to the fleet.   She was built of ten and twelve years' material and classed fourteen years A1.   Her registered tonnage was 1,102 gross and 1,045 net ; whilst her measurements were : length, 190 feet 4 inches ; breadth, 34 feet 2 inches, and depth of hold, 22 feet 1 inch.

In appearance the *Star of India* was a typical Blackwaller, with built-out quarter-galleries, big stern windows, long poop, and much-cluttered-up main-deck.

Her plain sail area was a moderate one, but large stunsails and other flying kites added a knot and a half to two knots to her speed in favouring winds.

It is not generally realized how heavily a ship's canvas was curtailed when stunsails were done away with.   Stunsail-booms in the Blackwall frigates, both on fore and main topsail and lower yards, were quite half the length of the yards themselves, thus, when stunsails were set on either side, it was like doubling the size of the sail itself.

The *Star of India* was, of course, painted Blackwall fashion, black topsides and white strake, black masts and spars, except for white lowermasts, bowsprit, boom and gaff and doublings.   This was strictly in imitation of the Royal Navy, and the boats also were painted Navy fashion, black topsides and white bottom.

This fashion was carried on, after it had been abandoned in the Navy and the Merchant service, by a few conservative members of the Royal Yacht Squadron.   No fashion of paint ever looked smarter or more seamanlike.

On her maiden voyage the *Star of India* sailed for Calcutta direct from Dundee, under the command of Captain H. Morris.

"Star of India"
Built 1861 Blackwall Passenger Ship

Her best-known commander, however, was Captain C. Holloway, who had her for over ten years. With the opening of the Suez Canal, most of the Blackwall passenger ships, which had been carrying passengers and troops to India and back, round the Cape, were driven out of the trade by the P. & O. steamers using the Canal. Luckily for their owners, the beginning of the 'seventies found the Australian and New Zealand emigrant trade booming, and most of the London passenger ships were at once transferred to this run.

It is a curious fact that the strict discipline and Blackwall fashion of carrying on, which was such a characteristic of the Indian trade, was soon slackened, if not entirely relaxed, when the ships were sent out to the more democratic and easy-going Colonies. The lordliness and swagger of the Blackwall frigates gradually fell away from them. Midshipmen wearing brass buttons, stationed at the gangway of a Blackwaller in a Colonial port, had to put up with the ribald jests and scornful jeers of disreputable apprentices in well-patched dungarees aboard the neighbouring wool clippers of the Aberdeen, Glasgow Loch, and other lines. And encounters ashore between the Blackwallers and the North Country crews of the Aberdeen, Liverpool and Clyde ships were only equalled by their combined warfare against the waterside larrikins.

It was a happy, care-free life for man and boy in the Colonial trade of the 'seventies and 'eighties, and the finest ships in the world thronged the ports of Sydney, Melbourne and Adelaide.

After two or three voyages to Australia, Captain Holloway found himself, in the autumn of 1873, under charter to the Shaw Savill Company. At this date the *Star of India* was owned by the Merchant Shipping Company, the successors of old Joseph Somes and his sons. Somes, along with his chief rivals, Dicky Green and Duncan Dunbar, had died in the early 'sixties. For a short while the firm registered as " Somes Brothers " before changing its name to the impersonal Merchant Shipping Company.

On her first New Zealand voyage the *Star of India* sailed from London for Lyttelton on September 26th, 1873, with three hundred passengers in her 'tween-decks, consisting, according to one of them, of a very mixed lot of English, Irish, Scots, Swedes, Danes, Germans, and even Poles and Russians. Most of these emigrants had never seen blue water before, and when the ship ran into the usual gale in the Bay of Biscay, sea-sickness and fright added to the home-sickness of the passengers. Wives blamed their husbands for their miseries ; the husbands, I fear, too often replied with bad temper. The Cockneys swore in lurid Billingsgate, cursing themselves for being such fools as to leave dear old London ; the Paddys told their beads and looked at the pig-pens with tear-filled eyes, whilst the Northerners submitted to every discomfort with the hardihood of Vikings.

Then, with the coming of fine weather, happiness began to reign aboard. The women brought their sewing up on deck ; the men began to gamble in small groups in corners sheltered from the wind—pitch-penny was a favourite game—I doubt if " crown and anchor " or " house " had been invented at that date.

The chief excitement of the passage was an encounter with a ship on fire in the South Atlantic. This was the *Isabella Kerr*, bound from England to Calcutta with coal.

She was not only on fire, but she was short of food and water, added to which her captain was ill. The two ships sailed in company till abreast of the Cape, though the *Isabella Kerr* had to lower her topgallant sails or she would soon have run ahead of the *Star of India*, for she was a very fast ship. Captain Holloway and his doctor went off to the burning ship, and she was also supplied with provisions and water.

When the two ships parted company, the fire had been smothered, but it broke out again in the Indian Ocean, and the fine clipper had to be abandoned, her crew being taken off by a tea ship.

Meanwhile the *Star of India* continued her way to New Zealand and reached Lyttelton on January 1st, 1874, 97 days out from the London River.

In these days, such a trip, with its long days and rough nights, would be viewed with horror by the average traveller, yet most old Colonials have a very soft place in their hearts for the sailing ships which carried them out to the Land of Promise.

One of the passengers aboard the *Star of India* on this trip records that many of the women shed tears as they left the smart Blackwaller for the shore.   Most Blackwallers were happy ships, and the *Star of India* was no exception.

The following voyage she again took out some three hundred emigrants to New Zealand. This time she sailed from London on July 31st, 1874, and reached Wellington on November 10th, 1874, a passage of 102 days.   This trip was without incident, except for one of those tragedies which are generally due to drink.   One of the emigrants, in what is described as a fit of dementia, seized his child and leaped overboard.   Both were drowned before a boat could reach them.

After a steady, successful life under the red ensign, the *Star of India* was sold in the 'eighties to Captain Michelsen, of Sandefjord, and for the next half-dozen years she voyaged to and fro across the Atlantic barque-rigged and timber laden.

She eventually went the way of so many of the old British wooden ships which were forced in their old age to earn a hard living under Norwegian colours and a windmill pump, ferrying lumber across the stormy Atlantic.

Star of India was abandoned in mid-Atlantic in 1892, but she remained afloat for some time, being sighted to the South of the Line by the barque *Criffel*, which was bound out to Iquique from Cardiff.

No sadder end can be imagined for a fine ship than to become a derelict, drifting on the ocean currents, a lonely object, garbed in weed and tatters, helpless yet menacing, a terror to her sisters, until, at long last, the day comes when a slow dive to Davy Jones's locker spells " Finis."

THE "BRITISH MERCHANT."

B ETWEEN February, 1877, and August, 1880, Messrs. Harland & Wolff launched nine of the finest and fastest sailing ships ever built in the British Isles. These, taking them in their launching order, were : *Slieve More, Slieve Bawn, Star of Italy, Star of France, Slieve Roe, G. W. Wolff, Lord Dufferin, Dawpool* and *British Merchant.* Sinclair's *Slieves* and Lawther's *G. W. Wolff* were exact sister ships in their lines and sail plans. Corry's two *Stars* were just 100 tons smaller, owing to being given 3 inches less beam and 5 inches less draught. Then came *Lord Dufferin, Dawpool* and *British Merchant,* 30 tons larger than the *Slieves,* with 5 feet 8 inches more length and 2 inches more depth on the same beam and sail plan.

The last of this magnificent fleet, the *British Merchant,* was built to the order of that well-known and much respected Liverpool shipowner, James Beazley, who was managing director of the British Shipowners Company.

In August, 1880, when the *British Merchant* was launched, the Company's fleet consisted of seventeen iron ships, headed by the 1,800-tonners *British Ambassador* and *British General.* The line was noted not only for good management, but for liberal treatment ; thus there was great competition amongst officers, and also amongst foremast hands, to serve in these ships, where kind and just treatment and good food were the invariable rule.

James Beazley had only once previously had a ship built by Harland & Wolff, and this was the 1,230-ton *British Peer,* launched in 1865, which was noted for her speed. Unfortunately, Mr. Beazley decided to lengthen her in 1876, and this spoilt her.

There was one other Harland & Wolff vessel amongst the fleet, the *Lady Cairns,* which had been launched in 1869, and was bought by Beazley in 1873. She was also a very fast ship. Others of the fleet had also no mean reputation for speed, such as the *British Ambassador.* Thus the advent of the *British Merchant* from the famous Belfast yard was of very great interest to the British captains.

Before turning to her performances, I must give her measurements. Her registered tonnage was 1,742 tons gross, 1,698 net, length 262 feet 9 inches, breadth 38 feet 3 inches, depth 23 feet 3 inches. As regards her sail plan, she had the old-fashioned bowsprit and jib-boom, extending 65 feet outside the knightheads, fore and main lower and topmasts in one, fore and main lower yards 87 feet 11 inches, lower topsail 78 feet 6 inches, upper topsail 71 feet 6 inches, topgallant sail 54 feet and royal 40 feet. This sail plan was the same as that of the *Slieves,* except that there were no stunsails provided.

Captain Edward John Molony, who had previously had the *British Commodore* and the *British Statesman,* was given the command of Beazley's new crack. On her maiden voyage the *British Merchant* sailed from Liverpool on November 3rd, bound for Melbourne. On the second day out the weather set in dirty and thick from the south-west, and during the night of the 7th, when in 50° 7′ N., 12° 9′ W., the *British Merchant* lost her bowsprit in collision with the German ship *Marguerite*. Luckily, no other damage was done, and the ship was able to proceed, but with the wind strong at S.W. and the sea rough, it was some days before a jury-spar could be fixed, and this gave the ship a poor run to the Equator, which was not crossed until December 2nd. The rest of the passage passed more or less uneventfully, though a man was lost overboard whilst running the easting down. With a jury-rig forward, Captain Molony had to be careful, and his best run was only 290 miles, made the day before the ship passed Cape Otway.

The *British Merchant* entered Port Phillip Heads at 2 a.m. on January 22nd, 79 days out from Liverpool. Captain Molony's comment on this passage was as follows :

" Taking into account the fact of losing the bowsprit and the S.W. winds in the North Atlantic, with not particularly good winds afterwards, the ship would have made a long passage if she had not been a remarkably good sailer."

After discharging at Melbourne the *British Merchant* loaded coal at Newcastle, N.S.W., for San Francisco, and sailing on March 15th, 1881, made the run across the Pacific in 57 days. This also was a fine performance, for she had insistent easterly winds for the first week, so Captain Molony kept her away north and passed between Fiji and New Caledonia. The trade carried her to 15° S., but then she had a fortnight of calms up to the Line, and Captain Molony wrote :

" A slow ship would have a very hard time crossing this belt. I would not take this passage except driven to it by steady easterly breezes after leaving the Australian coast."

At San Francisco the *British Merchant* loaded wheat and made the run home round the Horn to Queenstown in 101 days. From September 6th, in lat. 29° 16′ N., long. 37° 25′ W., *British Merchant* was in company with the smart Dale liner, *Borrowdale*, for six days, and again fell in with her on the 18th, the two ships arriving Queenstown within a few hours of each other.

This maiden voyage was a very satisfactory one in every way, the ship proving herself to be everything that was expected of her. Her outward cargo by weight and measurement totalled 3,557 tons. She crossed the Pacific with 2,560 tons of coal and 700 tons of ballast, and brought home from San Francisco 2,560 tons of wheat.

On her second voyage the *British Merchant* went out to Calcutta, making the run from the Tuskar to the Sandheads in 93 days. This was a fine performance, and she beat several well-known wool clippers, though Captain Molony records in his abstract :

" Was passed by the *Juno* at the Sandheads, the first ship that has passed the *British Merchant*."

This *Juno* was a 1,500-ton iron ship belonging to J. Steele, of Liverpool.

On this passage, whilst running her easting down, the *British Merchant* made a run of 330 miles in 40° S., 74° E., and another of 300 miles in 37° 42′ S., 85° 50′ E.

Loading jute in Calcutta the *British Merchant* had a very interesting race home with Corry's *Star of Italy*. The two ships left the Sandheads together on March 16th, and, with light winds and calms down the Bay of Bengal, were in company for a fortnight—" neither ship having the advantage in light winds." The Equator was crossed on April 5th, and from the 17th to the 22nd April the *British Merchant* made the following runs in the S.E. trades : 304, 272, 239, 224 and 288. In 44° E. *British Merchant* caught the usual sudden shift in a heavy squall from S.S.E. to W.S.W., which resulted in a strong westerly gale. The following day she fell in with the *Star of Italy* again, but in the fresh breeze the latter had the best of it, though she was carrying less sail. Then on May 13th, in 34° 5′ S., 26° 19′ E., the two ships were again in company for forty-eight hours. A fortnight later, in 15° 19′ S., 5° 48′ E., they spent another forty-eight hours in company.

"British Merchant"
Built 1880 General Trader.

Finally, they met in the Channel and had a last desperate race, in which the *Star of Italy* managed to reach Gravesend three hours ahead.

With unfavourable weather the passage of 112 days was not a bad one, though it must be confessed that it was the longest jute passage ever made by the *Star of Italy*.

On her third voyage, in 1882–3, the *British Merchant* made her first passage outwards round the Horn. After experiencing a pampero and the usual head gales off Cape Stiff, the Farallones were sighted at 4 a.m. on November 29th, and the anchor dropped in San Francisco Bay at 6 p.m., 114 days out, the ship having sailed 16,118 miles at an average of 141.3 per day, or six miles per hour.

On her homeward passage the *British Merchant* made one of the quickest runs of her career, and beat the famous *Thessalus*, which had the reputation of being one of the fastest sailing ships in the British Mercantile Marine. The *Thessalus* sailed from San Francisco on January 10th, and was followed by the *British Merchant* on January 21st. The latter crossed the Line on February 5th, 15 days out, and from February 24th, when she was in 46° 10' S., 131° W., to March 8th, when she was in 51° 53' S., 51° 28' W., the *British Merchant* made the following steady average : 275, 272, 270, 266, 255, 256, 244, 256, 234, 242, 224, 269.

On March 4th, in 77° W., a W.S.W. gale commenced, which carried the *British Merchant* round the Horn, but tried both her and her crew to the limit. On March 6th, when off the Horn, the sea was tremendous, with hurricane squalls out of the W.N.W. The *British Merchant* lost her bulwarks, her boats and one man washed overboard. Captain Molony, in his abstract, writes :

" Several other vessels met with disaster in this same gale, and more than one foundered."

The *Thessalus* was amongst these vessels, and also received a severe hammering.

On March 13th the *British Merchant* weathered out a sudden south-west gale, which for a couple of hours blew with hurricane force. This, however, carried the ship into the S.E. trades, and she crossed the Equator on March 29th. *British Merchant* was off the Fastnet at 8 a.m. on April 21st, when only 90 days out. Unfortunately she had to stand off for a hard south-east and east gale, and did not pass the Saltees Light till 1 p.m. on April 25th. She had covered 16,872 miles in 95 days, averaging 177 miles per day, or 7.4 knots. This, at that date, was the quickest passage recorded between San Francisco and Liverpool. The *Thessalus*, it is interesting to note, was off the Lizard on April 25th, and after a hard beat up-Channel anchored off Gravesend on the 29th, her passage being 105 days to the Lizard.

On June 8th, 1883, on her fourth voyage, the *British Merchant* left the Princes Dock, Liverpool, at 2 p.m., on her second passage to Melbourne. Again the weather was none too favourable for a fast run. The ship was 29 days to the Line, and her best run in the westerlies was only 284 miles. However, from July 22nd, when she was in 34° S., 30° W., she only had four runs under the 200 all the way to Port Phillip Heads, which were passed at 2 p.m. on August 25th, 78 days out.

Captain Molony again loaded coal across to San Francisco, making the run of 8,616 miles in 64 days from Newcastle. After discharging she went back to Newcastle for another coal cargo, making the run of 6,871 miles in 48 days. Her next passage was from Newcastle to Wilmington, May 7th to July 11th, 1884, 8,379 miles in 65 days. From Wilmington, Captain Molony went up to San Francisco and loaded a grain cargo for Havre. The *British Merchant* made a longish run for her, but she was rather foul after being twenty months out of dock. She left San Francisco on October 26th, 1884, and was off the Start on February 27th, 124 days out.

On his fifth voyage, from Liverpool to Calcutta, Captain Molony was obliged to leave the ship, ill, on June 30th, 1885, in Simon's Bay. The *British Merchant* was taken on by Captain D. C. Lewis, who made the good run of 35 days from the Cape to the Sandheads, the whole passage taking 105 days from Liverpool. Captain Lewis brought the ship home from Calcutta with jute to Dundee in 130 days. Captain Molony rejoined at Dundee on March 30th, 1886.

On her sixth voyage the *British Merchant* loaded in London for San Francisco, and sailing on May 5th, 1886, passed the Farallones at midnight on September 5th, 123 days out. The ship was again loaded for Havre, which port was reached at 7 a.m. on March 24th, 145 days out, after a very unpleasant time in the North Atlantic. On February 26th, in 26° 58′ N., 44° 47′ W., the *British Merchant* lost her boats and had other damage to her decks in a very heavy sea. The Scillies were made on March 23rd in a very heavy gale from the south, and with the night as black as pitch, with torrents of rain and the wind shifting to west in a hurricane squall, Captain Molony was compelled to heave-to for a few hours with the islands under his lee.

This time the ship was almost a year at home, but eventually left London for Sydney on February 23rd, and made the run out in 89 days. The passage was without incident except for April 13th, when the ship was in 42° S., 7° E. The wind backed from west to north-east and blew a fresh gale, with the barometer falling until it reached the very low reading of 28.8. The wind then died right away, and Captain Molony, in expectation of an S.W. shift, ordered the upper topsails to be furled. Sure enough, after thirty minutes' calm, the wind came from the south-west with hurricane force. The men were still aloft passing the gaskets round the upper topsails, but the wind was too much for them, and the topsails, together with the foresail, were blown to ribbons and completely lost. After blowing a hurricane for eight hours the wind fell light, and was easterly for the next twelve days, after which fair westerly winds carried the vessel round Tasmania to her port, the *British Merchant* anchoring in Sydney Harbour at 10 a.m. on May 22nd.

Captain Molony crossed the Pacific from Sydney to San Francisco in 59 days. San Francisco was left on October 24th, 1888, with a full cargo of grain, and the *British Merchant* had a light weather passage home, during which she never had to furl her topgallant sails.

In the South Atlantic the Down Easter *T. F. Oakes* was spoken on January 5th, 78 days out from Astoria for Falmouth, the *British Merchant* being 73 days out. On January 9th she spoke the *Drummuir*, which had sailed from San Francisco a day ahead of her.

The *British Merchant* was 95 days to the Line, and would have made a long passage of it but for her smart sailing in the North Atlantic, the ship being only 23 days from the Equator to Queenstown, which was reached on February 19th, 1889, 118 days out.

On her ninth voyage, in 1889, the *British Merchant* made the good run out to Calcutta from Newport of 85 days, but she was beaten by Alexander's *Glenlui*, a ship built by Royden in 1884, and a little over a hundred tons bigger than the *British Merchant*. The *Glenlui* made the run out in 79 days, and was only 25 days from the Cape to Calcutta.

Loading jute, Captain Molony was abeam of the Bishop Light 104 days out, and docked in Victoria Dock on December 9th, 110 days out.

On her tenth voyage the *British Merchant* made the following passages :

London, February 6th, 1890, Melbourne, April 28th ..	81 days
Newcastle, June 19th, San Francisco, August 19th ..	61 days
San Francisco, October 20th, Off the Wolf, February 16th	119 days
Hull, February 27th..	130 days

On her eleventh voyage the *British Merchant* went out round the Horn from London to Port Townsend in the good time of 118 days. On her grain passage this year she sailed from Tacoma on September 27th, 1891, and on December 18th, in 26° 13′ S., 26° 21′ W., lost her fore and main topgallant masts and all sail in a sudden squall of Force 8, which gave no warning; yet, in spite of being crippled, the ship anchored at Dunkirk at 5 p.m. on February 6th, 132 days out.

In 1892–3 the outward passage was made from Liverpool to Melbourne in 81 days, the ship's best run being 309 miles in the Roaring Forties. Loading coal at Newcastle, the *British Merchant* made the run to Colombo in 51 days. From Colombo she went to Wallaroo in 45 days, and then loaded at Port Augusta for Queenstown.

This was the year when there was so much ice in the South Atlantic. The *British Merchant* passed Cape Horn on April 16th, and on the 24th fell in with the ice in 47° 43′ S., 52° 26′ W. Here she spoke the *City of Madras*, the two ships threading their way amongst the icebergs for the next three days. Queenstown was reached on June 17th, 104 days out.

This voyage terminated Captain Molony's connection with the *British Merchant*, for he now left her to take over the big *British Isles*, the last vessel built for the British Shipowners Company. He was succeeded in the command of the *British Merchant* by Captain W. Thompson. The ship's career under the Red Ensign, however, was nearly over, and in 1896 she was sold to D. Cordes & Co., of Bremen, and renamed the *Arthur Fitger*. She continued to sail under the German flag until 1908, when she caught fire while lying in Shilshole Bay, Seattle, with a load of timber aboard. After the fire had been put out the ship was bought by Captain Griffiths, of Seattle, and converted into a towing barge, with her name changed to *Quatrino*.

The end came on October 15th, 1909. In tow of the tug *Goliath* she was being taken to Cordoba with 3,000 tons of Nanaimo coal. The light on Green Island was out, and the pilot, mistaking the surveyor's beacon on Grey Island, headed the tug between the two islands and, of course, piled his tow up, the poor old ship becoming a total loss.

INDEX OF SHIPS' NAMES.

GENERAL INDEX.